IDEOLOGY AND REVOLUTION
IN SOUTHEAST ASIA
1900–1980

IDEOLOGY AND REVOLUTION IN SOUTHEAST ASIA 1900–1980

Political Ideas of the Anti-Colonial Era

Clive Christie

Routledge
Taylor & Francis Group

LONDON AND NEW YORK

First Published in 2001
By Routledge
2 Park Square, Milton Park, Abingdon, Oxfordshire OX14 4RN
711 Third Avenue, New York, NY 10017

First issued in paperback 2015

Routledge is an imprint of the Taylor and Francis Group, an informa business

Typeset in Sabon by LaserScript Ltd, Mitcham, Surrey

British Library Cataloguing in Publication Data
A catalogue record of this book is available from the British Library

Library of Congress Cataloguing in Publication Data
A catalogue record for this book has been requested

ISBN 13: 978-1-138-86326-2 (pbk)
ISBN 13: 978-0-7007-1308-0 (hbk)

Publisher's Note
The publisher has gone to great lengths to ensure the quality of this reprint
but points out that some imperfections in the original may be apparent

Contents

List of Maps

Preface and Acknowledgements

The ideas and debates that engaged the main political actors and thinkers of Southeast Asia during the nationalist and anti-colonial era deserve more attention than they have received in the post-nationalist period. Admittedly, many of the better histories of individual states of Southeast Asia in the twentieth century examine the ideological background to the nationalist struggles and political conflicts of the post-independence period within those states. Cross-border comparisons and studies of ideological trends across the entire region have, however, been lacking; and in recent years, as a general theme, the political ideas that dominated the anti-colonial period have been increasingly pushed to the background.

In part, this has been a consequence of the decisive discrediting, since 1980, of Marxism-Leninism as a political and theoretical force. This side-lining of the question of ideology also reflects a fashion in academic social and political sciences that has placed increasing emphasis on recent theoretical formulae at the expense of the theoretical positions of the actual political participants of the period under study. Already the Cold War has been largely shorn of its essential ideological dimension, and is increasingly treated – by those who have no wish to delve into what they now consider to be the minutiae of defunct ideological battles – as a conventional big power confrontation.

In these circumstances, retrieval of the ideological perspective has become, in my opinion, a vital task. I have accordingly attempted here what amounts to a history of political ideas in Southeast Asia during the anti-colonial era: a presentation of the ideas and debates that had the greatest impact upon political movements and regimes of the first eighty years of the twentieth century.

Given the breadth of geographical coverage in this book, I have, of necessity, ventured beyond my own areas of linguistic competence. I thus owe a particular debt of gratitude to all those scholars of Southeast Asia who have over the decades undertaken the arduous task of translating and collecting the various writings and speeches of the main political actors and thinkers of the era covered in this book.

My special thanks go to my wife, Jan Wisseman Christie, who sacrificed much of her valuable time in going through my typescript and making the whole work presentable for publication.

CHAPTER ONE

Introduction

It is one of the uncontested clichés of our time that we now live in a 'post-colonial' era. If we simply define colonialism as a European phenomenon, then the above cliché is true in the strict historical sense. If, however, we understand 'post-colonialism' to be the description of an age that has in a sense 'transcended' the colonial experience, then the accuracy of the definition is far more questionable. The recent rhetoric of 'Asian values', for example, had its foundation in a classically anti-colonial mode of thinking. Ultimately, the attempt to assert 'Asian values' is based on a rejection of the so-called 'universal values' declared in the aftermath of the First and Second World Wars, and founded in the French 'Declaration of the Rights of Man and of the Citizen' of 1789. This assertion of universal human rights depending on universally accepted human values has been seen by the proponents of 'Asian values' as nothing less than an attempt by the 'colonial' West to maintain global authority via ideological hegemony.

It could, indeed, be said that anti-colonial modes of thinking dominate not only the current debate over Asian values, but also the debates on the global economy, international relations and 'multiculturalism'. Since this is the case, it would probably make more sense to replace the generally accepted division of twentieth century global history between a 'colonial' and 'post-colonial' era, and instead distinguish between a 'colonial' era – lasting roughly up to 1945 – when 'colonial' modes of thinking generally influenced political discourse relating to the colonial regions; and an 'anti-colonial' era – roughly from 1945 to the present day – during which an anti-colonial world view that had begun to emerge in the early decades of the twentieth century, has come to dominate large areas of political debate and rhetoric.

It is certainly true to say that anti-colonialism has formed the core of the political thinking of Southeast Asia in the twentieth century. From the attempts of the Southeast Asian intellectual elite to respond constructively to the overwhelming reality of European power at the beginning of the century, to the efforts at the end of the century of certain Southeast Asian leaders to assert 'Asian' as opposed to 'Western' values, anti-colonialism – used in the very broad sense as a response and challenge to the power and ideas of the West – has overshadowed the ideological debates of Southeast Asia.

Anti-colonialism, therefore, forms the fulcrum for any attempt to write an ideological history of Southeast Asia in the twentieth century. The experience of, or, in the case of Thailand, the shadow cast by Western global dominance affected the very disparate cultures of Southeast Asia in similar ways, as did the progressive collapse of colonial rule after 1945. There is, in fact a remarkable similarity – taking into account cultural and historical differences – in the ideological debates and conflicts throughout the region stimulated successively by the existence of colonial power, the growing challenge to colonial power, the process of the removal of colonial power, the establishment of independent states, the ideological crises that emerged within these 'independence regimes', and the attempt to establish what might be called genuine 'post-independence' regimes.

Bearing this core theme of anti-colonialism in mind, this book represents an attempt to analyse the ideological background to the endeavours of Southeast Asian intellectuals, writers and political leaders to respond to Western dominance; to come to terms with what was seen as the 'malaise' of traditional Asian societies; to formulate effective strategies of resistance to the West; to create a political and ideological base for the newly emergent independent states; and – in broader terms – to reflect on and understand the long-term historical significance of the relationship between the West and Asia. This book thus focuses upon ideas rather than events; and upon clearly defined ideologies rather than mere agendas.

This is, of course, an ambitious project, and there is an obvious danger of simply being overwhelmed by the material available to aid the coverage of such a broad theme. It has therefore proved to be imperative to confine the scope of the book to the discussion of contemporary texts and documents – books, articles, speeches, or policy declarations – produced by the main political 'actors' themselves. To reduce what might otherwise become fruitless speculation, the discussion of ideological sources and influences is confined where possible to references directly made in the above documents and texts.

Another major problem has been that of deciding upon the figures whose ideological and political thinking should be given prominence. It will become apparent that priority in this book has been given to the ideas expressed by the main – albeit contending – nationalist figures and political leaders who played active roles in the political arenas of the various Southeast Asian nations. From the Western perspective, this may seem to be a distorted approach: historically, the conduct of politics and speculation about the ideological foundations of politics have rarely been united, except in the largely mythological realm of the philosopher-king. It should, however, be borne in mind that the period of Western colonial rule severed the ideological links between the pre-colonial states and the independent states that emerged after 1945. So, while the leaders of the nationalist movements and the founders of the independent states of Southeast Asia were not merely accepting extant political systems from the colonial rulers, neither were they simply re-establishing regimes or dynasties in the pre-colonial mould. Like the protagonists of Machiavelli's *Prince* or the founding fathers of the United States, they were laying the constitutional and ideological foundations of new states – even if, in the case of Southeast Asia, these states had venerable historical antecedents. The political philosophies that guided such leaders as Sukarno, Ho Chi Minh, or Aung San may have been derivative and occasionally muddled, but they had – because of the peculiar circumstances of the time – an immediate and important impact.

Readers will rapidly note that revolutionary theory – particularly that derived from the ideological framework of Marxism-Leninism – had an overwhelmingly influential role during this anti-colonial period. In fact, it could be argued that the Marxist ideological viewpoint on revolution, nationalism and socialism constituted the most important unifying world-view that linked the anti-colonial movements of the region between 1919 and 1980. It need hardly be pointed out that this Marxist world-view has, since the 1980s, become deeply unfashionable. But this makes it all the more important to reconstruct – almost in the archaeological sense – a way of thinking, the intellectual foundations of which a 'post-Marxist' generation may find difficult to understand.

General books of this kind are read in many ways, and some readers will wish to concentrate their attention on certain countries or themes. It has proved to be necessary, therefore, to clarify in each case the ideological antecedents of a particular movement, regime, or individual political thinker, even if this involves the risk of repetition. It will, in any case, become apparent that the same basic political ideas may be interpreted very differently in different national and historical contexts. At the same time, it will become apparent that the political thinkers of twentieth-century Southeast Asia looked for inspiration, not to each other, but to their larger Asian neighbours, or to the West itself. This can be explained, in part, by the fact that an already linguistically and culturally diverse region was further fragmented by the colonial domination of no fewer than six Western powers.

On the issue of nomenclature, it has been decided in general to use the spelling system that prevailed at the time that relevant political thinkers and actors were writing. This will avoid confusion in the use of references or documents. In some cases, it was felt that the modern spelling – such as

'Sukarno' rather than 'Soekarno' – could be used without causing confusion. In other cases, such as the use of 'Sjahrir' rather than 'Syahrir', it was felt that the early spelling form would cause less confusion. In all cases, however, the guiding rule has been the maintenance of consistency.

It will be noticed that the bibliography is used strictly as a reference bibliography. In other words, only those books, documents, articles or pamphlets that are directly cited in the text are included in the bibliography. This is designed to enable ease of reference, and is also determined by the fact that a full bibliography, including all the works that might be relevant to an ideological history of the whole of Southeast Asia in the period between 1900 and 1980, would be simply unmanageable. Where possible, attempts have been made to refer readers in the first place directly to documents that are used in the text, rather than to the general edited work that contains the document. This, it is hoped, will enable readers to form a clearer idea of the exact documents used – documents which may, in any case, be more easily available to some readers in collections other than those cited in the bibliography.

Most of the translations and collections of documents used in this book were produced in what might be called the 'Heroic Age' of Southeast Asian scholarship in the 1960s and 1970s. This book is in no way intended to supersede this massive academic endeavour, but rather to direct attention back precisely to the political and social ideas embodied in those collections of documents. They constitute an indispensable source for our under-standing of the world-view of the anti-colonial era.

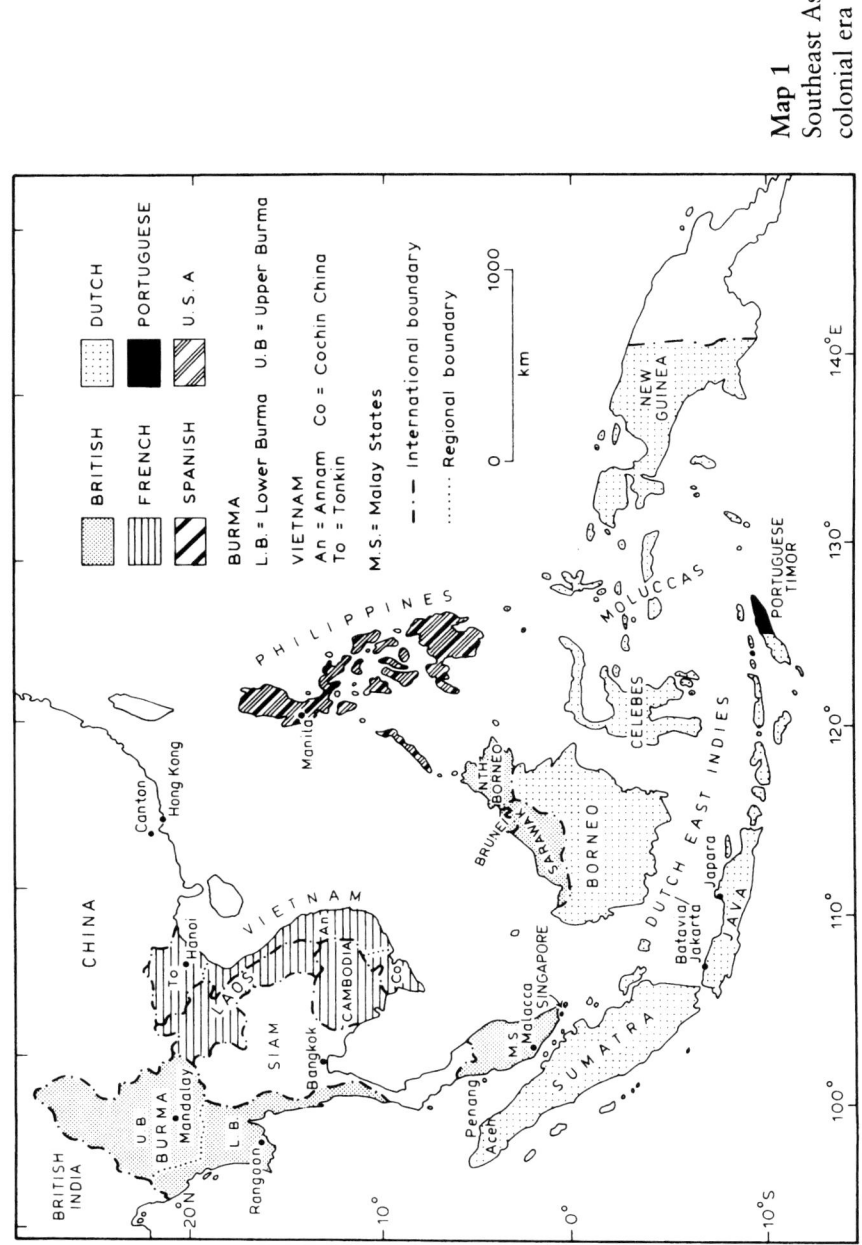

Map 1
Southeast Asia in the colonial era

CHAPTER TWO

Colonial Rule and Southeast Asian Responses

The last years of the nineteenth century saw a gradual transformation of the colonial situation throughout most of Southeast Asia. As colonial control was consolidated in the region, Britain, France and the Netherlands attempted to elaborate a justification for colonial rule and what might be called a 'philosophical' basis for that rule. This was driven by two imperatives, one moral, and one practical. The nineteenth century had seen the gradual 'democratization' of western and central Europe, and the growth of the notion that governments had a primary responsibility to protect the rights and welfare of their citizens. In this new political and social climate, it became increasingly difficult to justify colonialism simply in terms of the accumulated wealth and power that it conferred on the colonizing power. So colonialism acquired a stated moral imperative: the notion that a colonial power had a duty to confer upon colonized societies all the benefits of Western civilization, and thereby gradually 'raise' them up from their backwardness. This involved, among other things, the greater provision of educational opportunity, the extension of health care, the improvement of labour conditions, and the construction of roads, railways, canals, harbours and so forth.

This new era of colonial reform – in the Netherlands Indies, it was called the 'Ethical Policy' – highlighted a fundamental contradiction in colonial policy. While, on the one side, the colonial powers sought to change and reform the regions that they governed, on the other, they almost invariably depended on the support of an indigenous administration that had its roots in traditional society, and derived its justification for rule on the values of that traditional society. This dilemma was to some extent resolved by the fact that the colonial powers generally drew a distinction between general welfare reforms, which were available to the society as a whole, and access to Western education and technical expertise, which was limited to the sons (and occasionally daughters) of the traditional indigenous elite. A key objective of this new reform policy, therefore, was the gradual development of a 'partnership' or 'association' between the colonial power and an increasingly Westernized elite. The Westernization and modernization of the colonial regions, therefore, would ideally only operate in a limited way, without disturbing the hierarchies of traditional society. Across Southeast Asia, local responses to colonial rule during this reform era took different forms, but tended to be generated largely from within educated indigenous elites, who looked outwards, rather than backwards, for their inspiration.

The survey below considers a range of examples of local elite reactions, at the turn of the century, to colonial rule and what colonial rule hypothetically had to offer. Unfortunately, perhaps the most insightful Southeast Asian analysis of the 'colonial condition' – that contained in the two novels written in the Philippines by José Rizal (1861–1896), entitled *Noli Me Tangere* (1886) and *El Filibusterismo* (1891) – lies outside of the scope of this book, since Rizal was executed before the turn of the century. In his novels, Rizal demonstrated that the maintenance of colonial authority ultimately depended, not so much on naked power, but on an acceptance – by both the colonial power *and* the colonized people – of the innate superiority, and thereby right to rule, of that colonial power. The maintenance of this colonial 'prestige' meant, of course, that any plans for 'partnership' could only be applied within strict limits, and on condition that the notion of colonial superiority remain intact.

Rizal's novels illuminated the manner in which prestige, the essential prop of colonial power, entirely contaminated the relationship between ruler and ruled. In order to maintain prestige, it was necessary in the last resort for even the most liberal colonial power to violate the very values on which its civilization was based; at the same time, even the most 'liberated' colonial subject was forced to live within a system that depended on the notion of his inherent inferiority. Rizal's characters discovered that it was ultimately impossible to live as spiritually free human beings within the colonial relationship. Since the conversion of the colonial relationship into a true partnership between peoples sharing the same values was inconceivable, true freedom and equality could only be obtained through the complete removal of colonial power. Even then it was difficult to escape the moral cancer induced by the colonial condition, since the process of forcibly removing a colonial power would itself necessitate the violation of the very moral values that those seeking liberation espoused (Rizal 1961, 1968).

COLONIAL RULE AND RELIGIOUS REFORM

Colonial rule had a profound impact on the religions of Southeast Asia. This in turn had political consequences, not only because the pre-colonial political systems and values had been based on those religions, but also because the organizations for the propagation of religious reform that emerged in Southeast Asia at the end of the nineteenth century and the beginning of the twentieth became crucially important in the social, educational and political fields at the beginning of the anti-colonial era. Classic examples are the Young Men's Buddhist Association (YMBA) formed in Burma in 1906, and the Sarekat Islam (Islamic Association) and *Muhammadiyah* movements, formed in the Netherlands Indies just before the First World War.

It would be quite wrong to assume that the European colonial influence simply stimulated efforts to 'modernize' and in a sense 'Westernize' the established religions of Southeast Asia. In some senses, the reverse is true. Western scholarship of the nineteenth century played a major role in reviving interest in classic religious and literary texts, and thereby encouraged a return to, and re-examination of original sources. This is true of Sanskrit-Hindu, Pali-Buddhist, Chinese-Confucian and Arabic-Islamic texts in particular. Colonial scholarly interest in traditional Asian religion and literature is encapsulated in the series entitled *Sacred Books of the East*, edited by Max Muller, in James Legge's collected translations of the Chinese classics, and in E.W. Lane's monumental Arabic-English Lexicon, among many other examples. In fact, the colonial presence stimulated a religious *revival* as well as religious reform. This renewed interest in the textual origins of the respective religions necessarily involved a fundamental re-examination of their ethical and philosophical foundations – a return to their rational and spiritual core – thereby creating a new basis for inspecting current religious practice.

A good example is provided by the movement of Buddhist revival of the late nineteenth and early twentieth century. In 1891, a convert to Buddhism, Anagarika Dharmapala, founded the *Maha Bodhi* society in Ceylon, and a year later began publishing the society's influential journal, entitled *The Maha Bodhi and the United Buddhist World*. Subsequently, branches of the *Maha Bodhi* society were set up in Akyab, Rangoon, Bangkok, and other places in East Asia and Europe (Dharmapala 1965: xxxv-xliii). The stated objectives of the society were to stimulate a general interest in Buddhism, to disseminate an awareness of its fundamental principles, and to strengthen religious contacts between different parts of the Buddhist world (Dharmapala 1965: 635–42). Anagarika Dharmapala openly acknowledged the debt that the Buddhist revival owed to Western scholarship and – more particularly – to the now largely forgotten epic poem on Buddha's life and mission written by the British teacher, journalist and orientalist, Sir Edwin Arnold (1822–1904). Anagarika Dharmapala described Arnold's poem, *The Light of Asia*, as an 'incomparable epic', which had become 'the handbook of thousands of admirers of the Lord Buddha both in the East and the West' (Dharmapala 1965: 647). Furthermore, he went out of his way – he was to change his mind later – to assert that British rule provided a benevolent environment in which

Buddhism could flourish, even going so far as to state that, 'it is my belief that India after the extinction of the Buddhist empire [of Asoka] has had no beneficent government equal to the present one' (Dharmapala 1965: 648).

A favourable attitude to British government did not, however, imply any kind of deference to Western values. An examination of what was probably the most influential book of the Buddhist revival, P. Lakshmi Narasu's *The Essence of Buddhism* (1907), demonstrates that this revival brought about a renewal of confidence in Buddhism as a self-sufficient ethical and philosophical system that was perfectly attuned to the modern world. Narasu particularly emphasized the essential rationality of Buddhism. Its whole ethical structure, he asserted, was based firmly on reason, not revelation or dogma (Narasu 1907: 37). From the starting point of the Buddha's explicit rejection of the moral framework that provided the Hindu justification for the caste system, Narasu argued that Buddhism accepted the fundamental spiritual equality of human beings, and repudiated the concept of inherent moral superiority or inferiority of different groups of human beings (Narasu 1907: 88). He was, moreover, at pains to point out that, 'nowhere in any of the utterances of the Buddha do we find anything to show that he made any difference between man and woman' (Narasu 1907: 91). Overall, Narasu's book sought to demonstrate that the elucidation of the fundamental texts of Buddhism had helped to rediscover a comprehensive rational philosophy that was inherently democratic and egalitarian, and, moreover, more cosmopolitan in spirit than the modern secular ideologies of the West.

Developments of a similar nature were occurring in the Islamic world at the same time. By the end of the nineteenth and the beginning of the twentieth century, important sections of the intellectual elite of the Islamic world had come to accept Western colonial rule – however reluctantly – as a period that would at least give Islam a breathing space for reflection, reform and rejuvenation. Two key figures in this period of Islamic renaissance were Jamal al-Din al-Afghani (1838–1897) and Muhammad Abduh (1849–1905), both of whom moved extensively through the Islamic world, but were mainly centred on the Middle East. Since, however, their views had a decisive impact on the Islamic reform movement of Southeast Asia at this time, it is important to outline some of their basic ideas on Islam. A common theme that united both of these scholars, and indeed dominated the whole Islamic reform thinking of the time, was the notion of the fundamentally rational philosophic basis of Islamic doctrine and law.

Jamal al-Din al-Afghani attributed the spectacular failure of the Islamic world to resist the power of Europe primarily to its attitude toward science. What Muslim leaders and scholars of the time failed to comprehend, he insisted, was that the dominance of Europe did not depend on any innate characteristics within Western civilization, but rather on the fact that Western civilization had succeeded in harnessing the power of science.

Science, however, had no motherland; ultimately it was science, not the West that had reduced Islam to subjection (Donohue 1982: 17). The trouble with modern Islam was that it had tried to maintain a distinction between science on the one side, selected parts of which it had tried to appropriate, and faith on the other. Afghani asserted that this discrimination between science and religion was wholly artificial, and, moreover, damaging to Islam. Science could not be divided into what was 'acceptable' and 'unacceptable', 'Islamic' and 'non-Islamic': in the last resort, 'the father and the mother of science is proof' (Donohue 1982: 19). Science depended on a comprehensive philosophical base of reason; but the scholars of Islam had, in effect, deprived science of that philosophical base in the Islamic world (Donohue 1982: 18). This had not only doomed the Islamic world to backwardness, but was in the most profound sense un-Islamic, since the *Qur'an* and the *Hadith* (recorded sayings and deeds of Muhammad), which were the formative elements of the *shari'ah* or prescribed law of God, were fully consonant with reason, and formed a philosophical foundation on which science – *all* science – could flourish. Afghani's criticism of Islamic scholarship of the time was that it had prevented Islam from forming, as it should have done, the *fons et origo* of all human knowledge, but had rather treated Islam as a formulaic creed to be learned by rote. It had trapped Islam in an age of theological dogma, at a time when Europe had already moved on to the age of reason (Donohue 1982: 16–17).

Afghani's theory of government was equally radical. Following the argument of the famous Islamic historian and philosopher, Ibn Khaldun, as well as the fashionable nationalist theories of Europe, Afghani accepted that there was a natural tendency of peoples of similar ethnic identity to band together for mutual protection against outsiders, and thereby form collective societies and states. This was the social tendency that Ibn Khaldun had termed *'asabîya*. Afghani denied, however, that there was any innate law or blood instinct that drew people of the same ethnic group together: rather *'asabîya* was a utilitarian reaction to circumstances (Donohue 1982: 20). The great and fundamental achievement of Muhammad, argued Afghani, was that he had created a government and society that superseded the mundane links of blood and kin, and had instead submitted itself collectively to the universal law of God based on the *Qur'an*. This was the *umma*, or community of Islam, governed by Muhammad himself, and his *khalifa* or designated successors thereafter (Donohue 1982: 21).

Whereas states and societies based on blood-kin relationships divided humanity, the concept of the *umma* potentially united all groups of humanity under the moral guidance of God. Even if the Islamic state had, after the golden age of Islam, broken up into separate emirates or sultanates, the same basic principles applied: such states should not be based on the ethnic principle, and should ultimately be held together by a moral purpose under the law of God. An important reason for the decline of the Islamic world was the fact that these Muslim states had lost this moral imperative, and had therefore lost their intrinsic *raison d'être*. The first consequence of this moral failure had been a return to ethnic solidarity, or tribalism. The second – and more fatal – had been the establishment of European political dominance. The route to the regeneration of the Islamic world, therefore, lay, not in the establishment of nation-states in the European mould, but the re-creation of the true Islamic state based on the *shari'ah* (Donohue 1982: 23).

Muhammad Abduh, whose thinking was of equal, if not greater, importance in Southeast Asia, pursued the same theme of the relationship between Islam and human reason. The fundamental point made by Abduh in this respect was that, while the laws of reason did not and could not encompass the whole truth of divine revelation embodied in the *Qur'an*, the *Qur'an* and the *Hadith* – collectively the *shari'ah* – contained within it the laws of reason that could be apprehended by humanity. Therefore, while Islam was ultimately based on faith, it was always consonant with reason (Donohue 1982: 24). The backwardness of the Islamic world, therefore, was not in any way due to the intrinsic nature of Islam, but rather to the fact that Islamic civilization was still trapped in an age – long gone in Europe – where faith was bolstered by revelation and dogma, to the exclusion of the essential ingredient of reason. This was the fault of the exponents of Islam, not Islam itself. Like Afghani, therefore, Abduh was advocating the simultaneous *revival* and *reform* of Islam. The *shari'ah* contained within itself a far more comprehensive basis of reason that any other philosophical system, providing as it did for the absolute equality of all the races of humanity, and for absolute equality of all human beings under the law of God (Donohue 1982: 27).

The main religious links between Mecca and Egypt – which together comprised the heartland of Islam at this time – and Southeast Asia were the *haj*, or pilgrimage prescribed by Islam, and the continual movement to and from the Middle East of religious scholars and teachers. The principal 'clearing-house' of this interaction was the port-city of Singapore, and it was there that the movement for Islamic reform in Southeast Asia had its natural headquarters. A number of Islamic journals emerged during this period, mainly in Singapore, but also in Penang and other urban centres in the Malay States, Sumatra and Java. One of the most important of these reforming journals was *Al-Imam*, which was published in Jawi – that is, Malay written in Arabic script – from 1906 to 1908. Despite its relatively short period of existence, *Al-Imam* stands out, both because of the fact that illustrious scholars such as Sheikh Tahir Jalaluddin and Haji Abbas Muhammad Taha were connected with it, and because of the fact that it was one of the most effective transmitters of the reforming ideas of Afghani and Abduh (Roff 1967: 56–90).

Al-Imam's crusading campaign for reform coincided with the general concern over the backwardness of the Islamic world. Its specific anxiety, however, was directed at the Muslims of Southeast Asia, particularly the Malays of Sumatra and the various states of peninsular Malaya – the heartlands of Malayo-Islamic culture. The Malays, it was felt, faced an exceptional crisis, since this heartland region had in the course of the later nineteenth century been flooded with immigrants from the Chinese mainland who were manifestly more adaptable to the challenges of the modern society and economy that was rapidly emerging. The self-regeneration of the Muslim-Malay people through the agency of a reformed Islam had become a matter of extreme urgency: almost, it seemed, a matter of survival (Abu Bakar 1981: 258–64).

Following the general analysis of Afghani and Abduh, *Al-Imam* pointed to four key areas for the renovation of Malay Islam. The first essential task was that of the removal from the essential body of Islamic law and doctrine – embodied in the *Qur'an*, the *Hadith* and the *sunna*, or the collective codes of behaviour of the Islamic community in the time of Muhammad – of various non-Islamic accretions that had, over the centuries, insinuated themselves into the way that Islam was followed and interpreted. The most locally significant of these accretions were Malay *adat*, or pre-Islamic custom, and various unorthodox mystical practices that had taken root in Islam over time (Abu Bakar 1981: 68).

The second task was that of liberating Islam from the fossilized dogmatic legal tradition followed by the Islamic scholarly establishments of the various Malay states. Like Muhammad Abduh, the reformers of *Al-Imam* wished to push aside the whole body of blind legal precedent that clung like barnacles round the original principles of Islam, and to renew the direct link between divine revelation and human reason. This would have involved reasserting the principle of *ijtihad* or 'reasoned discussion' as the primary means of operating and interpreting Islamic law (Abu Bakar 1981: 81).

The main target of concern for the Malay Islamic reformers, however, was in the area of education. As in the rest of the Islamic world, Islamic education in the Malay region had tended to degenerate into mere rote-learning and recitation – made worse by the fact that Malay-speaking pupils, and sometimes even their teachers, had only a dim understanding of the meaning of the Quranic verses they were chanting (Roff 1978: 62–65, 67–68). Like Abduh, the reformers associated with *Al-Imam* wanted Islam to become the philosophical foundation of all education, the essential rational basis for understanding the world as a whole (Abu Bakar 1981: 268–70).

Most controversial of all, perhaps, were *Al-Imam*'s prescriptions for political reform in the Malayo-Islamic world. This issue was particularly sensitive, because Britain had, after 1874, established protectorates over a number of the Malay sultanates of the peninsula, and had thus acquired a vested interest in the maintenance of the status and authority of the sultans over their respective Malay subjects. This was a clear case of Western colonial rule propping up, rather than reforming or removing, the hierarchies of traditional pre-colonial society. For *Al-Imam*, the very fact that these sultanates had been forced to submit themselves to British supervision was the inevitable consequence of their previous failure to fulfil their primary task of obeying and enforcing Islamic standards of justice and government. The solution, argued *Al-Imam* in a number of issues, was to supplement the purely personal authority of the Sultan – an authority that was at the mercy of the vagaries of personality – with a properly constituted system of representation. Although it was not stated explicitly, it must have been in the mind of *Al-Imam*'s moderate reformers that such a system of representation would not only assure political continuity and strengthen the rights of the *umma* within a state, but would also accord with the fundamentally egalitarian principles of Islam (Abu Bakar 1981: 245–46, 274, 276).

KARTINI AND THE CULTURAL REVOLUTION IN JAVA

In the sprawling archipelago of the Netherlands East Indies, the Dutch made only selective use of the type of 'protectorate' system that the British imposed step-by-step on the sultanates of the Malayan peninsula. In the areas of more direct Dutch colonial rule, they 'co-opted' the traditional hereditary elite who had governed at the provincial and local level in the various pre-colonial states, incorporating them into the colonial adminis-tration. Up to the level of the 'Regency' or *kebupaten*, therefore, local government was in the hands of the largely hereditary traditional elite. This indigenous layer of administration was, however, supervised from above by Dutch officials operating at the 'Residency' level.

In the late nineteenth and early twentieth century, Dutch colonial policy underwent a radical change. The main aim of the new, 'ethical' policy was to give access to Western education and expertise to the children of this hereditary indigenous elite, either in Dutch language schools in the East Indies, or in the Netherlands itself. The primary objectives of this policy were to 'modernize' and thereby improve the efficiency – at a fractional extra cost – of the whole administration, and to strengthen the governing partnership between the Dutch and the indigenous elite. Through this alliance, it was intended that the Netherland's 'civilizing mission' would percolate through to the population as a whole without endangering the essential colonial structure.

The writings between 1900 and 1904 of Raden Ajeng or Princess Kartini (1879–1905), the daughter of an eminent member of this indigenous Javanese aristocracy, demonstrate both the liberating force of this new policy, and at the same time its inner contradictions. Kartini's family were traditional rulers in the Kudus-Demak-Japara region in the northern coastal part of central Java (see map 1), a stronghold of Islamic-Javanese culture, which was a rich compound of deeply embedded indigenous and Hindu-Buddhist characteristics and Islam. Kartini's grandfather, however, ensured that the children of the family received a Western education (Coté 1992: xii-xiii). For the female members of this family, however, this Western education was only available up to the age that *adat* (local custom) determined that they should be secluded at home – essentially in *purdah* – until the time that a marriage could be arranged for them.

Kartini's literary outpourings were fuelled by a sense of protest against this fate. After having a world opened up to her at a Dutch-language school, Kartini was thereafter compelled, along with her sisters, to remain effectively imprisoned within the family compound between 1891 and 1903, with the exception of a few, treasured excursions. She was given a lifeline, however, by the friendly relationship that she and her sister Roekmini established with Rosa Abendanon-Madri, the Spanish wife of J.H. Abendanon, who in 1900 had been appointed the Director of Education, Industry and Religion for the Netherlands Indies government – a post that lay at the heart of the reform project of Dutch colonialism at that time (Coté 1992: xxv-xxvi).

Kartini's letters, written from her family home in Japara to Rosa Abendanon-Madri in Batavia, reveal her thoughts and her ambitions. Her ultimate ambition was to get a proper education in the Netherlands, where she hoped to train as a teacher, while her sister Roekmini could train either as an artist or a midwife (Coté 1992: 65). As it became apparent to her that these aspirations were considered to be utterly inappropriate for daughters of the Javanese aristocracy, her sights were lowered to the hope of furthering her and her sister's education in Batavia, the capital of the Netherlands East Indies, with a view thereafter to establishing a school for 'the daughters of native rulers' (Coté 1992: 231). The impenetrable barrier of *adat*, however, prevented even this modest project. Although she and Roekmini did eventually manage to set up a small local school, all these plans ultimately disintegrated with her arranged marriage, in 1903, to the regent of Rembang, and her premature death in 1904 (Coté 1992: 427).

Beyond this essentially tragic story of unfulfilled aspirations, however, it is possible to discern in Kartini's letters, and in a memorandum that she addressed to a visiting Dutch official in 1903 – boldly entitled 'Give the Javanese an Education!' – the clear outlines of a systematic critique of traditional society and the colonial relationship, and a plan for educational and cultural reform.

From the outset Kartini denied that she in any way rejected her Javanese identity, or that she and her sisters intended to become, as she put it, 'more European than Javanese in our hearts' (Coté 1992: 536). But Kartini's own bitter experiences – and her acquaintance with Western culture –

unavoidably gave her an insight into what she saw as the stultified nature of Javanese society. In Kartini's eyes, Javanese aristocratic culture valued show and symbol above substance. Traditional culture had become a fossilized badge of status, not a living force that could illuminate the lives of those who lived within it. This was amply indicated, so far as Kartini was concerned, by traditional Javanese literature, which largely consisted of privately preserved heirlooms, containing arcane mystical works written in an ornate and inaccessible allegorical language (Coté 1992: 536).

Perhaps most limiting of all was the traditional Javanese attitude to knowledge. Kartini described this as a '*dukun* mentality': to the *dukun*, or practitioner of traditional medicine, knowledge was power, to be hoarded for profit, not disseminated for general enlightenment (Coté 1992: 532). Kartini observed that this '*dukun* mentality' even affected Javanese attitudes to Western education and knowledge. Far from seeing Western-acquired ideas and skills as a means of opening a debate on native society, the underlying spirit of enquiry was ignored while the power Western knowledge conferred was used to reinforce status (Coté 1992: 121). The fossilization of Javanese culture and attitudes, and its inadequate reaction to the opportunities offered by the modern world, were encapsulated for Kartini in the treatment of women (Coté 1992: 179).

Kartini did not, however, confine her strictures to Javanese society. In the course of her correspondence, she became all too aware of the fact that the Dutch concept of reform was limited to those measures that would bind the elite to the colonial project without disturbing the existing structure of native society (Coté 1992: 205–7). During the brief period between her marriage to the regent of Rembang and her death, she was in a position to witness the workings of the colonial administration at close hand. From this vantage point, she could see the extent to which the native rulers were trapped by the colonial system. They were, on the one hand, forced to carry out policies that the best among them knew were unfair and laid excessive burdens on the people – as, for example, the innumerable taxes on items of everyday life demanded from the peasantry. On the other hand, the native administrators were prevented from carrying out manifestly necessary reforms – for example, the banning of opium consumption – that would endanger government revenue (Coté 1992: 518–19). Her overall conclusion was that the colonial government, despite its reforming rhetoric and talk of 'association' with the educated indigenous elite, ultimately depended on 'prestige' – the maintenance of an unbridgeable distance between ruler and ruled – and that this 'prestige' would be threatened by genuine and thoroughgoing reform in indigenous society (Coté 1992: 539).

Kartini's plan for educational reform took as its starting point the notion that learning from the West should not simply be a matter of acquiring knowledge and expertise. Even more necessary was the inculcation of what she saw as the underlying *spirit* on which Western education and knowledge were based: namely, the liberating force of altruism and enquiry. In its first stage, this essentially moral endeavour for the changing of the world view of native society would necessarily be confined to the elite class. This, she realized, was the only practical course in a society with such an ingrained sense of social hierarchy, and equally ingrained habits of deference (Coté 1992: 529–30).

The immediate priority, she argued, should be the education of the daughters of the nobility. With the educational liberation of the mothers of the elite, the foundation would be laid for what would amount to – although Kartini never used such language – a deep-rooted cultural and social revolution (Coté 1992: 530). Built on such a solid social and moral basis, in which altruism would prevail over the hoarding of knowledge, these educational reforms would then percolate through the entire society (Coté 1992: 544–47). In this way, traditional deference to the indigenous nobility would gradually be replaced by a new relationship based on respect and 'solidarity' (Coté 1992: 529, 532). At the same time, the ultimately degrading relationship, based on 'prestige', between the Dutch and the indigenous elite would be replaced by growing mutual understanding and respect – and thus a genuine partnership would emerge (Coté 1992: 539–40).

Kartini knew only too well that these ideas seemed hopelessly idealistic and even dangerous, not merely to the Dutch and indigenous administrators in general, but also to dearly loved members of her own family. She was painfully conscious of the fact that growing demands for reform would inevitably break the links of trust and deference that had bound together the generations in traditional society. As she put it: 'It is very sad, we are engaged in estranging ourselves from our lives, loosening bonds, which till now have meant our greatest happiness' (Coté 1992: 320).

THE STRAITS CHINESE OF SINGAPORE: CULTURAL REFORM AND IMPERIAL PARTNERSHIP

The island of Singapore, where the British East India Company set up a trading station in 1819, was developed thereafter as a major entrepot mainly by a fruitful combination of Chinese labour and entrepreneurial skills presided over by British administration. The Chinese immigrant community that established itself in Singapore during the course of the nineteenth and early twentieth centuries came principally from the coastal regions of South China stretching from Hainan Island to the province of Fukien. From the early years of the foundation of the port, the so-called 'Straits Chinese' – Chinese whose families had settled for some time, and quite often intermarried with Malays in the Straits region of the Malayan peninsula and Sumatra – assumed a natural intermediary role between the British administration and business interests on one side, and the immigrant

Chinese groups on the other. Their knowledge of Malay, English and the Chinese dialects made them invaluable for facilitating business transactions, and as mediators in the endless problems and tensions that arose, both among the Chinese immigrants of numerous dialect and clan groups, and between the Chinese community as a whole and the administration (Song Ong Siang 1967: 81–82, 87–90).

Generally, as the more successful Chinese immigrants learned English, an elite Chinese community began to coalesce around a distinct English-speaking Straits Chinese identity. Some of the members of this English-speaking group converted to Christianity. The most evident signs of the 'Westernization' of this community during the course of the nineteenth century, however, was the increasing acquisition – by male members of the community at least – of a British education, either in the Straits Settlements of Singapore or Penang, or in Britain itself. This Westernization went hand-in-hand with a determined quest for self-improvement in ways that took a distinctly nineteenth century form. In 1882, a 'Celestial Reasoning Association' was formed for the discussion of philosophical and moral topics and the improvement of English; in 1885, following the imperative *mens sana in corpore sano*, a Straits Chinese Recreation Club was formed; and, in 1889, the Chinese Christian Association took over many of the functions of the Celestial Reasoning Association, particularly when, in 1908, a Reading Club and Drama section was added to the Association (Song Ong Siang 1967: 210, 216, 254–56).

In this pre-First World War period, intellectual leadership of the Straits Chinese was provided, not by Confucian scholars of the old school, but by British-educated professional men, most prominent among whom was Song Ong Siang, a barrister born in 1871, and Lim Boon Kheng, a doctor born in 1869. *The Straits Chinese Magazine*, which was started in 1897, provided a forum for their political, social and cultural ideas, and for their overall reform project for the Straits Chinese community. The principal ideas of the Straits Chinese reformers of this period are outlined in the excerpts collected in Song Ong Siang's *One Hundred Years' History of the Chinese in Singapore*, first published in 1923, and in Lim Boon Kheng's *The Chinese Crisis from Within*, which he published in 1901 under the pseudonym Wen Ching.

Like Kartini in Java, the contributors to the *Straits Chinese Magazine* in Singapore were concerned by the fact that Western education, although it had created a new outward-looking professional stratum attuned to the modern world, had not generated fundamental cultural or 'moral' reform within the broader community. The Straits Chinese reformers, like other Southeast Asian reformers of the time, felt that the expertise offered by Western education had been imbibed, but not the philosophical base for the revolution in ideas that had transformed European civilization. As a crucial step to bring about a more fundamental change, *The Straits Chinese*

Magazine urged that a modern education be made available to the *nyonya*, or female members, of the Straits Chinese community. Their suggested educational programme may have been restricted – emphasizing as it did a combination of languages and domestic skills – but the ultimate objective of this liberation of women from what was described by *The Straits Chinese Magazine* as their 'pernicious bondage' was far-reaching: 'There can be no general improvement in the social condition of the race until the women are refined and elevated by a sensible education and by the increase in social amenities which only enlightenment can ensure' (Song Ong Siang 1967: 357–58).

The Straits Chinese reformers were by no means suggesting, however, an abandonment of Chinese culture and tradition. Their reform plans were based on the idea of a fruitful relationship between European and Chinese ideas, and Lim Boon Kheng in particular strongly advocated that a reformed version of Confucianism should serve as the moral base of an educated and enlightened Straits Chinese society. For Lim Boon Kheng, this Confucian revival would necessarily require the detachment from the body of Confucian ideas of its ossified carapace of scholasticism and ritual, and its redefinition as a living and all-embracing moral, social and political philosophy (Song Ong Siang 1967: 286; *Straits Chinese Magazine* 1904: viii(1), 30).

The long-term objective of the ideas promoted by *The Straits Chinese Magazine* was not just the liberation of a formerly ritual- and tradition-bound society, but to provide the basis for a wholesale reformation that would enable the Straits Chinese to play an increasingly *political* role within the British Empire. The leaders of their community had already achieved eminence in the economy and civil society of Singapore. But the Straits Chinese reformers felt that the community still lacked the essential 'citizenship' values – a combination of social altruism and a sense of public responsibility – that would enable and entitle it to become genuine partners in empire (*Straits Chinese Magazine* 1900: iv(4), 86; 1903: vii(3), 109). A reformed Confucianism was considered to be a particularly appropriate means of supplying the missing ingredient of what Lim Boon Kheng called 'moral education' (Song Ong Siang 1967: 286).

Placed as they were at the crossroads of three identities – Chinese by origin, Malayan by settlement, British in political terms – it was perhaps natural that this self-confident, wealthy and well-educated Singaporean elite should seek to redefine the nature of empire itself. What they ultimately envisaged was a British Empire bound together by a common loyalty and core values, and in which a shared role in the government of the empire would be open to the elite of all races and cultures – so long as they had received the requisite education and loyally subscribed to the agreed objectives and values of that empire (*Straits Chinese Magazine* 1897: i(2), 72; Song Ong Siang 1967: 480). This radical vision was, in many ways, well ahead of its time: more attuned, perhaps, to our modern global world of migration, cultural complexity and mixed identity than to the nationalist era just over the horizon in Southeast Asia.

The Straits Chinese viewed the British Empire as a potential moral force for good in the world – but only if it was able to substitute the principle of racial equality for the prevailing concept of white racial superiority. This viewpoint assumes particular significance in Lim Boon Kheng's analysis of the Chinese crisis in 1900, *The Chinese Crisis from Within*, which he published in 1900 under the pseudonym Wen Ching. Although this book focuses upon China rather than Southeast Asia, it presents a highly significant analysis of the general relationship between the West and Asia at the time, and of the opportunities and pitfalls that lay ahead in the development of this relationship. In its polite way, it is a critique of Western colonialism.

By 1900, China was disintegrating. Lim Boon Kheng ascribed responsibility for this state of affairs primarily to the Manchu dynasty, particularly the Manchu court dominated by the Empress Dowager. In 1898, after the humiliating defeat by Japan in 1894–5 had revealed the true extent of the weakness of the Empire, the Emperor Kuang-Hsu had initiated a thoroughgoing reform programme led by the leading proponents of fundamental political change, Kang Yu-wei and Liang Ch'i-ch'ao (Wen Ching 1901: 49–58). However, the forces of reaction within the court and the administration soon ousted the reformers. Thereafter, growing internal weakness and anti-foreign activity culminated in the so-called 'Boxer' Rebellion, in which the Manchu government colluded with secret societies to oust the foreign powers from China (Wen Ching 1901: 266). The inevitable result, given the inherent weakness of China at this time, was the defeat of the 'Boxers' and the tightening of European, American and Japanese control over China.

Following the lines of the liberal Chinese intelligentsia of the time, Lim Boon Kheng argued that China would never be able to reform itself unless it was liberated from the Manchus, a non-Han (ethnic Chinese) people whose elite formed a top layer of government. He also, however, explicitly blamed China's troubles on the Western imperial powers, including Britain. Over the century, these powers had steadily encroached on Chinese sovereignty, seizing slices of coastal territory, forcing unequal tariff and judicial agreements on the Chinese government, and providing backing for extensive missionary activity. Lim Boon Kheng pointed out that these intrusions upon Chinese sovereignty had weakened the authority and status of Chinese administrators and unfairly disadvantaged Chinese commerce within its own borders (Wen Ching 1901: 289–94, 300–1).

Lim Boon Kheng argued that the Christian missions in particular had had a disastrous effect on Western-Chinese relations. By converting the poorer and less-educated elements of society, the missions had helped to create a *deraciné* community that no longer had any place in, and was thereby an implicit threat to, the traditional social order of provincial China. Worse, the fact that the missionaries, in order to convert such people, had promoted a superstitious and simplistic version of Christianity, meant that the status of Christianity – and, indeed, of the West itself – was lowered in the eyes of educated Chinese (Wen Ching 1901: 317, 320, 324–25). This deepened the mutual misunderstanding between China and the West. While on the one hand, European behaviour towards the Chinese was manifestly dictated by an innate sense of racial superiority, the Chinese were confirmed in their view that Western supremacy depended on 'brute force' alone (Wen Ching 1901: 284).

Lim Boon Kheng concluded that Britain, in its relations with China, had reached the point at which it would be forced to make a choice between moral imperatives and *realpolitik* – and that this choice would affect the future of the British Empire in Asia as a whole. He urged the British to reject the temptation simply to exploit a weak China for the sake of commercial gain and a short-term perception of imperial interest. Rather, he wrote, the British Empire should seek to show that its political superiority was based upon 'moral right', and that on this basis it should help China to reinstate the kind of constitutional monarchy that had begun to take shape during the reform period of 1898. This would have involved the removal of the stranglehold of the Empress Dowager and the Manchus, and the accession to power of outward-looking and reform-minded patriots of the Kang Yu-Wei/Liang Ch'i-Ch'ao mould (Wen Ching 1901: 269). Encouraging an orderly, gradual reform programme working from the top down – Lim Boon Kheng described his model for China as 'constitutional oligarchy' – would avoid the danger of blind reaction on one side, or revolutionary anarchy on the other (Wen Ching 1901: 328). With some prescience, Lim Boon Kheng warned that if Britain failed to identify itself with the forces of moderation and constitutional change in China, it would in the future be faced by a combination of anti-Western and revolutionary forces (Wen Ching 1901: 282–83, 285).

PHAN BOI CHAU AND 'PAN-ASIANISM'

When Japan and Tsarist Russia went to war in 1904 over the issue of the control of the Manchuria-Korea region, the Straits Chinese reformers urged the creation of a Sino-Japanese alliance, based on mutual respect, to prevent further European encroachments in East Asia (*Straits Chinese Magazine* viii, 1 : 40). It was also during this decade before the First World War that the Vietnamese writer and patriot, Phan Boi Chau (1867–1940), turned his hopes to the creation of some kind of 'Pan-Asian' anti-colonial alliance. The Straits Chinese saw a Sino-Japanese accord as a means of strengthening and rejuvenating China. Phan Boi Chau's world-view was more radical: he believed that the combined power of Japan and mass of China could act as an anti-imperial 'dynamo' that would energize Vietnam, and ultimately generate an irresistible Pan-Asian force that would drive the West out of Asia altogether.

If one word could sum up Phan Boi Chau's ideas, it would be 'resistance'. He was the quintessence of the restless 'political agitator' that so disturbed the peace of mind of early twentieth-century colonial governments. Born into a mandarin family, Phan Boi Chau never managed to liberate himself from the traditional mindset of the Confucian elite of Vietnam, even though he emerged into adulthood at a time when the Vietnamese state and its society were disintegrating in the face of the French imperial advance. In the crucial period of the Can Vuong ('support the dynasty') revolt of 1885 and the establishment of the French Protectorate, Phan Boi Chau divided his time between studying for the mandarin exams and engaging in various forms of patriotic activity. Thereafter, he dedicated his whole life to the objective of building a strong and effective resistance movement against the French.

Phan Boi Chau felt that the Vietnamese people were trapped between their own inertia and backwardness on one side, and the crushing power of the French on the other. Like other patriots who had witnessed the failure of the Can Vuong movement, he believed that resistance to the French could only succeed if the Vietnamese masses could somehow be mobilized. Like others of his class and generation, however, he was sure that the people as a whole could only be educated, and hence made politically aware, under the leadership of the traditional elite (Marr 1975: 16–17). The problem with this programme lay in the fact that the whole traditional Vietnamese political apparatus – from the monarch in Hué to village elders – had been co-opted into the French imperial system, through their establishment of a protectorate regime over the Nguyen dynasty. Although Phan Boi Chau recruited disaffected members of the royal family and court to his anti-colonial network, by the early 1900s it was apparent to him that the traditional Vietnamese elite – in his eyes the only conceivable lever that could raise Vietnamese society out of its torpor – had been fatally compromised by the protectorate system (Marr 1975: 17–19). As he put it in his prison memoir, he felt himself helpless before 'the distressing sight of the disintegration of the capital, the loss of the country, and the shame of lords who have become servants' (Marr 1975: 20).

It was in this situation that Japan's stunning victory in the Russo-Japanese war of 1904–5 burst upon his political consciousness. 'For me', he wrote, 'it was like a new and strange world opening up' (Marr 1975: 23). The guns at Port Arthur may not have disturbed the sleep of the mass of the Vietnamese people, but they did rouse such members of the intellectual elite as Phan Boi Chau from their Confucian dreams. Phan Boi Chau felt that the most important impact of the Japanese victory was its transformation of the world-view of the Vietnamese intelligentsia of his generation. Hitherto, their political debates had focused solely on the relationship between Vietnamese monarchy and the French Protectorate. Now they were able to place that local confrontation within the much wider global perspective of 'the competition and struggle between the Europeans and the Asians, between the white-skinned people and the yellow-skinned people' (Marr 1975: 23). Vietnam was but part of what was nothing less than a Darwinian struggle for racial survival.

Although Phan Boi Chau's practical attempts to hitch Vietnamese nationalist fortunes to Japan's power – by arranging for the education of selected Vietnamese youth in Japan and building Pan-Asian links – failed during the years between 1905 and 1911 (Marr 1975: 30–39), he was once again roused to action by news of the outbreak of the Chinese Revolution against the Manchus in 1911 (Marr 1975: 50). His revived dreams of a Pan-Asian alliance – headed by Japan and a newly liberated China – that would free Asia from colonial rule, was embodied in his *Modest Proposal for an Asian Alliance*, written at this time. China, however, collapsed in chaos soon after 1911, and Phan Boi Chau himself was arrested and imprisoned in Canton by an unsympathetic Chinese provincial governor (Marr 1975: 54). It was there, in 1914, while he was waiting for what seemed his inevitable extradition to French Indochina and subsequent execution, that he wrote his *Prison Notes*. They amount to a personal political testament and a meditation on the fate of Vietnam (Marr 1975).

Phan Boi Chau's efforts to build a nationalist movement and Pan-Asian anti-colonial network may have failed to get off the ground, but his contribution to the Vietnamese nationalist world-view was nevertheless of great importance. Even if his schemes were naive, he helped to give an international perspective to the Vietnamese nationalist struggle, and to place that struggle in the wider context of Asian anti-colonialism. Underlying his thinking there was also a marked sense of urgency – a fear that, in the global Darwinian struggle between the races, Vietnamese culture and identity might soon be extinguished altogether (Marr 1975: 39).

In this fear he was joined by his contemporary compatriot and fellow nationalist, Phan Chau Trinh (1872–1926). For Phan Chau Trinh, however, the main threat to Vietnam's cultural and political survival came from the monarchy and the mandarinate, not France or the West. In his famous 'Letter to the Government of Indochina' written in 1907, Phan Chau Trinh argued that it was the fossilized, corrupt and decadent mandarin system that had left Vietnam helpless before the French, and during the ensuing decades continued to preside over a Vietnam that had become 'like a sick man, dying from an incurable disease' (Nguyen and Huu nd.: 470). The one true service that France could have performed for Vietnam was to remove the traditional political system altogether and – on the basis of its own proclaimed 'civilizing mission' – lay the basis for fundamental reform and revival. Instead, the French had used the protectorate system to keep the Vietnamese people trapped inside the rotting hulk of the monarchy and the mandarinate. Phan Chau Trinh concluded in his letter that the French were deliberately using the protectorate to keep the Vietnamese in a state of weakness and backwardness – thus, as he put it in the Darwinian language of the time, 'making our race degenerate' (Nguyen and Huu nd.: 471). For Phan Chau Trinh, however, the solution did not lie in the weaving of Pan-Asian fantasies, but in a determined effort to challenge the mutually beneficial conspiracy of power and survival that bound together France and the mandarinate, and embark on a grass-roots programme of educational, social and political reform (Nguyen and Huu nd.: 471).

CHAPTER THREE

~·~

The Impact of Marxism-Leninism on the Anti-Colonial Movements of Southeast Asia, 1900–1940

By the beginning of the twentieth century, the colonial empires of Southeast Asia faced a growing dilemma. At the very time that Britain, France and the Netherlands were consolidating their respective empires in the nineteenth century, these nations were also transforming themselves into modern democratic states. The moves made by these empires at the beginning of the twentieth century to broaden imperial rule into a 'partnership' with Western-educated native elites, and to open up educational and welfare facilities in the Southeast Asian colonies, represented – in some cases rather lame – attempts to resolve this fundamental contradiction between the democratic principle that was beginning to form the basis for domestic politics, and the authoritarian principle of racial prestige that underpinned colonial rule.

This contradiction became even more acute during the course of the First World War. On the one hand, the importance of empire was made manifest: the resources of empire – not least the abundant man-power that could be recruited for the war effort in Europe and the Middle East – gave France and Britain the means to sustain their all-out global struggle against an intrinsically more powerful Germany. On the other hand, Britain, France and (from 1917) the United States tried, as democracies, to give a moral dimension to their cause by asserting as one of their basic war aims the granting of the right of national self-determination, or at the very least the right of 'autonomous development', to the various nationalities within the Austro-Hungarian and Ottoman Empires.

In the 1917 'Montagu Declaration', Britain began to apply these principles to its own Empire. The Declaration stated that British policy towards India would henceforth be based on 'the increasing association of Indians in every branch of the administration', and 'the gradual development of self-governing institutions with a view to the progressive realisation of responsible government in India as an integral part of the

British Empire' (Christie 1998: 83). This was, of course, a limited concession expressed in opaque language. It did, however, amount to both an acknowledgement of the extent to which Britain depended on Indian and imperial support in the war effort, and an acceptance of the general principle that the ultimate goal of imperial policy was to move towards 'responsible' self-government', albeit within the framework of the imperial structure.

It is not surprising, therefore, that when Germany and her allies were defeated in 1918, the most politically advanced colonial and semi-colonial regions should demand for themselves the same right to national self-determination that was given, for example, to Poland, Czechoslovakia, or Yugoslavia. The 1919 Paris Peace Conference was bombarded by demands for the recognition of the national rights of – among other peoples – the Arabs, the Indians and the Chinese. It was in this spirit that a group of Vietnamese patriots resident in France submitted to the French Government in 1919 a request for the recognition of basic rights for the people of Vietnam. One of the principle signatories of this remarkable document was a young Vietnamese who at this time used the pseudonym Nguyen Ai Quoc, and was later to be known as Ho Chi Minh (Ho Chi Minh 1994: 22–23).

This Vietnamese document is, in the light of later history, notable for the moderation of its demands. Although it asserted 'the sacred right of the people for self-determination', it did not request the immediate application of this principle to Vietnam. Rather, it laid claim to the intermediate rights of assembly, press freedom, increased educational opportunity, the application of the rule of law rather than rule by decree, the granting of amnesty for exiles (including Phan Boi Chau) and political prisoners, and the establishment of an elected colonial component in the French parliament (Ho Chi Minh 1994: 23). The fact that these demands were ignored, both by the French and the other Allied powers, was to have a fateful consequence for Southeast Asia, since Nguyen Ai Quoc was in 1920 to become a founder member of the French Communist Party, subsequently becoming an agent for the Comintern, or Communist International, and then in 1930 playing the key role in the creation of the Indochina Communist Party.

The colonial powers, particularly France and the Netherlands, failed seriously to apply the principle of self-determination – or to form a new relationship that would have replaced outright subjugation with some form of partnership – in their Asian colonies during the period following the First World War. This failure on the part of Europe's liberal democracies explains the attraction that Marxism-Leninism exerted over the generation of Asian nationalists who emerged at the end of the First World War. Marxism-Leninism's anti-imperial world-view, and its conviction that only socialism could truly liberate the colonial world and create a new, prosperous and just world order, attracted a following in Asia soon after the Russian

Revolution dramatized the ideology on the world stage. The disappointments of the decades between the wars created the conditions for the emergence of communist parties throughout Southeast Asia. In fact, the fundamental principles outlined by Marx influenced not only the communist movements of Southeast Asia, but also the nationalist movements of Southeast Asia as a whole. Marxism-Leninism's emphasis on the fundamental link between capitalism and imperialism on one side, and nationalism and socialism on the other, leaked out of the rhetoric of Southeast Asia's communist parties into that of anti-colonialist movements in general – and continued to do so till the 1970s.

THE MARXIST WORLD-VIEW

The Marxist-Leninist theory of imperialism evolved naturally from Marx's analysis of history and society. Karl Marx (1818–1883) was simultaneously a moral philosopher and a social scientist. His work compares the *actual* state of the vast mass of humanity through history – so obsessed with the everyday struggle for survival that they have neither the leisure nor the means to express their innate humanity in social or cultural terms – and the possibility of creating a new structure of society that would enable all of humanity to achieve its human potential. This underlying, almost utopian, quality in Marx's thought should not be ignored if Marxism's innate appeal to a generation of Southeast Asians is to be understood, even though it was progressively buried beneath what the Marxist writer Bertolt Brecht described as 'the dry, indecorous vocabulary of dialectical economics' (Brecht 1976: vol. 2, 225).

Marx, as a social scientist, attempted to uncover the fundamental laws underpinning human societies and their historical evolution. Following Charles Darwin, the natural scientist, Marx the *social* scientist argued that the basic structure of human societies was determined by the relationship between humanity and its material environment. The uncertainty of this relationship, and the scarcity of natural resources, inevitably necessitated a competition between humans for use and control of these resources. This competition, in turn, provided the dynamic for the development and change of societies through history: competition for resources inevitably led to inequality, with successful groups within society gaining control of a disproportionate share of these resources; societies would therefore tend to be divided into hierarchies of power and wealth, and this in its turn would lead to a diversification of status and economic function – in other words, to the creation of distinct 'classes'. It is for this reason that Marx argued that all societies except the most primitive – in which competition for resources had not yet become an issue – were class-based societies. Economic circumstances at any particular stage would favour a particular class, who – via their domination of the economy – would acquire surplus wealth that would enable them to dominate all aspects of that society. Consequently, the latter's political structure, social organization, culture and beliefs would reflect the interests and 'world-view' of that dominant class. There would, however, always be pressure and competition from below, from the less advantaged classes of society: a condition, that is, of perennial 'class struggle'. As underlying economic circumstances gradually changed, however imperceptibly, so the relative power of the competing classes would change, leading to new forms of class domination. This unending process of struggle between classes for control of wealth and power provided, Marx concluded, the basic dynamic for the evolution of human societies through history.

However, Marx argued that, from the seventeenth century onwards, a qualitative change began to affect western European societies. This change was initiated through a comprehensive 'rationalist' revolution that enabled humanity, first to understand, and then to dominate natural forces. This transformation of humanity's perspective on the world laid the basis for the scientific and technical revolution, and the revolution in commerce, production and administration, generally referred to as the 'industrial revolution'. Marx argued that this massive upheaval – an upheaval that for the first time gave human societies a chance to dominate their environment – did not spring simply from a revolution of the intellect. It was powered by a new class that had emerged within traditional feudal society: an urban class whose wealth was based on commerce and industry rather than land. Governed in its activities by the rational laws of profit and loss, and increasingly untrammelled by the restraints that bound traditional society, this 'bourgeoisie' harnessed the energies unleashed by this revolution in order to accumulate wealth and concentrate power to a degree unheard of in other societies.

This was the basis of the so-called 'capitalist' society that Marx described in his key work, *Das Kapital*. Marx's attitude to this new capitalist system was profoundly ambiguous. On the one hand, Marx the social scientist recognized that an industrial revolution, financed and driven by the bourgeoisie, was an absolutely necessary precondition for the creation of an economy that could overcome the problems of scarcity, and therefore could potentially meet the fundamental economic needs of all its members. Only capitalism could prepare the way for a world where humanity as a whole – not just a tiny proportion of it, as in previous societies – could achieve their full potential as human beings. On the other hand, Marx the moral philosopher was aware of the appalling human cost of this transformation: the uprooting and dislocation of entire communities, and the destruction of a traditional life that at least provided some consolation and dignity in a world of poverty.

The key point made by Marx in *Capital* was that the benefits of industrialization were not shared by the entire society. On the contrary, power and wealth were increasingly concentrated in a tiny bourgeois class, and traditional society's hitherto complex social structures were now simplified or 'rationalized' into a stark confrontation between a bourgeois or 'capitalist' class that 'owned' the economy, and the mass of people, collectively termed the 'proletariat', who had failed in the ruthless struggle of profit and loss, but whose labour powered the modern economy. The intermediate classes of shop-keepers and skilled artisans, known as the petite- or 'petty'-bourgeoisie, and the small-holding peasantry, were essentially remnants of previous traditional economies and societies, and were destined either to rise to the ranks of the bourgeoisie, or sink into the masses of the proletariat.

This new industrialized society was qualitatively different from previous, non-industrialized societies. However, its social structure was, like previous societies, based on class. As in all class societies, therefore, the class confrontation between a bourgeoisie who wished to engross all the benefits of the economy for its own use, and a proletariat who aspired to use the benefits of industrialization for the society as a whole, meant that the social structure was inherently unstable. This instability was sharpened by an underlying 'contradiction' between capitalism's productive power on the one side, and the mechanism of the market on the other. The streamlining of productive forces, driven by ever-intensifying competition, poured ever more goods into the market. At the same time, producers were forced to reduce costs in order to make their products more competitive. This led to the progressive cutting of wages, and thereby to the impoverishment of the very market on which the dynamism of production depended. This contradiction, in its turn, led to crises of overproduction, and cycles of boom and slump that would get worse at each cycle, since each period of overproduction would lead to yet another cutting of wage costs that would further impoverish the market. This fundamental flaw of capitalism, Marx predicted, would ultimately bring about the disintegration of the entire capitalist system.

The most significant 'contradiction' within capitalism, however, lay in the fact that the more successful the capitalist system became, the more it empowered the proletarian class that would ultimately produce an entirely new market and social structure. Capitalism created a mass labour-force, concentrated this labour-force in the towns and in the factories, dragged this labour-force out of the traditional and into the modern world, and forced it to become organized in the routines of industrial production. It therefore created the basis on which this work-force, or proletariat, would develop an awareness of the yawning gulf between its solidarity and potential power, and its actual status within capitalist society – as well as a consciousness of the difference between the intrinsic capacity of the industrialized economy to transform society, and its current use purely for the benefit of a tiny ruling class. The increasingly acute crises of capitalism would, therefore, eventually merge with the growing 'class consciousness' and political organization of the proletariat. This would culminate in the breakdown of the capitalist system, and its replacement by a new system. The new system would by no means destroy the industrial structures created by capitalism, but rather would use that industrial framework as the essential basis for a rationally-organized social system that would base production, not on profit, but on the needs of the whole society – that is, 'socialism'.

MARXISM AND IMPERIALISM

Marx did not view his prediction of the emergence of a socialist society as a vague prophecy or a utopian wish: he believed it to be the inevitable outcome of a comprehensive scientific explanation of the laws governing the structure and evolution of human societies. These same scientific laws, according to Marx, explained the modern phenomenon that was of most immediate interest to Asian anti-colonialists: namely, nineteenth century European imperialism.

In Marxist terms, imperialism was a natural outcome of the explosion of economic activity engendered by capitalism. The age-old desire to expand trading-links, generally seek new sources of raw materials and find new markets was now powered by all the strength and resources of industrialized society. Modern imperialism was not only 'pushed' by the laws governing capitalist competition, but also 'pulled' by the vast imbalance of power, particularly in the nineteenth century, between the industrialized and non-industrialized worlds. The bourgeoisie, moreover, had transformed the traditional state into the modern nation-state, which was not merely an expression of identity, but, much more importantly, an instrument of capitalist power and expansion. The bourgeoisie then used the power of the modern nation-state to force open and monopolize new markets and sources of wealth; consequently – within an astonishingly short space of time – European imperialism dominated the entire globe.

Marx's views on the nature of imperialism echoed his analysis of the impact of capitalism: if capitalism was a blind force driven by no moral imperative but by profit – which would nevertheless create the essential preconditions for the just and prosperous society of the future – so imperialism was a brutal but ultimately 'progressive' agent of history. Just as capitalism's creation of a mass proletariat was building the very class that would destroy and supersede capitalism itself, so imperialism – which was after all an extension of capitalism – was unwittingly summoning out of torpid traditional societies modern forces that would eventually challenge imperial rule. For example, Marx and Engels argued that the British were, in pursuit of their own economic interests, creating in India the basis of a modern economy, since, inevitably, Britain's search for new resources and markets meant that the forces of economic and social change were penetrating all aspects of traditional society, and undermining the legitimacy and authority of the structures and ideas that had held that society together (Marx 1975: 27). They cited, as an example of this effect, the fact that the Indian army and the Indian railway system created by British imperialism was uniting and in a sense empowering India in a way that had never before been the case (Marx 1975: 30–32).

While Marx held no illusions about the brutal impact of European imperialism on the traditional societies of Asia and Africa, he did – as a true child of the optimistic Victorian age – view European imperialism as a historically 'progressive' force in the long term. Later followers of Marx, benefiting from detailed analyses of the workings of nineteenth century imperialism, viewed its historical role in a different light. Although they accepted that imperialism could have the economic effect of 'jolting' traditional societies out of backwardness, they also pointed out that imperial powers often attempted to preserve intact the political and social structures of traditional society as a means of maintaining administrative continuity and social stability. The effect of this imperial strategy was to create a dual economy, in which a modern economic sector coexisted with a traditional sector that was not only untouched by imperialism, but was deliberately held in a condition of social and economic stasis.

LENIN: REVOLUTION, THE COMMUNIST PARTY, NATIONALISM AND IMPERIALISM

In the latter part of the nineteenth century, it appeared that Marx's predictions of ever intensifying capitalist cycles of boom and bust in Europe, leading to ever sharpening class confrontation between the bourgeoisie and the proletariat, had been avoided: first, through the expansion of empire and thereby the creation of new markets; and, secondly, through the ameliorating impact of 'bourgeois-democracy'. During this period, democratic rights were gradually extended to the lower classes within an expanding parliamentary system: partly as a result of this, social welfare legislation beneficial to the working-class, or 'proletariat', was put in place, and working-class organizations such as trade unions were able to operate more and more freely. All these developments halted the slide into increasing impoverishment and class alienation of the proletariat envisaged by Marx. This led many Marxists to conclude that the transformation from capitalism to socialism would not take the form of a revolution, but rather of an 'evolution', through which the embryo of socialism would naturally and relatively peacefully emerge from the shell of capitalism. In these circumstances, the task of 'social democracy' – that is, the organizations striving to bring about a socialist society – was to work within the existing 'bourgeois-democratic' parliamentary system, acting as a kind of pressure group promoting the interests of the working class, and thereby pushing society towards its inevitable socialist goal (Lenin 1902: 172).

This was the origin of the great twentieth century divide within Marxism between what was to become 'parliamentary socialism' on one side, and 'Marxism-Leninism' or 'communism' on the other. The key figure in this ideological split was Vladimir Ilyich Lenin (1870–1924), a leading Russian Marxist. Lenin argued that it was inconceivable that capitalism and the bourgeois class would voluntarily preside over their own demise through some kind of evolutionary process. It therefore followed that the 'ameliorative' actions of bourgeois democracy were designed precisely to 'blunt' working-class consciousness, and thereby perpetuate the capitalist system with a measure of working-class consent. The task of 'social democracy', therefore, was to maintain a clear distance from 'bourgeois democracy'. This meant actively affirming the separate class interests of the proletariat, the assiduous development among the proletariat of an awareness that their interests and those of the bourgeoisie were irreconcilable, and ultimately a recognition of the need to prepare for a *seizure* of power by revolutionary means (Lenin 1902: 231–38).

This view of the ultimate necessity of revolution raised the question – fundamental to an understanding of what was to be called 'Marxism-Leninism' – of the role of the leadership of the party that represented the interests of the proletariat. In immediate terms, Lenin argued that this party should avoid at all costs merely acting as a representative or ambassador of proletarian/working-class interests within the framework of bourgeois democracy. Such a party, even if it occasionally took a militant stand by supporting the occasional strike, would soon find itself 'buried' within the capitalist system (Lenin 1902: 174–78).

The position taken by Lenin – particularly in his polemical essay entitled *What is to be Done?* (1902) – was that a workers' party did not exist merely to promote the immediate or day-to-day interests of the proletariat. Rather, it should have a *long-term* perspective on the class struggle as a whole, and therefore be able to educate the working class to place their aspirations in the context of far broader historical developments. In effect the party of the working class should act as a force of history. This required that the party should be led by people who had an intellectual grasp of Marxist theory, and could use that overall theory to guide political practice. In the first instance, therefore, intellectuals from the bourgeois class – people like Marx and Lenin who had liberated themselves from their bourgeois class perspectives – would have to play a key educative role within the party. In a sense the ultimate task of the party was not to 'proletarianize' the intellectuals, but rather to 'intellectualize', in the first instance select members of the proletariat, but eventually the proletariat as a whole (Lenin 1902: 222).

The vital task of such a leadership was to understand that, although Marx had outlined the basic laws underlying the evolution of the class struggle, the global development of this class struggle was extremely 'uneven' and complex. While capitalism – via imperialism – had become a global phenomenon, there were within that universal force huge differences in relative stages of economic development, and thereby in the class structure of different societies. Moreover, the capitalist phenomena of nationalism and imperialism had an unpredictable impact on the relationship between classes at a global level.

This required an ability to understand the deeper historical forces at work behind political events, and thereby to harness or manipulate political circumstances and events precisely to 'progress' those deeper historical forces towards the ultimate goal of socialism. This in its turn required that the party of the working class be guided by a tightly organized, theoretically equipped, disciplined 'professional revolutionary' leadership (Lenin 1902: 222). This leadership would avoid, on the one hand, the temptation of simply working within the institutions of bourgeois democracy; and on the other, the temptation – based on the notion that historical developments could in a sense be 'pre-empted' – of encouraging terrorism and 'propaganda by the deed' in premature attempts at revolution (Lenin 1902: 222). Rather, a professional revolutionary leadership would *use* the institutions of bourgeois democracy, which were designed to preserve capitalism, precisely as a long-term means of 'disintegrating the system' (Lenin 1902: 207), Use of, or militant action against, the institutions of bourgeois democracy would depend on circumstances: likewise, class alliances – for example with parties of the peasantry or the petty-bourgeoisie – would be formed or rejected according to a calculation of the balance between short-term advantage and long-term developments.

Lenin viewed nationalism through the same theoretical prism. Like Marx, Lenin viewed the nation-state as a phenomenon of the capitalist system – a means of concentrating the power of the state to pursue the economic goals of the bourgeoisie. Additionally, by instilling a sense of patriotism in the respective working classes of nation-states, it divided the international working class and blunted class consciousness. On the other hand, both Marx and Lenin viewed the nation-state as a necessary and inevitable stage in the development of capitalism, the precondition of socialist society (Lenin 1914: 595). Equally, in the complex global situation, a distinction had to be drawn between the nationalism of imperialist states that oppressed other nationalities and colonial peoples, and the nationalism of those oppressed peoples. The struggle of the latter for 'national self-determination' may be led by the bourgeoisie of that oppressed nation; but the global effect of a national struggle of this kind would be to weaken the very imperial structures on which the survival of capitalism, and thus of nationalism, ultimately depended. In this complex and uneven international network of relations between classes and nations, once again a determination of the overall interests of the working class depended on a comprehensive theoretical perspective.

During the First World War, Lenin came to the view that imperialism was not simply an extension of the capitalist system, but was *the* primary driving force of capitalism (Lenin 1917). By the early twentieth century, wrote Lenin, the competitive dynamic within capitalism had weeded out or absorbed many smaller businesses, and created a new phase, 'monopoly capitalism', in which huge combines, linking industry, banks and commercial enterprises, competed for access to and control over a global market (Lenin 1917: 694–95). Since these combines were normally formed on a national basis – French, British, American and so forth – the concept of the 'national interest' of imperial powers was virtually identical to the actual economic interests of these huge monopolies. In this late imperial era, international political competition and capitalist economic competition had become one and the same thing (Lenin 1917: 721–22). The natural outcome of such global economic competition was the ultimate form of competition – world war.

LENIN, THE RUSSIAN REVOLUTION AND THE BIRTH OF ASIAN COMMUNISM

Thus, for Lenin, the First World War was the inevitable outcome of the inherently competitive-antagonistic dynamic within capitalism itself. As such, this 'capitalist civil war' offered an ideal opportunity for parties representing the proletariat to unite the working class of Europe, and convert the war between imperialist nations into a revolutionary struggle between classes. Initially, however, the war served to demonstrate the capacity of imperialism to generate patriotic feelings among the working classes of France, Germany and Britain, and thus *divide* rather than unite the European proletariat (Lenin 1917: 723). More than this, the most prominent European social-democratic parties succumbed to patriotism, rejected Lenin's class perspective, and supported the war efforts of their respective countries. It was at this point, indeed, that we can place the beginning of the definitive split between parliamentary social democracy, or the 'Second International', and what was to be known as 'communism', 'Marxism-Leninism' or the 'Third International'.

The long duration of the war, however, placed a huge strain on European societies and economies. In these circumstances, it was perhaps inevitable that the economically weakest and politically least developed of the Great Powers, Tsarist Russia, should by 1917 have cracked under the strain. Russia was a country in a process of transition to industrialization, and large parts of its society were still in a pre-industrial, feudal phase of development. Although it had a large empire, it was at the same time economically dependent on French and English capital – virtually a 'colony'. In these semi-developed circumstances, autocracy remained supreme, and the structures of bourgeois democracy had hardly emerged. As Russia floundered in leaderless turmoil through 1917, Lenin argued that the party of the Russian proletariat – what was called the 'Bolshevik' or, later, Communist Party – should by-pass the weak parliamentary institutions of bourgeois democracy, form a 'worker-soldier-peasant' alliance within the local ad-hoc 'soviets' or councils that were springing up throughout Russia, and, under Bolshevik leadership, use the soviets to seize power (Lenin 1919: 473).

The events of the Russian Revolution were to have an enormous significance for the subsequent development of Asian communism. In classical Marxist terms, Lenin's seizure of power was premature: 'revolution' could only occur in highly developed industrialized societies where a mass proletariat, forming the vast majority of the population, would – as it were – 'burst through' the outdated and restraining shell of capitalism. Lenin's justification, however, was that levels of proletarian class consciousness were not mechanically linked to levels of economic development: on the contrary, it was often precisely a working class that was undergoing the early traumas of industrialization – as in Russia or parts of Asia – that was likely to have the sharpest class consciousness (Lenin 1919: 474). Lenin's most important argument, however, was that the now-universal phenomenon of capitalism had to be understood as a whole. Seen from this global perspective, the Russian Revolution was not an isolated event, but rather the seizure of a 'bridgehead' in the advance towards world revolution (Lenin 1919: 474–75). For Lenin, the Russian Revolution only had validity as part of a far wider process: Russia had been the weak link in an interconnected chain of global capitalism that would now unravel.

In the meantime, Russia – thrust as it was into the temporary centre of world revolution – had the duty to create the bases for a socialist system that would eventually supersede capitalism globally. First and foremost of its tasks was the creation of the 'Union of Soviet Socialist Republics' (USSR) or Soviet Union, which – in theory at least – replaced the old Tsarist Empire with a voluntary federation of sovereign and socialist nation-states. The overall development of these disparate states, which were at different stages of economic development, was to be guided by a new party representing the interests of the working class throughout the Soviet Union – the Communist Party of the Soviet Union, or CPSU. The USSR was to serve as a 'living prototype' of a non-antagonistic, mutually-supportive, socialist and international system (Stalin 1947: 197–98).

The other organization created after the Russian Revolution was the 'Comintern' or Communist International, whose first meeting took place in the Soviet Union in March 1919. This organization was designed to coordinate all international revolutionary forces, oppressed classes and oppressed nations in the global struggle against capitalism (Lenin 1920: 655). The task of this new Communist ('Third') International, or Comintern, was outlined in one of the most influential of all Lenin's writings, *Preliminary Draft of Theses on the National and Colonial Questions*, published in 1920. The fundamental point made by Lenin in *Theses* was that there was a natural link of interest between the proletarian revolutionary movements of the industrialized world, and the 'national-liberation' movements of the colonized world. Both had an interest in overthrowing the joint forces of capitalism and imperialism (Lenin 1920: 655). It therefore followed that the primary task of the Comintern was to build international revolutionary solidarity between these two struggles. Crucially, this demanded that the communist parties of the imperialist nations should aid national-liberation movements in their respective colonial areas (Lenin 1920: 656–57). In general, although these colonized areas were part of the global capitalist web, they were themselves passing through the transitional phase between feudalism and capitalism. It therefore followed that the Comintern should generally aid the emergence of 'bourgeois-democratic' classes and institutions within these colonized areas (Lenin 1920: 657).

The point that Lenin was making was that, while the bourgeois were now playing a 'reactionary' role in the industrialized world by attempting to hold back socialism, in the more backward colonial areas they were generally still playing a 'progressive' role in historical terms, by pushing for national independence and the destruction of the native feudal class on which colonial rule depended. Lenin urged that the forging of revolutionary alliances in the colonized areas should depend, above all, on a proper appraisal by the Comintern of local circumstances and stages of economic development. In particular, he warned against the temptation to support anti-colonial movements whose aim was *not* to push their societies forward into the modern world, but rather to *revert* to the traditional, pre-colonial world (Lenin 1920: 657).

The Comintern's objective, in other words, was to build alliances of all revolutionary classes in the colonial regions. The composition of these class alliances, and the decision as to whether a particular class could play a revolutionary role at a particular time, would depend on a 'correct' appraisal of the global and local situation at that time. Apart from the proletariat, no class was *inherently* revolutionary, nor was any other class *inherently* reactionary: the revolutionary or reactionary status of a class depended on ever-shifting historical circumstances. Lenin insisted, therefore, that the Comintern should never allow the proletariat of any country – however embryonic and weak – to be completely merged or swamped within a class alliance whose membership would be ever-shifting. A separate communist movement, ultimately embodied in the formation of a communist party, should protect the specific interests of that working class, and at the same time seek to 'revolutionize' anti-colonial elements, and guide them to the ultimate goal of 'victory over capitalism' (Lenin 1920: 658).

It is no exaggeration to state that Lenin's *Theses* formed the foundation stone for Southeast Asian communism, and that subsequent debates over strategy took place within the boundaries of the basic ideological framework that Lenin provided. Nguyen Ai Quoc – later called Ho Chi Minh – explicitly cited the *Theses* as the 'path which led me to Leninism', and converted him to communism. 'At first', he conceded

> 'patriotism, not yet communism, led me to have confidence in Lenin, in the Third International. Step by step, along the struggle, by studying Marxism-Leninism parallel with participation in practical activities, I gradually came upon the fact that only socialism and communism can liberate the oppressed nations and the working people throughout the world from slavery' (Fall 1968: 24).

THE COMINTERN AND THE DEVELOPMENT OF ASIAN COMMUNISM, 1921–1927

The years following the formation of the Comintern saw the practical development of a global revolutionary network and an increasingly complex debate within the ideological framework established by Lenin, who died in 1924. The centre of the Asian revolutionary network was Canton in South China (see map 1), which in the early 1920s became the base for a revolutionary alliance formed between the Chinese Nationalist Party – or Kuomintang (KMT), as it was then known – and the Chinese Communist Party (CCP), which had been set up in 1921. This alliance was directed against the colonial powers, who had a substantial grip on the economy and even parts of the territory of China. It was also directed against the still formidable bastions of feudal society in China, and against the elements of the Chinese bourgeoisie that supported the colonial-capitalist system. Canton was also, however, the headquarters of a large Comintern network that extended throughout East and Southeast Asia. It was during the 1920s and 1930s that Marxist-orientated revolutionary organizations were set up in Southeast Asia, among them the three main communist parties of the region – the Partai Kommunis Indonesia (PKI) in 1921, the Indochina Communist Party (ICP) in 1930, and the Malayan Communist Party (MCP), also in 1930.

Lenin had hoped that the Russian revolutionary 'bridgehead' would stimulate revolution in the European heartland of capitalism. As it became increasingly evident, in the years immediately after the First World War, that this hope would not be immediately realized, the Comintern's attention turned to Asia. In Lenin's last article, 'Better Fewer, but Better', written in 1923, he asserted that the 'Imperialist war', the Russian Revolution, and the dismal failure of the colonial powers to make good on their general rhetoric of 'self-determination', had created a new revolutionary environment in which the traditional societies of Asia had been 'dislodged from their groove' (Lenin 1923: 853). The Soviet Union's pivotal position between the capitalist and colonized worlds, and between Europe and Asia, had energized Asia and created two hostile camps, with the combined revolutionary camp of the working class in the developed world and of the 'masses' of the colonized world gradually encircling the shrinking capitalist camp (Stalin 1947: 192–93, 195).

Although this notion of 'two camps' was based on the idea of a global *class* confrontation, there was also in Lenin's vision of 1923 the sense of a definite *geopolitical* shift in the locus of world power. Lenin wrote:

'... the upshot of the struggle will be determined by the fact that Russia, India, China etc., account for the overwhelming majority of the population of the globe. And it is precisely this majority that, during the past few years, has been drawn into the struggle for emancipation with extraordinary rapidity, so that in this respect there cannot be the slightest shadow of doubt what the final outcome of the world struggle will be. In this sense, the complete victory of socialism is fully and absolutely assured' (Lenin 1923: 854).

This geopolitical perspective was shared by Asian communists of the time. In the course of the 1920s, China had become revolutionized. At the same time in the Pacific, Britain drew away from its hitherto close ties with Japan, and appeared to be drawing closer to the United States. In these circumstances, it is not surprising to find the key Southeast Asian communist writers of this period – Nguyen Ai Quoc/Ho Chi Minh of Vietnam, and Tan Malaka of Indonesia – forming an almost pan-Asian view of an impending confrontation between the 'White' and 'Yellow' races in Southeast Asia (Ho Chi Minh 1925: 134; Gunn 1995: 9, 41–42).

It was the Comintern that had the task of co-ordinating international revolutionary strategy. In this early period, the main problems that it faced were those of harmonizing the interests of the working-class revolution in the capitalist world and of the 'national-liberation' movements in the colonized world. On this topic, a significant shift can be detected between the position of Lenin and that of his successor in the Soviet Union, Joseph Stalin. Whereas Lenin had stated that only those anti-colonial movements that were 'progressive' – that is, not seeking to re-establish the pre-colonial *ancien regime* – should be supported, Stalin asserted that Comintern support for anti-colonial movements should depend, not on their internal, 'subjective' characteristics as inherently 'progressive' or 'reactionary', but on the extent to which they 'objectively' threatened global capitalism. In other words, a reactionary anti-colonial rebellion could be supported if it severely weakened the position of a colonial power. This emphasis on the international as opposed to the local revolutionary perspective may have been ideologically justifiable. It did, however, raise the question, which was to become crucial for the world communist movement in ensuing decades, of *who* was to determine the overall international revolutionary perspective (Stalin 1947: 194–95).

A study of Nguyen Ai Quoc/Ho Chi Minh's writings during the early- to mid-1920s makes clear his unease concerning the actual as opposed to theoretical operation of this revolutionary alliance between the White working class and the Asian masses. For all the rhetoric of 'revolutionary solidarity' and the repeated emphasis of the Comintern on the duty of the communist parties of Europe to aid revolutionary activity in their respective colonies, Nguyen/Ho could not help observing that European communist parties gave a low priority to the colonial regions, and were often lukewarm in their support for anti-colonial activity (Ho Chi Minh 1960: 12–14, 144). While in class terms, he argued, imperialism provided the basis for solidarity between the equally oppressed White proletariat and Asian masses, it also encouraged a sense of racial distinction between the 'superior' Whites and 'inferior' colonial peoples. So long as this 'race consciousness' prevailed over 'class consciousness', imperialism would continue to recruit the White working class to suppress the colonial peoples, and, conversely, recruit Vietnamese, Senegalese or Indian troops to aid European wars (Ho Chi Minh 1960: 75–78). This race/class dilemma remained a focus of concern for Nguyen/Ho in the years leading up to the formation of the Indochina Communist Party.

The other critical problem for the Comintern in the co-ordination of anti-colonial revolution was the question of the class composition of revolutionary movements. In 1925, Stalin outlined the three major 'stages' of revolution in the colonized world. In colonial regimes of the first stage, under which industrial development was still negligible, a local bourgeoisie would hardly have emerged: in such circumstances, 'revolutionary elements' in general should encourage the creation of a 'mass' anti-colonial movement without distinction between classes (Stalin 1947: 216–17). In colonial regimes of the second stage, under which the economy has been substantially developed, an urban bourgeoisie and a small working class would have emerged: in this situation, the bourgeoisie would split between an element working within the imperialist economy, and a 'national-bourgeois' element seeking to remove alien domination of the economy, and therefore supporting the national revolution. Here, a distinct communist party should be formed to represent the present and future interests of the working class, and this party should build an anti-colonial alliance with the national bourgeoisie; always ensuring, however, that this alliance be kept firmly on the revolutionary path (Stalin 1947: 216–17). In colonial regimes of the third stage, under which the economy and industry was highly developed, the bourgeoisie as a class would become increasingly locked into the global capitalist-imperialist economy, and would therefore cease to be revolutionary. In these circumstances, the communist party and the working class should play a leading, co-ordinating role in the revolution, and should seek to win to their side all disaffected classes – particularly the peasantry – and eventually seize power in the manner of the Bolshevik Revolution of 1917 (Stalin 1947: 217–18).

Although Stalin's 'three-stage' programme became the general 'line' in Southeast Asia, Tan Malaka's blueprint for revolution in Indonesia, published in 1925 under the title *Naar de Republiek Indonesia* ('Towards an Indonesian Republic'), reveals the problems of applying this line in practice. Tan Malaka (1897–1949), the foremost Indonesian communist intellectual of this period, had played a key role in the early years of the Partai Kommunis Indonesia (PKI), or Indonesian Communist Party, and he subsequently worked as a Comintern representative in Canton. His party *apparatchik* position did not, however, affect the originality of his thinking. Tan Malaka was among the later followers of Marx to challenge Marx's notion that imperialism – intentionally or otherwise – *necessarily* forced the social and economic modernization of colonized areas. In Indonesia, according to Tan Malaka, Dutch capitalism coexisted with indigenous feudalism through the operation of a dual economy. All of the social, political and economic traits of traditional society had been left undisturbed – had, indeed, been reinforced in political terms – by Dutch colonialism, while the capitalist economy thrived in a number of more or less completely separate enclaves (Gunn 1995: 12, 15, 19). Consequently, Dutch colonialism had had a marginal impact on the feudal class structure of Indonesia, and no significant bourgeois class had emerged.

According to Stalin's 'three-stage' formula, it was questionable whether in such a society a communist party should be formed, let alone be allowed to play a leading role. But Tan Malaka argued that, in the absence of an effective bourgeoisie, a communist party had the duty of leading and forcing along the revolutionary momentum (Gunn 1995: 27). The appropriate revolutionary strategy, he continued, was that of building a mass movement based on the varied discontents of the different sections of society. In this respect, he urged – against the view of Lenin – that *all* anti-colonial elements, even those such as Islam that were inherently anti-communist, should be incorporated into the mass movement (Gunn 1995: 4). The revolution itself, wrote Tan Malaka, should not take the bald form of a seizure of power by the communist party – a move that could easily be countered, leaving the party to be isolated and destroyed by the Dutch – but a process of 'encircling' the colonial regime through strikes, demonstrations, and other forms of mass action that would eventually and cumulatively disintegrate the colonial economy (Gunn 1995: 30–32).

Tan Malaka then addressed the question of how – once the colonial regime had collapsed – Indonesia could pass through the industrial-capitalist phase towards socialism. His fundamental premiss was that a liberated Indonesia would have to link itself to the global socialist system created by the Soviet Union (Gunn 1995: 25). More immediately, however, the Indonesian Communist Party would have the task of co-ordinating economic and political policy, and controlling the 'commanding heights' of the economy. Beneath this, small-scale capitalism – the life-blood of economic development at this stage – would be encouraged, while thoroughgoing land reform would enable the peasantry to gain agriculturally viable plots of land (Gunn 1995: 20–21). In essence, therefore, a competition would be set up between the socialist principle embodied in the communist party's planned control of the commanding heights of the economy, and the 'bourgeois-capitalist' principle of private property that would operate at the lower levels. Unlike the ruthless economic competition of pure capitalist societies, this would be a peaceful competition, in which the socialist principle of co-operation and mutual benefit would gradually predominate throughout the economy (Gunn 1995: 19–20, 26).

In his analysis, Tan Malaka was one of the first communist thinkers of Asia to tackle the basic question: How can we achieve industrialization – the essential precondition of a socialist society – without first experiencing the injustices and class struggle of capitalism? Tan Malaka thus brought to Asia the notion that the capitalist phase of development could occur within a planned framework controlled by the communist party, if not by-passed altogether.

SOUTHEAST ASIA AND THE ERA OF COMMUNIST DOGMATISM, 1927–1935

In 1926 and 1927, premature and badly organized rebellions in Java and Sumatra headed by the PKI – rebellions which Tan Malaka had strenuously opposed – were easily crushed by the Dutch. In 1927, too, growing tension between the Kuomintang (KMT) and the Chinese Communist Party (CCP) culminated in a massacre of communists in Shanghai, the near destruction of the Chinese Communist Party in South China, and the expulsion of the whole Comintern network from Canton.

Thereafter, the Comintern and the Soviet Union were forced to realign their international strategy and readjust the ideological underpinnings of that strategy. The failure of the Indonesian communists was easily ascribed to 'adventurist' elements who had failed to build the base for sustained revolutionary activity. It was agreed by the Comintern that the Chinese Communist Party, on the other hand, had allowed itself to be too closely merged into, and subordinated to, the KMT-CCP alliance, and had thereby lost its class perspective and its understanding that any alliance with the bourgeoisie must be temporary and strictly conditional (Bukharin 1928: 232–33).

The basic class 'lesson' that was drawn from these events was that while the phase of 'bourgeois democracy' – that is, the phase of liberating the economy and the nation from foreign control and economic backwardness – was necessary for colonized nations, the bourgeoisie of these nations were 'ambiguous' and 'vacillating' in their world-view and therefore in their allegiances (Third International 1928: 238). They hovered, as it were, between the global revolutionary and capitalist camps, and, while they might at a particular stage find that their interests coincided with global revolution, they would – as capitalism steadily entrenched itself in the colonized states – decisively move into the capitalist camp, and be satisfied with moderate reform and limited independence within the overall capitalist system.

The new political 'line', therefore – elaborated both by the Comintern and by Stalin himself – was that, first and foremost, communist parties and movements all over the world should heighten their 'proletarian conscious-ness'. They would thereby become more acutely aware of the dangers of being mired in the institutions of the 'bourgeois-democratic' period, and of forgetting that the goal of communists was to guide and push society towards the ultimate goal of socialism (Stalin 1953: 241–42). In the colonized world, it was thus, paradoxically, necessary for the communist parties to take over leadership of the nationalist movement, and themselves to guide societies through the anti-colonial and bourgeois-democratic phases. The bourgeoisie must be effectively by-passed, although the communist movements could form a broad class alliance – strictly under the leadership of the communist parties – with the peasantry, the 'petty-bourgeoisie' and the 'broad masses of the exploited' (Third International 1928: 239).

This political line was echoed by the 'theses' of the newly-formed Indochina Communist Party in 1930. Not only was the Indochina Communist Party to take the lead in anti-colonial activity, but it also aimed for a 'soviet'-style revolution to establish a 'worker-peasant and soldier' government, after which a radical reform programme would be initiated (Ho Chi Minh 1930: vol. 2, 147–48). Unlike Tan Malaka's prescription for a post-revolutionary Indonesian society, this reform programme would not merely have involved the seizure of the commanding heights of the economy hitherto controlled by colonial capitalism, but also a much more thoroughgoing state control and regulation of the economy as a whole. What was envisaged, in other words, was a rapid, forced-pace march towards industrialization and socialism simultaneously, with central planning of the economy enabling the Indochina Communist Party to compress severely – or even by-pass altogether – the phase of property-owning capitalism (ICP 1930: 110).

MARXISM-LENINISM AND THE CONUNDRUM OF THE PEASANTRY

The Indochina Communist Party (ICP) was formed in 1930, after the impact of the world economic slump had begun to hit Southeast Asia. In the course of 1930 and 1931, the party tried to co-ordinate the storms of upheaval and protest that had spontaneously broken out throughout Vietnam, particularly in the north-central regions. ICP leadership undoubtedly gave coherence and organization to these rural and urban protests. On the other hand, attempts by the ICP to follow their own recently formed political 'line' – by setting up local worker-peasant soviets and waging simultaneously a *nationalist* struggle against the French and a *class* struggle against the landlords and land-holding peasantry – had the predictable effect of destroying patriotic unity and dividing the Vietnamese peasantry. In the wake of the brutal repression of these rebellions, the ICP was decimated. It was not able to recover its strength and coherence for nearly a decade.

During the ICP's years in the wilderness, two prominent figures of the party, Truong Chinh and Vo Nguyen Giap, produced an in-depth study of the culture, discontents and aspirations of the Vietnamese peasantry, published in 1937 under the title *The Peasant Question* (Truong Chinh and Vo Nguyen Giap 1974). This work was in many respects a remarkable study. Marx himself had mistrusted the peasantry as an instinctively reactionary social class, always ready to lend a hand in the repression of the working class. As a Russian, Lenin could not but have a greater awareness of their revolutionary potential. But the tendency of Marxism-Leninism had always been to categorize and prescribe policies for the peasantry, never truly to attempt to understand peasant culture and consciousness. It was, in fact, precisely a dogmatic approach of this kind that had led the ICP to antagonize a significant section of the peasantry in the 1930–31 revolts, with such disastrous consequences. In 1925, Tan Malaka, acutely conscious as he was of the vast cultural gulf that divided the Western-educated Marxist intellectuals from the peasantry, had urged communists to make the effort to 'descend to the people' (Gunn 1995: 1–2). *The Peasant Question* represented just such an effort.

Truong Chinh and Vo Nguyen Giap began their study with the recognition that the peasantry had played a – perhaps *the* – decisive role in the major upheavals of modern history, the foremost of which were the French and Russian Revolutions. The conundrum of the peasantry lay in the fact that their historical role had been uneven: after 'blazing' into action at key moments, they had then relapsed into torpor (Truong Chinh and Vo Nguyen Giap 1974: 8). Herein lay the dilemma for revolutionaries in countries where the peasantry formed the vast majority of the population. While on the one hand the political consciousness of the peasantry was unreliable and unpredictable, on the other hand they were the absolutely indispensable key to revolutionary success (Truong Chinh and Vo Nguyen Giap 1974: 20, 25).

The solution to the riddle of the peasantry, according to *The Peasant Question*, first required an understanding of the peasant mentality. The peasantry were dispersed and isolated: as such, they lacked the basic precondition for a collective consciousness, or organization for collective action. In these circumstances – and given their often precarious economic conditions – their instincts tended to be deferential, supersititious, suspicious and fearful of change, respectful of hierarchy and tradition, and, in sum, fatalistic in their outlook (Truong Chinh and Vo Nguyen Giap 1974: 7–8, 21–22, 25). Their economic circumstances varied widely, ranging from the substantial peasant-proprietor who was virtually indistinguishable from the minor landlord, to the landless 'vagabond' who could only scrape a living by seasonal work in the towns and on other people's land. Given this fact, a unified peasant 'consciousness' could not be defined. Like the bourgeoisie, peasants 'vacillated': their 'revolutionary' and 'reactionary' instincts were determined by a wide and ever-shifting set of variables. The one constant feature, however, was their attachment to land: to the basic idea, that is, of private property. As such, of course, their basic outlook tended to be non-socialist (Truong Chinh and Vo Nguyen Giap 1974: 19–21).

On the other hand, peasant life was continually faced by almost unendurable hardships, some of which sprang naturally from the hazards of agrarian life, but most of which were imposed on them from outside (Truong Chinh and Vo Nguyen Giap 1974: 9). *The Peasant Question* set out systematically to categorize these impositions: the taxes of all types – direct and indirect – levied by the colonial government; the rent demanded by landlords; the cycle of debt in which vast numbers of the peasantry were enmeshed; the unequal impact of an alien colonial legal system whose operations they did not understand; and the myriad 'obligations' that were imposed on them by a corrupt system of local government that was dominated by local landlords.

Truong Chinh and Vo Nguyen Giap recognized that the communists could not hope to win over the peasantry unless they gained a true understanding of the inner mechanisms of peasant life. Above all, this would involve an understanding of peasant culture, and a realization that, while that culture may not articulate its discontents in the language of Marxism-Leninism, it had its own time-honoured and often hidden ways of expressing its grievances. By way of example, Truong Chinh and Vo Nguyen Giap cited the continuing popularity amongst Vietnamese peasants of the famous epic poems, *The Tale of Kieu* and *The Warrior Wife's Lament*. Although these poems were valued as expressions of national culture in general, it was also certain that elite Vietnam read these poems in entirely different ways from the peasantry (Truong Chinh and Vo Nguyen Giap 1974: 102). At one level, these poems could be read as exemplary tales of female submission and loyalty; at another level, however, they could be understood as expressions of resentment against the injustices inflicted upon women and other oppressed elements by feudal society. The basic condition of Vietnamese women as depicted in these poems could be understood as a metaphor for that of the peasantry as a whole: both were dominated by the sense that they had no control over their fate (Truong Chinh and Vo Nguyen Giap 1974: 101). The basic task of communists, therefore, was to give the peasantry 'confidence in themselves'; a confidence that would enable them to seize control of their own destiny (Truong Chinh and Vo Nguyen Giap 1974: 14). If this could be achieved, the peasantry could indeed become an 'invincible force' in Vietnamese history (Truong Chinh and Vo Nguyen Giap 1974: 21–22),

*   *   *

The above analysis provides some insight into the appeal that Marxism-Leninism must have exerted on young intellectuals in the late colonial era. It was not just that Marxism-Leninism provided a coherent framework for anti-colonialist activity: to those living in societies that had for centuries been trapped in deference, custom and tradition, it also transmitted the liberating news that their backwardness and subjugation was not the result of an immutable 'fate', but of the operation of clearly discernible human forces that could ultimately be challenged and defeated:

Today everywhere, from the hundred-storeyed cities
Over the seas, cross-ploughed by teeming liners
To the loneliest villages, the word has spread
That mankind's fate is man alone . . .' (Brecht 1976: vol. 2, 234).

CHAPTER FOUR

~~~~~~~~

Southeast Asian Nationalism Before the Second World War: The Ideological Foundations

The broad outlines of the socialist analysis of politics and history described in the previous chapter provided the ideological underpinnings for nationalist thinking in Southeast Asia up to, and beyond, the period of independence. The non-communist Southeast Asian nationalists focused their interest in socialism on its general explanation of capitalism and imperialism, not on the tightly-defined doctrines of Marxism-Leninism and the 'Third International'. At the same time, Southeast Asian communist movements – particularly the Vietnamese communists – gradually came to accept the central importance of nationalism as a political force.

The core appeal of the general Marxist analysis of politics lay in the fact that it provided a framework for the linking of nationalism, socialism and democracy – a linkage which dominated Southeast Asian nationalism up to the 1970s, albeit in many different ways. These links were succinctly explained in Jean Jaurés' *Studies in Socialism*, published in English in 1908. Although Jean Jaurés died before the split between the Second and Third Internationals at the end of the First World War, his essentially 'pre-Leninist' views on Marxism remained influential among some later non-communist nationalists in Asia, Sukarno in particular. Jaurés accepted that the nation-state and nationalism were phenomena of the capitalist era – instruments through which the bourgeoisie in different states could concentrate political power in pursuit of their respective economic interests. He also argued, however, that the socialist revolution of the future should not take the form of a 'rupture' – the break-up, that is, of the economic, social and political institutions created by capitalism – but should, rather, be a 'conquest' by society as a whole of these institutions (Jaurés 1908: 13). The bourgeois nation, therefore, should not be obliterated by socialism; instead, a bourgeois phenomenon should be transformed into a socialist phenomenon, and the 'socialist nation' should provide an immediate and practical means through which the first stages of socialist society could be

45

built (Jaurés 1908: 6–8). In the same way, the institutions of 'bourgeois democracy' and the abstract concepts of democracy that had been promulgated in the bourgeois era should not be pushed aside, but should instead be given their complete meaning and value through the addition of socialist principles. Socialism, concluded Jaurés, was the 'full and decisive interpretation of the Rights of Man' (Jaurés 19–20).

The details of the debates surrounding the nationalist idea in Asia in general, and Southeast Asia in particular, were determined by the specific circumstances and realities of European imperial power. As noted in chapter 2, Chinese reformers like Kang Yu-wei and Liang Ch'i-ch'ao agonized at the turn of the century over the measures that would need to be taken to enable China to modernize and strengthen itself in the face of outside threats. Coming as they did from the traditional intellectual elite, their initial plans for reform were strictly based on the notion that change should come 'from above': it was hoped that, with the creation of new, Westernized, institutions of government, and a transformed and Westernized education system, the process of reform would gradually percolate down in an orderly manner to the population as a whole.

The miserable failure of the Chinese reform movement led Liang Ch'i-ch'ao (1873–1929) to embark in 1902 on an entirely new train of thought. In his essay 'The Renovation of the People', Liang Ch'i-ch'ao acknowledged that the 'renovation' of Chinese civilization required something far more fundamental than the reform – however radical – of institutions: what was needed was a force that would mobilize the entire society. The key to what Liang Ch'i-ch'ao described as the 'renovation of the people' was to be the same force that had united and energized the people of Europe, and given them the dynamic impetus that enabled them effectively to conquer the world: nationalism (Liang Ch'i-ch'ao 1902: 221–22). For China as for elsewhere, Liang Ch'i-ch'ao claimed that the innate strength of nationalism as a unifying and mobilizing force lay in the fact that it could be built on an already existing sense of identity, inherited culture and tradition, and a shared historical experience. On this sure basis, a China whose energies and masses were concentrated by a conscious policy of nationalism could confront with confidence the challenges and ideas of the modern world (Liang Ch'i-ch'ao 1902: 223).

Two points of particular importance emerge from this analysis. The first is that Liang Ch'i-ch'ao did not treat the phenomenon of nationalism from the point of view of inherent 'rights', but rather from that of power. Although the notion of the 'right to self-determination' is implicit in Liang Ch'i-ch'ao's thinking, his interest in nationalism focused on the right to national liberation, not as an end in itself, but as a *means* of mobilizing the whole society and dragooning the masses into the modern world. This, in turn, implied a very different view of culture and tradition from that held by the previous generations of Chinese intellectuals. For the previous generations, Chinese traditional culture and values either served as an essential, living foundation on which all reform would have to be based; or, for the radicals, as an encumbrance from which a reformed China would have to be liberated. The new generation of nationalists, however, did not view traditional culture and values primarily as inherent phenomena, either to be built on or rejected; they were treated, instead, as symbols – as 'badges of identity' – that could unite the people.

The acknowledged 'father' of Chinese nationalism, however, was Dr. Sun Yat-sen (1866–1925). Sun Yat-sen did not receive a traditional elite education, and in this respect his ideas represent a decisive break with the classical foundations of Chinese political thought. Despite his undoubted importance in the history of modern Chinese – and indeed Asian – political thought, it has to be acknowledged that his ideas lacked a clear and consistent theoretical foundation, and often displayed a sublime indifference to contemporary Chinese realities. These weaknesses were noted by his contemporaries, Chinese and foreign alike.

As with all his Chinese contemporaries, the starting point of Sun Yat-sen's political thinking was the task of renovating China. Unlike the turn-of-the-century moderate reformers, however, Sun urged that the first task was the removal of the Manchu dynasty, and indeed the complete elimination of the control over the Chinese political system exercised by the 'alien' Manchus. For Sun Yat-sen, national and democratic goals were inextricably linked, since the removal of the dynasty would both restore China to the ethnic Chinese or *Han* people – the essential nationalist task – and, at the same time, pave the way for the creation of 'people's sovereignty', or democracy. National sovereignty, therefore, implied popular sovereignty. But, Sun Yat-sen added, such popular sovereignty or democracy would be meaningless unless it involved a general improvement in what he called 'people's livelihood'. He therefore advocated a general plan for the redistribution of land via compensation, and an equalization of land holdings (Sun Yat-sen 1905: 228). Although his plans changed over time, this general programme of 1905 – which linked the acquisition of national independence, the establishment of a republic based on popular sovereignty, and the promotion of social justice through the redistribution of wealth – remained more or less constant factors. This broad notion that national, democratic and social objectives should be inter-locked had a profound influence on the development of Southeast Asian nationalism.

Another striking general feature of Sun Yat-sen's political thinking was his view that democracy could only be introduced into China by stages. In the first stage of the national revolution, a period of military rule would 'eradicate' the traces of the previous regime; in the second period of so-called 'tutelage', the military and political leadership would gradually introduce democratic structures, starting at the local levels; and in the third and final stage, a fully democratic system would be installed (Sun Yat-sen

1905: 229). After the Russian Revolution, the structure of the Leninist-style communist party provided Sun with an exemplar of the kind of political 'tutelage' that he had envisaged; and, in 1921, he modelled his renovated Kuomintang nationalist party on this communist prototype. Sun Yat-sen never, however, abandoned his essentially non-Marxist political schema, which he felt to be appropriate to the condition of China and Asia. Indeed, Sun Yat-sen saw nationalism and anti-imperialism as the dominating forces in the global revolutionary storm that had been unleashed by the Russian Revolution, and that had been given concrete political shape by the KMT-CCP-Comintern alliance formed in Canton in the early 1920s (Ssu Yu-teng 1969: 266).

It would be quite wrong, however, to imagine that all Asian thinkers embraced the concept of nationalism, and the ideological paraphernalia that accompanied it, as beneficent. In Indonesia during the inter-war years, for example, a fierce debate took place among Islamic scholars concerning the desirability of supporting the nationalist idea. While some agreed that Islamic and nationalist forces had a common cause in challenging *kafir* (unbeliever) colonialism, more orthodox elements looked upon nationalism as unacceptable idolatry (*shirk*) of a purely human creation – the nation – at the expense of the divinely ordained community (the *umma*) that united all Muslims, irrespective of race or place (Noer 1979: 255).

Perhaps the most systematic Asian criticism of nationalism came from the Indian writer and philosopher Rabindranath Tagore, who in 1917 published a book entitled *Nationalism*. Tagore's analysis approached the subject of nationalism from a position that was far removed from the essentially Western-influenced approach of many other Asian intellectuals of the time. His *point d'appui* was not political or economic, but ethical, religious and cultural.

Rabindranath Tagore did not view European global dominance simply in economic terms. He drew a distinction between the push of European economic and political power on one hand, and, on the other, the attraction exerted globally by the universal values underpinning European civilization. Tagore did not suggest that European civilization was in any way intrinsically superior to those of Asia; he merely pointed out that the intellectual and philosophical revolution that Europe had undergone in the modern era had enabled it to breathe new life and meaning into its core cultural values. Asian and Indian civilizations, by contrast, had not experienced this type of moral or ethical revolution. The ethical foundations of India's civilization, for example, remained trapped in a sclerotic caste system that had, in effect, become a system of racial discrimination (Tagore 1917: 3–12, 97–98). It was for this reason that, while Asia and India might seek to resist the imposition of European power, the more enlightened elements amongst their elites were irresistibly drawn to the values of a civilization that appeared to have universal validity. For

Indian thinkers, Britain's beneficial values included not only the (fundamentally Christian) notion of ethical freedom and equality, but also the more modern values of the rule of law, moral responsibility and altruism (Tagore 1917: 110).

However, continued Tagore, the West had gained global dominance, not through moral power, but through power alone. The organizing body for this exercise of power was the nation; the generating spirit was nationalism. European nationalism had recruited all the scientific, technological and industrial gains that had emerged from its revolution in ideas, and harnessed them to the ideological conception of the nation. For Tagore, the modern nation was not a naturally evolved, living organism, but, as he put it, 'the aspect of the whole people as an organized power' (Tagore 1917: 110). Such a constructed nation did not just ignore the core values that supported Western civilization: in the name of 'national rights' and 'national interests', it created an ideological framework that justified behaviour that was the very antithesis of these core values. Moreover, although nationalism invoked 'roots', 'culture' and 'tradition', in practice the past was merely uprooted from its ethical foundations and used to power the national idea (Tagore 1917: 42). A living tree was hacked out and shaped into a battering-ram. It was with horror that Tagore saw Asia – instead of absorbing the European values that could enrich and bring new life to their own civilizations – trying to recreate the very ideological force that had enslaved and demeaned it. For Tagore, the greatest danger of nationalism lay in the fact that, while it 'rediscovered' and idolized traditional cultures and civilizations, its imported ideological framework, in fact, irreparably alienated populations from the true ethical foundations of their own civilizations (Tagore 1917: 77–78, 81, 112–21).

Tagore's views, along with those of Mahatma Gandhi and Swami Vivekananda, had a profound influence on the Javanese intellectual Dr. Soetomo (1888–1938). In 1908, Soetomo became one of the founders of Budi Utomo (roughly, 'High Endeavour'), an organization created by members of the Javanese elite, primarily to encourage educational, cultural and social reform. Budi Utomo served as a prototype for more overtly political organizations in ensuing years. Soetomo's political views were not outlined systematically, but they were expressed generally in his *Reminiscences (Kenang-kenangan)* of 1934, and in a series of essays collected in 1932, and given the general title *Poespa-Rinontje* ('a garland of flowers'). He did not so much reject nationalism outright, as attempt to subsume it within a much wider cultural and political programme for Indonesia. His primary concern was that the core moral values of Indonesian society – and when Soetomo referred to Indonesia, his main focus was undoubtedly on Java – should be retained, and strengthened, during the process of rapid change that the country was undergoing. His fear was that, in the rush of youth to gain a Westernized, technically orientated education, these moral values – indeed moral values generally – would be discarded, and Indonesia would become a spiritually bereft, inferior imitation of the West (Veur 1987: xlvii).

Soetomo argued that it was the duty of the educated elite to sustain this broad moral perspective, and disseminate it through society as a whole. Although Soetomo's thinking was ultimately less radical than Kartini's had been (see chapter 2), he agreed that this project required above all the development of a sense of social responsibility and altruism among the privileged indigenous classes (Veur 1987: 241). Guided by such spiritual *satriya* (responsible aristocrats), the whole of society could be bound together in a sense of common obligation and common purpose. Soetomo compared such a society to a *gamelan* orchestra, in which each sector of society would contribute to the harmony of the whole (Veur 1987: 236, 262).

Soetomo's fundamental aim, therefore, was not so much the encouragement of an anti-colonial confrontation with the Dutch colonial power, but the development within Indonesian society of what the Indians called *satyagraha*, and the Indonesians *daya kebatinan*: namely, 'inner spiritual power' (Veur 1987: 246–49, 258). Of course, this almost exclusive concern with the nature of Indonesian society, rather than with the colonial relationship, meant that Soetomo's vision tended to ignore the reality of Dutch power. But if Dutch power was ultimately based on White racial 'prestige', and if such prestige depended on a notion of *moral* superiority, then clearly the development of what might be called 'moral self-confidence' among Indonesians would alter the colonial relationship. Colonial self-confidence in the right to rule would evaporate, and the way would be paved for *merdeka* (national freedom) in the fullest sense: a freedom that would be spiritual as well as merely political. For Soetomo, the achievement of *Indonesia Merdeka* ('Free' Indonesia) was dependent on a much broader goal – the creation of *Indonesia Mulia* (a 'Noble' Indonesia).

Against this background of the general Asian debate over nationalism, it is worth examining the impact that the nationalist idea had on two very different Southeast Asian societies: the fully colonized Netherlands East Indies, and the 'semi-colonized', semi-independent state of Siam.

THE BASIS OF INDONESIAN NATIONALISM: SUKARNO AND HATTA

In the course of the 1920s and 1930s, although the Indonesian nationalist movement itself was generally weak and divided, and unable to make much political headway in the face of the intransigence of the Dutch, the core of a national ideology and strategy was nevertheless created. Two Indonesian political activists played a key role in the nationalist debate of this time:

Sukarno of Java (1901–1970), and Mohammad Hatta of Sumatra (1902–1980). During this period, the ideological differences between these two were more a matter of emphasis than of substance. The main point on which they agreed – and where they differed from more conservative figures such as Soetomo – was that true independence could not, and indeed should not, be gained via negotiation for some form of 'partnership' relationship with the Dutch.

Moreover, if Soetomo virtually ignored the Dutch colonial presence in his quest for spiritual self-strengthening within Indonesian society itself, for Sukarno the colonial relationship, and the need to base Indonesian nationalism on an anti-colonial perspective, lay at the very heart of his political thinking. This was evident in his first major polemic, entitled *Nationalism, Islam and Marxism*, written in 1926, after the communist and Islamic sections of the nationalist movement had split, and just before the communist PKI destroyed itself by launching premature and badly organized local rebellions (see chapter 3). Sukarno asserted that the success of the nationalist movement absolutely depended on the building of unity between the different ideological elements of the Indonesian nationalist movement: and that the key to such unity was the common focus on anti-colonialism (McVey 1969). He pointed to the alliance in China between Sun Yat-sen's KMT and the Chinese Communist Party as an example of how nationalist and communist elements could unite in a common anti-colonial purpose (Feith 1970: 357–58). He conceded that there were fundamental ideological differences between Marxism and Islam, but argued that the Islamic rejection of the principle of usury accorded with the Marxist objective of ending the system of 'surplus-value' that formed the basis of the capitalist economy. In other words, according to Sukarno, both Marxism and Islam were fundamentally anti-capitalist, and therefore anti-colonialist. Moreover – whatever their differences – Marxism and Islam shared a common purpose against a colonial power that was not only oppressive in racial and economic terms, but that also effectively subjugated Islam to Christianity (Feith 1970: 359–60).

In 1930, Sukarno comprehensively and systematically outlined his political philosophy in the defence speech that he delivered in Bandung, where he was facing the charge that the party he had formed in 1927 – the Partai Nasional Indonesia or PNI – was planning to overthrow the colonial regime by 'subversion' and force (Paget 1975). It is true that Sukarno, in this speech, had to balance his desire to assert his political views with the need to defend himself against the charge that he had behaved 'illegally'. But although this may have forced him to moderate some of his views – particularly on the whole question of 'armed struggle' against the Dutch – the fact remains that the overall views expressed in this speech, and indeed the imagery that he invoked, were repeated in different ways throughout his political career.

The centrepiece of the speech – delivered in Dutch, and later translated into Indonesian – was an analysis of imperialism. While Sukarno conceded that imperial conquest was a general feature of human history, he nevertheless argued that the character of modern European imperialism was qualitatively different. In general, he based his anti-colonial views on the Marxist theory of imperialism (Paget 1975: 9–11). He differed from orthodox Marxism, however, in his analysis of the impact of imperialism on a colonized society such as Indonesia. Although he accepted that imperialism had created the lineaments of a modern economy in Indonesia, he insisted – as had Tan Malaka a few years earlier – that this modernization had made little impact on the indigenous economy (Paget 1975: 26–29). Indeed, he added, the purely exploitative nature of Dutch imperialism meant that all sections of Indonesian society – from the labourer to the small-holding peasant and even the embryonic native bourgeoisie – had been steadily impoverished (Paget 1975: 35–41). Sukarno's basic point, therefore, was that capitalist-style colonialism did not – as Marx and Engels had anticipated – 'jolt' the native economy out of its subsistence torpor, and create new classes and greater class differentiation. Rather, class distinctions ceased to have any significance as the entire nation was impoverished and 'proletarianized' (Paget 1975: 78).

It was therefore a central tenet of Sukarno's that the concept of 'class struggle' was irrelevant in the Indonesian context. Just as the tyranny and injustice of the capitalist system stimulated 'class consciousness' among the proletariat in the West, so Sukarno argued that imperialism was stimulating 'national consciousness' in Indonesia and the colonized world (Paget 1975: 96–101). Suffering and impoverishment had united the people in a general sense of injustice, and reawakened the old folk yearnings for a 'saviour' – whether it be the *ratu adil* ('just king') or *Prabu Djajabaja* ('Prince Djajabaja') of pre-Islamic culture, or the *Mahdi* or 'expected one' of Islam – who would liberate them and initiate a new golden age (Paget 1975: 43–44, 47). This reconnection with the past, moreover, was no mere passive expectation: the memory of a glorious past, and the experience of a dismal present, had united and energized the people to struggle for a better future. This sense of the continuity of Indonesia's culture and history had become the essential source of the 'secret power' (*kekuatan rahasia*) of Indonesian nationalism, and the key to developing 'the spirit of the masses' or *semangat rakyat* (Paget 1975: 70, 116).

Sukarno implicitly disagreed with Marx and Engel's view that pre-colonial Asian cultures had become in some way fossilized. Sukarno asserted, on the contrary, that pre-colonial Indonesian civilization had had an inner dynamic and capacity for natural economic evolution – an evolution that had been stifled, not advanced, by Western colonialism (Paget 1975: 80). Imperialism, by stifling the 'natural' tendencies of evolution within indigenous society, had held Indonesia in a state of economic and social backwardness. Sukarno also asserted – as had Rizal in the Philippines more than a generation earlier – that the mystique of imperial rule was sustained by a deliberate cultivation of the sense of the 'inherent' racial inferiority of non-European races. This mystique of 'prestige' necessitated a continual undermining of the self-confidence of the native population (Paget 1975: 59, 91). Likewise, the imperialist regime was driven, by its instinct for self-preservation, to emphasise the differences within Indonesia: between regions, classes and religions (Paget 1975: 86).

Sukarno's nationalist strategy was based on these basic characteristics of imperial rule. The first and obvious response to imperialism's 'divide and rule' tactic was to insist upon national unity above all things: a unity that would override class, regional, religious and ideological differences. Just as important, however, was the need to rebuild the self-confidence and the self-reliance of the people as a whole: this required the mobilization of the entire people in a mass movement inspired by *semangat rakyat* or 'the spirit of the masses' (Paget 1975: 62–65). Like Liang Ch'i-ch'ao, Sukarno saw the drawing of the masses into the political arena primarily as a process of national empowerment. It naturally followed that Sukarno viewed any form of political co-operation with the imperial power, or engagement in any negotiating process, as not only futile but psychologically damaging. For Sukarno, the creation of a nationalist movement was not only a means to an end – complete independence – but an end in itself. The very process of building such a mass movement, and the development thereby of a sense of unity and power, were essential means of instilling self-confidence and self-reliance in a subject people. The inevitable deals, betrayals and disappointments of bargaining with the colonial power would vitiate this nascent *semangat rakyat* (Paget 1975: 93).

The nationalist movement, therefore, was for Sukarno a struggle for national self-discovery and self-empowerment, not a weapon of negotiation with the colonial power. Independence was not something that could be haggled over in piecemeal deals. The only possible answer to imperialism was total, unfettered national freedom. In his defence speech, Sukarno cited the views of the Italian nationalist Joseph Mazzini and the Irish Republican martyr Erskine Childers that independence, total independence, was the primary goal: only after this had been achieved could discussion begin on the ideological foundations of an independent Indonesia (Paget 1975: 49, 54). Like these nationalist activists and thinkers, Sukarno saw the nation as a living organism and a spiritual force. The nationalist movement, therefore, had the primary task of 'reviving' an already-existing entity and 'restoring' its spiritual power (Paget 1975: 53). This required the restoration of complete independence and complete unity.

Sukarno was careful, however, not to imply that armed force was required to achieve this goal. Here Sukarno turned to the 'Second International' socialist movement in Europe as a model. Just as the social-democratic parties of Europe – including that of the Netherlands itself – had built up a working-class party and ancillary working-class organizations within the legal framework of bourgeois democracy, so, Sukarno argued, a mass nationalist movement could steadily 'enlarge its sphere of authority' within the colonial area without either cooperating with colonial rule, or, on the other hand, providing the colonial authorities with an excuse to suppress or weaken it (Paget 1975: 67, 73–74). Ultimately Sukarno – to a degree like Soetomo – saw the basic issue as one of self-confidence and moral authority. As the nationalist movement gained in self-confidence, so the moral authority that lay behind colonial rule would drain away, and the colonial power would find itself weakened by the growing contradiction between its economic imperatives and its liberal and democratic values.

Mohammad Hatta belonged to the same nationalist generation as Sukarno. Hatta and Sukarno – along with Soetan Sjharir – were to become the main ideological guides of the 1945–49 Indonesian Revolution, and the founders of the independent Indonesian state. Although, after 1945, the political perspectives and general world-views of Sukarno and Hatta began to diverge – and this divergence contributed not a little to the post-independence instability of Indonesia – during the 1920s, there were great similarities in their general political philosophies and strategies. Their analyses of imperialism were similar, and they agreed on the strategy of 'non-cooperation' with the colonial power, and on the need to develop a sense of 'self-reliance' among the Indonesian people. However, there were between them, even in the pre-war period, differences of emphasis, of nuance, that are worth examining.

Hatta and Sukarno had a shared view that struggle and conflict lay at the heart of human history; and, moreover, that it was this conflict – this 'dialectic' of history, as Marxists called it – that provided the dynamism for change and progress. However, they had arrived at this shared view by different routes. Sukarno's vision of this dynamic turbulence was not explained in systematic terms. Rather – as in his defence speech of 1930 – he tended to invoke images from Java's pre-colonial religious mythology, particularly those relating to the mysterious and unpredictable powers lying underneath Java's own volcanic landscape (Paget 1975: 120–25). Above all, it was the Hindu god Krishna of the *Bhagavad Gita* who encapsulated in his words and deeds the confrontation of – and at the same time the balance between – on the one side, the operation of the disruptive forces determining human destiny, and on the other, the natural inclination to social harmony (Paget 1975: 94–95). The starting-point of Mohammad Hatta's political philosophy was a similar view that 'human society is ruled by the general law of conflict' (Hatta 1926: 38). However, his historical perspective was influenced, not just by Marx, but by other philosophers of the standard European tradition, ranging from Heracleitus of ancient

Greece to the nineteenth-century German philosopher, G.W.F. Hegel (Hatta 1926: 36–38).

Hatta's notion of the operation of the 'dialectic' (the progressive resolution through history of the confrontation between opposing forces and ideas) formed the basis for his analysis of imperialism. Like Sukarno, he accepted the basic Marxist position on the capitalist origins of the phenomenon of European imperialism. However, whereas orthodox Marxism emphasised the fundamental divide between capitalists of all races on one side, and oppressed classes of all races on the other, one can see in Hatta's thinking at this time a tendency to give greater significance to the *racial* divide between the White civilizations of Europe and the Non-White civilizations of colonized Asia and Africa. From this perspective, Hatta attached great importance to Japan's defeat of Tsarist Russia in 1904–5, and to Turkey's national resurrection following the break up of the Ottoman Empire in 1918 and Turkey's defeat of Greece in 1919–22 (Hatta 1923: 17–24). For the orthodox Marxist, these were victories of essentially reactionary states that had the incidentally 'progressive' effect of weakening global imperialism. For Hatta, they had a far greater significance: they were signs of a reawakened Asian civilization. In focusing upon this concept of a fundamental confrontation between civilizations, Hatta was more of a Hegelian than a Marxist. Like Hegel, he believed that civilizations embodied ideas. For Hatta, the confrontation between Europe and Asia was not simply a matter of race or economics: European civilization encapsulated the 'idea' of an innately individualistic, competitive approach to economic behaviour, while Asian civilization embodied the 'idea' of social and economic cooperation (Hatta 1930: 139).

It followed from this world-view that Hatta regarded the relationship between Indonesia and Dutch colonialism as inherently antagonistic. It was from this objective viewpoint that Hatta supported the line that the Indonesian nationalist movement should not cooperate or in any way 'associate' itself with the colonial power (Hatta 1926: 49–51). Sukarno shared this viewpoint, but his perspective was essentially *subjective*: for him, the primary value of non-cooperation lay in the fact that it was the key to developing Indonesian unity, self-confidence and self-reliance.

On the question of the independence strategy of the Indonesian nationalist movement, Hatta – like Sukarno – used the example of the Irish nationalist movement that had gained independence from Britain after the First World War. The different examples from that movement that they chose to highlight, are, however, significant. Sukarno chose Erskine Childers, the intransigent and romantic patriotic figure who was prepared to plunge Ireland into civil war rather than accept a truncated Ireland or a limited independence. Hatta, by contrast, focused upon the united *Sinn Féin* party of the period before its fatal divisions – which in 1918 won a massive electoral victory and then, instead of negotiating with Britain for independence, proceeded to set up the institutions of an independent Ireland as if British rule did not exist. This was for Hatta a model of the desired outcome of the peaceful non-cooperation strategy (Hatta 1930: 130)

Whereas Sukarno placed his main emphasis upon the building of a mass movement, Hatta focused on the guiding role, within the nationalist movement, that would have to be played by intellectuals, particularly those that had received an education in Europe. Just as Lenin had stated, in *What is to be Done?* (see chapter 3), that only intellectuals could liberate themselves from the limited perspectives of a particular class and thus gain a general perspective on the class struggle as a whole, so Hatta argued that Indonesian students in Holland, who had acquired a privileged view of the workings of imperialism both from the colonized and the metropolitan viewpoint, could understand its structure and its global significance (Hatta 1928: 211). Above all, they had the chance to escape from what Hatta called the 'colonial hypnosis': that notion of White racial superiority from which Asia would have to liberate itself in order to become truly free (Hatta 1928: 212–13, 244).

THAILAND: SOCIALISM, NATIONALISM AND DEMOCRACY

The Kingdom of Siam, later known as Thailand, was the only Southeast Asian country that was able to retain its independence during the colonial era. The reasons for this have been endlessly argued over, and can probably be summed up as a combination of good government and good luck. In the final period of colonial expansion in the last half of the nineteenth century, Britain's primary strategic interest was focused on Burma, which lay on the eastern frontier of British India, while France's priority was the Vietnam-Indochina region. By the end of the nineteenth century, Anglo-French colonial rivalry had been superseded by their common interest in restraining German ambitions in Europe; under these circumstances, an independent Siam formed a useful buffer – a sliver of independent Asia 'as thin as a piece of silk', as Liang Ch'i-ch'ao put it in 1896 – between the British and French spheres of influence.

Siam also, however, had the good fortune to be ruled, from the late eighteenth century onwards, by an astute and outward-looking dynasty. The primary explanation for the ability of the Chakkri monarchy to preserve Siamese independence during a period of imperial expansion lay in its capacity to make timely concessions to the imperial powers, while at the same time building the base for a modern administration and armed forces. Using educational opportunities available in Europe, a new Western-educated administrative elite was created, which was fitted into a state structure that had been reorganized along European lines.

However, despite these remarkable achievements, Siam was forced to pay a heavy price for its survival. The 'timely concessions' that it had to make to

Britain and France involved the ceding of large chunks of territory on its borders, and the surrender of a measure of sovereignty in the area of foreign trading relations and legal control over resident European foreigners. Furthermore, the top layers of the administration depended on a number of foreign advisers. Siamese independence was precarious and conditional, and her real status could have been described as 'semi-colonized'.

It is this background that helps explain the so-called 'Revolution' in Siam of June 1932, though the immediate stimulus was undoubtedly the drastic impact of the world depression, triggered in 1929, on Siam's economy. In the decades before 1932, Siam's Western-educated administrative elite increasingly resented the absolute control over policy exercised by the monarch and a small clique of favourites. For this new Westernized class, the system of absolute monarchy not only denied them the right to participate in decision-making, but – almost more importantly – it was also a humiliating symptom of Siamese backwardness. Along with a desire to democratize the political system along Western lines, there was also undoubtedly among this elite a nationalist aspiration to end what was seen as Siam's semi-colonial status and its vulnerability to Western interference and intervention, and – through the thoroughgoing modernization of its political system and society – to enter into the ranks of the 'civilized' nations (Thak 1978: 37).

In June 1932, a small faction of army officers and civilians calling itself the 'People's Party' seized power. They forced the monarch to acquiesce in the creation of a new system of government, in which the monarchy would play only a constitutional and ceremonial role, and affairs of state would be directed by the administrative class, temporarily acting on behalf of the people as a whole. In theory, this was a democratic and constitutional revolution along European lines, with royal sovereignty replaced by the principle that, as the constitutional agreement of December 1932 put it, 'sovereign power emanates from the Thai people' (Thak 1978: 98–99). In practice, a period of 'tutelage' was regarded as necessary – one during which the political elite that had seized power were to undertake reforms in welfare and education that would eventually enable the people as a whole to exercise their sovereignty (Thak 1978: 55).

The more radical elements of the 'People's Party' – influenced as they undoubtedly were by Marxist ideas – saw democracy and social welfare as completely interrelated. The most eminent of the former was Pridi Panomyong, who, in March 1933, proposed the introduction of a new national economic policy. Briefly, this would have involved the purchase by the state of all productive land, and the take-over by the state of most sectors of the economy. This nationalized economy would then have been run on the basis of central planning, and the population in general – with the exception of some who worked in specialized sectors – would effectively have become government employees who received state salaries and state-provided welfare and education, but who could be moved from job to job according to the general needs of the economy and the seasonal requirements of agriculture (Landon 1968: 265–66, 271–72, 274, 276–77). Although such a programme was manifestly socialist in its intent, Pridi Panomyong pointed out that it was not 'communist': the plan paid no attention to the issue of class; the state would not expropriate the land, but would give full compensation to property-owners in the form of government bonds; and the plan drew a clear distinction between the public sphere of the economy, and the private sphere of family life and the ownership of homes (Landon 1968: 272, 282–85).

Despite Pridi's disclaimers, the more conservative elements in the People's Party considered the plan to be essentially communist in its assault on the principle of private property. Not only was the plan rejected, but in April 1933 an 'Act Concerning Communism' was introduced, making it illegal to advocate 'the total or partial abolition of the right of private property' on the basis of the 'communist' principle that such property belonged to 'the community' or 'the state' (Landon 1968: 251–52).

Pridi subsequently made clear that the plan was based on a generally Marxist – though not specifically communist – analysis of Siamese society: in particular, the notion that Siam's 'semi-colonized' status meant that an imperialist-capitalist foreign-dominated modern economy existed side by side with a feudal indigenous political system and economy (Thak 1978: 58). The economic plan, therefore, was to be the centre-piece of a general strategy designed to modernize the economy, and at the same time develop a self-reliant and increasingly self-sufficient nation that could free itself from foreign economic control (Landon 1968: 280). The socialist task of providing for the welfare of all the people would have gone hand in hand with the nationalist task of *mobilizing* the whole population into a system where work would be directed to social welfare and national power rather than private profit (Landon 1968: 268, 276–77).

Though Pridi's plan was plainly utopian, it is important to note that many of its basic premises were part of the common currency of political thinking at that time – and mirrored the widely-held notion that there was an inextricable link between nationalism and socialism. Many Asian national-ists, for example, would have accepted Pridi's argument that the socialist principle, with its concern for public welfare, was more in tune with the spirit of nationalism than was capitalism, which was based on the notion of the primacy of private interest (Landon 1968: 273). More basic than this, however, was a general sense – particularly in the aftermath of the economic crash of 1929 – that the global capitalist system was entering a stage of terminal decline, and would sooner or later be replaced by a more rational, efficient and socially just system based upon social and economic planning.

Although Pridi Panomyong's socialist world-view was Western-inspired, he based his analysis of society upon traditional Buddhist principles, specifically upon the proposition that human society was held together by 'attachment' or desire – a desire at the more exalted levels for power, wealth and status, and at the more humble levels for freedom from hunger, disease and destitution. This attachment contributed to the 'impermanence of society': a situation in which societies were governed by an inner law of competition, anxiety and antagonism (Thak 1978: 58). Given that this state of 'impermanence' and instability was generated by 'desire', it followed that impermanence was greatly exacerbated in a system like capitalism that was based on private property and the pursuit of private interest. Orthodox Marxism saw the fundamental antagonism of capitalist society as the class divide between the property-owning bourgeoisie and the property-less proletariat. By contrast, Pridi described the general condition of the people in a private property-owning society in classically Buddhist terms: as an antagonism, not between classes, but between selfish desire that was generated by the concept of individualism and private interest on one side, and the concept of social welfare and social harmony on the other (Landon 1968: 292–93). What he emphasized was not so much a population's overall condition of misery or poverty, but rather the gap between their aspirations for permanent happiness and economic sufficiency, and the *impermanence* of any happiness which might be fleetingly achieved, but can be destroyed in a moment by bad weather, disease, accident or sudden death (Landon 1968: 264). Pridi's 'Buddhist socialism' was not designed to create a Buddhist utopia, but rather to reduce the psychological state of anxiety created by impermanence, thus giving a measure of security, and thereby spiritual contentment, to the population.

CHAPTER FIVE

Intellectual Responses to Colonialism Between the World Wars

In a speech delivered in 1928, the young Mohammad Hatta made the point that, for a colonized society, every aspect of life was 'politicized'. Culture in general, education, literature, social relations, family relations – all were permanently overshadowed by the overwhelming fact of the colonial relationship (Hatta 1928: 206–8). Thus any action in everyday life took on a political significance – even, paradoxically, an attempt to live a private life as if the colonial situation did not exist.

Nevertheless, there were in the years between the First and Second World Wars, Asian and Southeast Asian thinkers who, while they could not ignore colonial realities, tried to consider the future of their societies from a broad perspective that was as much cultural as it was political. In Southeast Asia, two of the major thinkers to take such a broad perspective were Pham Quynh in Vietnam and Soetan Sjahrir in Indonesia, their somewhat different approaches being shaped by the particular colonial circumstances they experienced.

PHAM QUYNH: CONSERVATIVE REFORMER

One of the most influential Asian examples of the cultural approach was provided by the Chinese intellectual Hu Shih, a Western-educated writer and academic who taught at Peking University during the inter-war years. Hu Shih's views on China represented an unusual mixture of cultural radicalism and – to a degree – social conservatism. He pointed out that the 'debate' between traditionalists and modernizers was in a sense irrelevant: neither the imposition of, nor resistance to, cultural change could be determined by the fiat of the intellectuals. Change was occurring through an infinitely complex social and cultural transformation: by 'inches and drops', as Hu Shih put it (Hu Shih 1919: 255). Fundamental upheaval in China meant, argued Hu Shih, that Confucianism – deprived of the social system that it had sustained – had simply, whether one liked it or not, become irrelevant (Hu Shih 1919: 253). In this environment of rapid and irresistible change, the task of the intelligentsia was not to prescribe this or that social or political solution, but to prepare Chinese society *as a whole* for the new world with which they would have to engage (Hu Shih 1919: 254). This required the creation of a 'new culture' based, not on the intricate classical Chinese literature and language that had dominated – and fossilized – Chinese education for millennia, but on a modernized and 'upgraded' version of a Chinese vernacular literary tradition that was embodied in novels, Buddhist literature, popular poetry and folk tales (Hu Shih 1922: 256). In short, Hu Shih advocated a thorough-going 'democratization' of Chinese culture as the essential precondition for coping with social and political change.

The eminent Vietnamese intellectual Pham Quynh played a major role in a similar linguistic and literary reform movement in Vietnam in the inter-war period. To an even more marked extent than Hu Shih, however, Pham Quynh's social and political outlook combined a reforming approach to literature with a traditionalist approach to politics.

During the inter-war period the French in Indochina failed to carry through any consistent plan for political reform, and relatively liberal periods were invariably followed by periods of repression. The problem of framing a consistent programme of political change was made particularly difficult for the French by the complexity of the colonial structure they had created in Indochina. In Laos and Cambodia, France had instituted a 'protectorate' system which enabled it to exert an overall control while maintaining intact the traditional systems of government. A similar French protectorate had been established in 1884 over the Vietnamese (or 'Annamite' as it was then called) monarchy in Annam (central Vietnam) and Tonkin (north Vietnam). The southernmost Vietnamese region of Cochinchina, however, was directly administered by the French as a colony of France. Thus, within the single nation of Vietnam, two opposed colonial systems and colonial 'philosophies' were applied at the same time. In Cochinchina, the policy of 'assimilation' intended – through the medium of a French administrative and educational system, the use of the French language, and the injection of French political values and culture – to create what would in effect be an Asian extension of France, peopled by 'brown Frenchmen'. In the protectorates of Annam and Tonkin, however, the policy of 'association' entrusted responsibility for political, social and cultural development to the indigenous monarchy and mandarinate, but within the overall framework of the French protectorate and global imperial system.

By the mid 1920s, France had decided, however, that the Vietnamese monarchy was effective neither as a system of political control, nor as a vehicle for gradual political and social change. During the early years of the century it had proved to be politically unreliable, since it had often acted as a focus for anti-French nationalist discontent. In the years after the First World War, the now-quiescent monarchy was increasingly seen by politically-conscious Vietnamese as a puppet of the French: as such, it lost all national credibility and thereby – so far as the French were concerned – its central role in the French colonial strategy. With the death of Emperor Khai Dinh in 1925, therefore, a new Convention imposed upon the Annamite court by the French effectively transferred political and economic responsibility directly to the French protectorate, confining the authority of the monarchy to court and ritual matters. The apparatus of Vietnamese government was maintained, but it was now directly controlled by the French *résident-supérieur* in Hué (Mus 1954: 314–16).

While the French laid the blame for the failure of the protectorate system on the monarchy, the monarchy itself ascribed equal if not greater blame to the French. Emperor Khai Dinh's personal testament of 1925 – a traditional summation of the successes and shortcomings of his reign – accepted that the Vietnamese monarchy and mandarinate had failed to adapt their conservative system to a rapidly changing world. On the other hand, he accused the French themselves of permitting – through their policy of making French education and Western ideas widely available to young Vietnamese, both in Vietnam and in France itself – the importation of destructive ideologies that had seriously destabilized the institutions and values of traditional Vietnam. In so doing, France had opened the floodgates to anarchic forces that would eventually overwhelm both the monarchy and the French protectorate (Mus 1954: 322). Throughout, the tone of this document – the valedictory statement of the last Vietnamese monarch to live entirely 'within' the traditional culture – was highly pessimistic, and its prescriptions for the future were curiously opaque, and even contradictory. On the one hand, in true traditionalist fashion, it urged at all costs the maintenance of *tôn-miêu*: continued respect, that is, for the tombs of the dynastic ancestors, and, by extension, for the institution of the monarchy itself. On the other hand, Khai Dinh admitted the need for reform of the institutions of government if anarchy and revolution were to be avoided (Mus 1954: 324).

In a context in which France took the view that political development required a *tightening*, not loosening, of the colonial regime, the scope for fruitful (and legal) political debate was limited. The attention of eminent Vietnamese intellectuals of this time was therefore mainly concentrated on cultural and social issues and, in particular, on the question of the role to be played in the future by Vietnam's traditional values. Perhaps the most important and definitive contribution to this debate was provided by Dao Duy Anh's books, entitled *An Outline History of Vietnamese Culture* and *A Critical Discussion of Confucianism*, both of which were published in the relatively liberal 'Popular Front' period of 1936–1938, when an anti-Fascist left-inclined coalition governed France (Marr 1979: 334–36). Dao Duy

Anh based his critique of Confucianism on its status and relevance within modern Vietnamese society. From this perspective, he concluded that the Confucian 'world-view' – whatever its intrinsic merit – had simply been 'transcended' in the Hegelian sense: that is, it had been rendered irrelevant by the deep-rooted Westernization of Vietnamese society that had already taken place. The artefacts of the modern world and the rhythms of work imposed by the modern economy were becoming part of Vietnamese existence right down to the village level. The schools taught *quoc-ngu*, or the Vietnamese language written using the Roman alphabet rather than Chinese characters, and a large-scale translation project had made Western literature available to the reading public. In short, Vietnamese society *as a whole* was now 'living within' a world that was more modern than traditional (Jameson 1993: 92).

Though some welcomed this shaking-off of the *ancien régime*, more conservatively-inclined intellectuals like Tran Trong Kim (1883–1953) dreaded its probable effect on Vietnamese society. What most alarmed Tran Trong Kim was the way in which this break up of traditional values and entry into the modern world had been effected. Blind economic and social developments had undermined from below a stable hierarchical structure in which leadership had been based – in theory at least, and often in practice – on a leading intellectual stratum backed by moral authority. A system had been destroyed from within, but no political leadership or social structure had been created to control or give coherence to the new society that was emerging. As Tran Trong Kim gloomily expressed it: 'we have lost the essence of our society, which has kept it stable for thousands of years' (Jameson 1993: 94–96).

At first glance, it might seem that Pham Quynh (1892–1945) contributed to this assault on traditional Vietnamese culture. Significantly, Pham Quynh was not a member of the traditional elite, and had not followed the normal scholar's path through the classical examination system. In 1908, he moved from the Protectorate School in Hanoi (formerly the School for Translators) to work in the Ecole française d'Extrême Orient, mainly as a librarian. In 1917, he founded *Nam Phong* ('South Wind'), which became the major literary and cultural journal of the inter-war period. *Nam Phong* played a vital role in promoting the romanized writing system of Vietnamese (*quoc-ngu*), in encouraging a new and more Westernized literary style, and in giving access – both in French and in Vietnamese translation – to French and European literature (Jameson 1993: 82). Pham Quynh, in addition, contributed to a massive translation project designed to make European classics of all kinds available to the Vietnamese reading public (Malleret 1934: 316).

Pham Quynh, however, combined this cultural radicalism with a deeply conservative world-view. In 1937, a collection of his essays written between 1929 and 1932 was published in Hué under the general title *Essais Franco-Annamites*. Emerging as they did from a period of political upheaval –

during which the communist and nationalist rebellions that had broken out between the years 1929–1931 had provoked a harsh French reaction (see chapter 3) – the essays are of considerable interest. They represent an attempt to create a framework of ideas that could harmonize Western and Asian values, and create a new political relationship between the French protectorate and Vietnamese nationalism.

As a first step, Pham Quynh set out to explain the deep-rooted historical causes for the establishment of the French protectorate. Modelling his analysis on that of the Chinese Confucian scholar and historian, Ssu-Ma Kuang (1019–1086), Pham Quynh attempted to identify the recurring patterns in Vietnamese history that would reveal the general political characteristics of the nation (Pham Quynh 1937: 57–65). In political terms, he detected a pattern of extreme oscillation between unity and anarchy. In times of national danger, the people and the state would coalesce in a remarkably effective manner under a strong dynasty that would 'emerge' to meet the crisis. In the ensuing period of dynastic decline, power would tend to leak away from the institutions of central government, and the basic unit of the political order – the village – would become the rock of social stability (Pham Quynh 1937: 57–65). It appeared to Pham Quynh that there was no guarantee of the continuity of social order intervening between the central state and the locality. Similarly, in the realm of political ideas, the body of Confucian precepts had failed to resolve the problem of long-term stability. Consisting as they did of a series of aphorisms and comments, they lacked a systematic framework of thought. Despite this lack of a systematic framework, however, Confucian precepts had, over the millennia, hardened into rules – what Pham Quynh called *la règle*. The Confucian system had thus tended to encourage an ossification of social and political thinking during times of peace, while during periods of anarchy, *la règle* dissolved into a conglomeration of well-meaning apophthegms that bore no relation to social and political reality (Pham Quynh 1937: 271).

It was the unfortunate fate of Annam/Vietnam, wrote Pham Quynh, that the most intense period of Western colonial expansion – the last half of the nineteenth century – had coincided with the period of decline of the Nguyen dynasty and of the overflow of Chinese social anarchy into north Vietnam. The key to the survival of Asian states, continued Pham Quynh, had been a combination of inner strength and resilience, guaranteed by adherence to indigenous political and social values, coupled with a supple ability to engage with the West. While Vietnam had possessed this combination under the Nguyen dynastic founder, Gia Long, it had progressively lost both strength and flexibility under succeeding rulers. During the last years of Vietnamese independence, the Nguyen dynasty had clung to a system, the foundations of which had already disintegrated: the dynasty and its elite had continued to act out a Confucian morality play in a social and political void (Pham Quynh 1937: 19–27).

French take-over was, therefore, not only inevitable, but in some ways useful. Pham Quynh argued that the French protectorate system, whatever its faults, both enabled Vietnam to absorb Western ideas within a stable framework, and gave it precious space in which to reform, reorganize and modernize itself (Pham Quynh 1937: 47–56). He believed that the first step in the rehabilitation of Vietnam should be taken in the realm of education and ideas. Like other Asian intellectuals of his time, he accepted the notion that there could be a fruitful interchange between the values embodied in Eastern and Western civilizations. At the same time, he believed that the core elements sustaining these civilizations were fundamentally different: the force at the heart of Western civilization was that of 'energy' or 'dynamism' – described in Vietnamese as *âu*, or the principle of 'activity'; the corresponding Asian – and here Pham Quynh meant primarily East Asian – value was that of 'wisdom' or 'stability', in Vietnamese, *du'o'ng* (Pham Quynh 1937: 89, 91).

The contemporary crisis of Vietnam, argued Pham Quynh, lay in the fact that this interchange of values, far from regenerating society, was in the process of destroying it. Carried to extremes, the values of both East and West could have a malign rather than beneficial influence. Eastern 'wisdom' and 'stability' could rapidly become fossilization and stagnation; Western 'energy' and 'activity' could create skyscrapers of political ideology without any secure moral or social foundations (Pham Quynh 1937: 86–96). In Vietnam, the French had signally failed to encourage the rejuvenation of the traditional political system: the fatal result was that a sclerotic society was now confronted by a new generation of semi-Westernized, semi-educated, 'deracinated' youth, who had imbibed radical and even revolutionary ideas that had no place in the Vietnamese tradition. The consequence – for Vietnam and even more so for its neighbour China – was an entirely destructive combination of anarchy and stagnation (Pham Quynh 1937: 117–36, 166–76).

It was the central belief of Pham Quynh that, before Vietnam could allow itself to be fruitfully 'impregnated' with Western ideas, it had to undertake an 'intellectual and moral reform' of its own core values and culture (Pham Quynh 1937: 488). First and foremost, this required an understanding of the essential difference between Confucian and Western ways of understanding the relationship between the individual, the society and the state. Whereas European political thought since 1789 had tended to begin with a definition of individual human rights, and build an ideal political system on the basis of those fundamental rights, Confucianism saw society as an organic entity, of which individuals formed an intrinsic part. Thus, whereas the 'political mentality' of the liberal West began with the rights of the individual, that of Confucianism gave priority to the welfare of society as a whole. The primary task of the Vietnamese governing elite and intelligentsia, therefore, was to ensure that traditional Vietnam's essentially

Confucian perspective was maintained during an era of inevitable political and social transformation (Pham Quynh 1937: 117–36).

In Confucianism, society was seen, not as a formless entity, but as a network of organic relationships beginning with the family and culminating in the state. These organic relationships did not merely link the components of a living society, but also – through the family and state ancestor-cults prescribed by the *Book of Rites* – linked the dead, the living, and the generations to come. In other words, society as a living organism was bound together by a pattern of mutual obligations, symbolized by ritual, that transcended time. The spirits of the ancestors had no life in themselves: their existence depended on the commitment of a living society to maintain ritual continuity (Pham Quynh 1937: 28–37).

In Vietnam, Pham Quynh continued, society was linked to the past not merely by its connection with ancestor spirits: it was rooted in an ancient landscape, and in a shared historical experience. The festival of *Tết* at the beginning of the Vietnamese New Year incorporated and symbolized all these organic connections. Through the rituals of *Tết*, links were reaffirmed between Vietnamese society and its natural environment, between members of individual families, and between components of the whole national family. This sense of the existence of an organic national family was further strengthened by the Vietnamese phenomenon of local village cults which were sanctioned by the emperor; and by the fact that Buddhist ceremonies for the welfare of 'lost souls' drew into the ritual network those who might have been excluded by the strictly Confucian family and state cults (Pham Quynh 1937: 35, 41–46). For Vietnam, nation, family, religion, ritual, and social and political philosophy were inextricably linked. The collapse of Confucian values, therefore, led not only to social anarchy but also to the disintegration of the identity of the nation itself (Pham Quynh 1937: 302–11).

Cultural rehabilitation, therefore, had to precede fruitful engagement with the West. Pham Quynh's campaign for cultural reform thus formed an intrinsic part of his overall national project. He saw the use of the *quoc-ngu* Vietnamese writing system as a means of strengthening and modernizing the national culture, and at the same time as a vehicle for engaging with the Western world without losing national identity (Pham Quynh 1937: 227–32). He viewed language reform as a perfect example of Vietnam's ability to ensure national survival through 'pliability'. While the Vietnamese language, including some aspects of its writing style, had to be 'Europeanized', at the same time Pham Quynh agreed with the French conservative thinker Charles Maurras that language was not merely a convenience, but also the 'soul' of a national and cultural identity. If, therefore, French was allowed to take over from Vietnamese as the 'modern' language of intellectual discourse, Vietnam would be 'deracinated', and social disequilibrium would be the certain result (Pham Quynh 1937: 215–23).

On condition that a modernized and reformed Vietnamese language could act as the medium of cultural exchange, Pham Quynh accepted that French civilization had much to offer Vietnam. It is significant, however, that he did not believe the modern political and social ideas of France to be relevant or applicable to Vietnam. Rather, it was the rational mental discipline that generated these ideas, gave shape to them and organized them, that Pham Quynh felt that Vietnam (and indeed Asia) desperately needed to learn, and to apply to their own society (Pham Quynh 1937: 266–74). What France, above all other Western cultures, had to offer were what he termed *la méthode* – the capacity to think clearly, and *la doctrine* – the ability to organize ideas into a rational framework (Pham Quynh 1937: 276–83). Carefully averting his eyes from the liberal and revolutionary trilogy of *liberté, égalité, fraternité*. Pham Quynh looked to another set of values buried more deeply in French civilization: 'order, clarity and logic' (Pham Quynh 1937: 273).

Pham Quynh placed the political reform of Vietnam in the context of this much wider project of national renovation. The starting-point of his political analysis was the acceptance that Vietnam needed the partnership with France – but that this partnership had to be redefined. The colonial relationship, propped up by the notion of innate racial superiority and 'prestige', needed to be replaced by a new relationship founded on mutual respect: what he termed a *politique d'égards* (Pham Quynh 1937: 350–58). The first step in a true *politique d'égards* was to be the full restoration of the original protectorate concept: France should enable Vietnam – led by an *élite clairvoyante* – to evolve and reform itself on the basis of its own political system and social values (Pham Quynh 1937: 190). On this firm foundation, the proper groundwork for a reformed monarchy could be laid, with a constitution, modern ministries, and a parliament in which the electorate would be expanded gradually as modern education spread (Pham Quynh 1937: 389–97). This constitutional monarchy would operate as a self-governing entity 'within the framework of the protectorate'. But Pham Quynh envisaged that the scope of self-government would enlarge over time until Vietnam effectively became a self-governing nation within a French 'commonwealth' in which the main ties would be those of economic and cultural affiliation rather than political control (Pham Quynh 1937: 501–9).

Given Pham Quynh's insistence on the need to assert and maintain Vietnam's national identity, his support for the institution of the protectorate and the concept of Franco-Vietnamese partnership may seem paradoxical. It was, however, entirely consistent with his world-view. During the inter-war period, what he called the *toxine de la démagogie* ('the poison of demagogy') had infected both the colonized world *and* Europe (Pham Quynh 1937: 344–49). The epicentre of this threat of global anarchy was communist Russia, itself a classic example, according to Pham Quynh, of the harm that could be done by European ideas, detached from their social and cultural roots, made formidable by modern techniques of political organization, and imposed upon a semi-oriental people, most of whom were still entrenched in a traditional world (Pham Quynh 1937: 271–72). In such a dangerous global environment, the survival of the values of both Europe and Asia demanded that like-minded nations should lend support to each other.

SOETAN SJAHRIR: BEYOND THE COLONIAL RELATIONSHIP

In the years between the wars, the Netherlands East Indies, like Indochina, experienced great social and political turmoil, and a similar oscillation in colonial policy between liberalization and repression. It was during this period that the concept of an Indonesian nation, linking all the islands of the colony, was given cohesion by the promulgation at the Second Indonesian Youth Congress in 1928 of a national language – *bahasa Indonesia* ('the language of Indonesia'), which was based on the demotic Malay that already served as the language of communication between the islands. During the decade of the 1920s, a national literature was effectively established, with the publication of a number of novels written in *bahasa Indonesia*. The themes of these novels reflected the subterranean cultural upheaval that was occurring in the East Indies at this time – in particular, the generational conflict between an increasingly Westernized youth of the educated elite who were being pulled away from regional affiliations and *adat* (customary law), and an older generation who failed to understand that a Western education would not simply confer status on their children and give them enlarged opportunities, but would change their whole world outlook (Alisjahbana 1966: 23–64).

It was during the decade of the 1920s, too, that Indonesian nationalist political organizations were created, and a mass nationalist movement began (see chapter 4). As a result, between 1929 and 1934, the Dutch colonial authorities took fright and clamped down on what they considered to be 'subversive' political activity. In 1933, towards the end of this period of Dutch backlash, a monthly literary journal entitled *Pudjangga Baru* ('New Writers') was founded. This journal dominated the Indonesian literary and cultural scene until 1942, and works published under its aegis provide an insight into the world-view of Indonesian intellectuals at this time.

This is particularly true of a novel entitled *Belenggu* ('Shackles'), which was written by the eminent Sumatran writer Armijn Pané (1908–1970), and published in three monthly parts by *Pudjangga Baru* in the course of 1940 (Freidus 1977: 41; Pané 1964; Pané 1985). Put simply, it concerns the relationship of a Jakartanese doctor with his wife and his mistress, and the 'ghosts' of the past that emerge out of the tensions created by this love-triangle. Read socially and politically, however, what is particularly fascinating is the *milieu* it describes. The world of the protagonists is one in which the social and cultural tensions that preoccupied an earlier generation of Indonesian writers – between tradition and the modern world, between regional and wider loyalties, between arranged marriages and individual choice – no longer have the same central significance. The protagonists of *Belenggu* inhabit a new, almost entirely Westernized, urban environment of doctor's rounds, telephone messages, charity bazaars, and increasingly quaint and irrelevant lamentations for the culture they have lost. But *Belenggu*'s characters are uncomfortable, uneasy with their lives. Armijn Pané describes a Western-educated elite struggling to find a role in a social milieu where the old rules and guidelines no longer apply. The chains (*belenggu*) that bind them are not those of custom and tradition, but rather of a reluctance to come to terms with a new age in which each individual has responsibility for charting his or her own life.

The novel is permeated by a sense of alienation. Although the characters in the novel live within a colonial system, Dutch colonialism – as an issue and as a social and political reality – only figures tangentially in the book, due largely to the censorship constraints against trespassing into the political arena. It is perhaps precisely because of these constraints that Pané attempted to depict a world in which the characters lived and behaved as if colonialism did not exist. As a result, the most powerful feeling conveyed by the novel is of a society suspended in a vacuum: on the one hand, the colonial relationship is ignored; on the other, the characters are haunted by the sense that they have lost contact with their own people. The one overtly political figure in the book, Hartono – who had been a member of Sukarno's nationalist organization before the latter's arrest – describes in the course of the story the collapse of his illusion that he could penetrate what he calls the *rahasia massa*, or 'secret of the masses' (Pané 1964: 89). In fact, the main relationship of the book – that between the doctor, Sukartono, and the *kroncong* singer Yah – is of particular significance in this respect. This ultimately doomed love affair symbolizes an attempt by the intelligentsia to engage with the 'masses', not at the level of abstract political formulae, but at the everyday level of a shared popular culture – embodied in the demotic musical form of *kroncong* music – where 'heart and mind' could unite (Pané 1985: 107).

Perhaps the most eminent product of this period of cultural alienation and political *stasis* described in *Belenggu* was the Sumatran politician and intellectual, Soetan Sjahrir (1909–1966). In 1934, shortly after launching himself into Indonesian nationalist activity, Sjahrir was arrested by the Dutch for 'political subversion'. He was held in internal exile, first in Dutch New Guinea, and then on the remote eastern island of Banda, until 1942. During this period, he wrote a series of letters to his wife in the Netherlands. These letters, edited by his wife in diary form, were published in Dutch in 1945, and subsequently translated into English and published in the United States under the title, *Out of Exile* (Sjahrir 1949). In many ways, Sjahrir's was the most radical analysis of the dilemma facing the Western-educated Asian intellectual in the late colonial era. However, while his world-view clearly had Marxist characteristics, Sjahrir attached greater value to the Western democratic version of socialism than to the communist variety.

What made Sjahrir's reflections at this time so radical was his outright rejection of the commonly-accepted notion – even by a Marxist-influenced thinker like Mohammad Hatta – that Asian civilization possessed intrinsic values that were distinct from those of Western civilization. It therefore naturally followed that he rejected the then fashionable idea that the task of the Asian intellectual was to generate a dialogue between the values of the two civilizations, out of which a 'synthesis' might emerge (Sjahrir 1949: 67–68). His basic position was that capitalism, along with its subsidiary instrument, European imperialism, had created a *universal* culture (Sjahrir 1949: 178). For Sjahrir, the much-vaunted 'enduring' values of the East – characterized as 'harmony', 'stability', 'patience', or collectively as 'spiritual values' – were in fact the last redoubt of doomed and dying feudal-traditional cultures (Sjahrir 1949: 160). The modern axis of global confrontation between values was not that between Europe and Asia, but between the two forces that were contending for the inheritance of a capitalist system that was itself beginning to disintegrate: namely, fascism on one side, and democracy and socialism on the other (Sjahrir 1949: 161–62).

Sjahrir fully recognized that the 'spirit of the West' could – in either its old, capitalist form, or its new, fascist manifestation – be both brutal and destructive (Sjahrir 1949: 145). He nevertheless asserted that it was not only futile, but actually harmful, to suggest that Asia was intrinsically 'spiritual' and 'pacifist', in contrast to a Western civilization that was inherently 'materialist' and based on force (Sjahrir 1949: 18, 145). Such attempts to occupy the moral high-ground as a compensation for weakness and backwardness would merely encourage Asians to stay in a twilight spiritual world, evading the challenges of the modern world (Sjahrir 1949: 77–78). Sjahrir was impatient with what he saw as a dreamy nostalgia for ancient kingdoms and remnants of a dying culture. What Asia and Indonesia needed was a willingness to engage wholeheartedly with what he called the 'Faustian' spirit of the West which, with 'its resilience, its vitality, its rationality', had global validity (Sjahrir 1949: 144, 146).

Paradoxically, argued Sjahrir, the main impediment to Asian engagement with this modern spirit was colonialism itself. Colonialism would never have survived on the basis of force alone: its real mainstay had been the cultivation of the notion that White civilization was inherently different from, and innately superior to, that of Asia (Sjahrir 1949: 189). It was for this reason, of course, that colonial powers had been quite happy to encourage the maintenance of traditional values and political systems in colonized Asia, and to highlight essential cultural differences. After the First World War, however, the West – trapped by its own liberal rhetoric – had itself lost confidence in the assumptions that sustained the colonial systems (Sjahrir 1949: 157), leaving colonial rule to be shored up by force alone. Colonial power without the essential underpinning of prestige could not be sustained for long. Neither, however, could colonialism reform itself or adapt to a changing world, for the simple reason that any thoroughgoing, genuine reform of the colonial system would involve the elimination of its original economic and ideological *raison d'être*. Unable to adapt to the modern world, but with enough residual power to crush any challenges to its authority, colonial rule had become an immovable dying hulk (Sjahrir 1949: 181, 191–94).

Like Rizal before him, Sjahrir noted the bizarre situation created by colonialism, in which a Western education was made available to a colonial people, but in which those few who imbibed the values implicit in this education could have no role in colonial society. When Sjahrir returned to the East Indies from the Netherlands in 1932, he found himself looking at indigenous society through Western eyes. As he put it himself, he could understand the motives of a character in a Dostoevsky novel far better than he could the psychology of the Malay phenomenon of *amok* (Sjahrir 1949: 64, 23–24). People like him could never slot back into a society in which they were expected to defer to White colonial authorities, whose claim to superiority they could not accept, and whose education was often inferior to that of the indigenous intelligentsia (Sjahrir 1949: 24). As Sjahrir put it, in a society in which colonial relationships 'corrupt and vitiate life', the 'educated native' lost not only his political freedom, but something much more profound – his psychological freedom (Sjahrir 1949: 189).

Sjahrir agreed with Hatta's perception that the colonial relationship infected and distorted every aspect of social life and political behaviour. Partly as a result of this, he could not accept the view of 'non-cooperators' like Sukarno and Hatta, that it was possible to conduct 'democratic life' by ignoring the colonial political framework (Sjahrir 1949: 204–5). For Sjahrir, even non-cooperation was in the end a covert form of engagement with the colonial power, since it was based on the premiss that, if a sufficiently powerful mass movement could be developed by the non-cooperating nationalists outside the colonial political framework, the colonial authorities could eventually be compelled to make concessions. In other words, the non-cooperators anticipated that the bluff underlying colonial rule could be called; that, ultimately, the Western imperial powers would in the last resort – if confronted by a choice between wholesale repression and negotiation – give priority to their liberal values over the logic of colonial rule. Sjahrir, basing his opinion on the nature and the mechanics of colonial society he observed during his period of internal exile, was convinced that this was wishful thinking (Sjahrir 1949: 208).

Sjahrir felt that one of the most destructive aspects of colonialism was that it distorted the world-view of the colonized. For him, as noted above, the major global confrontation of the inter-war years was that which pitted fascism and militarism against democracy and socialism. This was an ideological conflict that was international in its scope, superseding regional, cultural or racial differences. The civil war in Spain between fascist and republican forces, and the war in China between militarist Japan and nationalist China, were linked elements of this ideological conflict, the outcome of which would have global repercussions (Sjahrir 1949: 115–16). However, Indonesian nationalists – like those of many parts of Asia – remained trapped in the essentially outdated mind-set of the confrontation between colonialism and anti-colonialism, between 'the West' and Asia. Since the world-view of Indonesian nationalism was exclusively anti-colonial, the Spanish conflict was largely ignored as irrelevant, and – because the Western powers, albeit inadequately, supported China in its war with Japan – Indonesian nationalists were instinctively sympathetic to Japan (Sjahrir 1949: 186–88, 196).

Anti-colonialism was stunting the Indonesian nationalists' ability to see the world clearly, but for this colonialism bore a large share of the blame. For Sjahrir, the tragedy was that the Western colonial powers had missed a golden opportunity. In an age when colonialism had long outlived its historical 'moment' and, as he put it, 'more profound antitheses have come to the fore', the West had had an ideal chance to replace the antagonistic and outdated relationship of colonialism with a global democratic alliance, based on equal partnership, against modern forms of tyranny that threatened Asia just as they did Europe (Sjahrir 1949: 211). Unfortunately, the failure of the West in Spain and in China demonstrated that the Western colonial powers were quite unable to adapt to new international realities (Sjahrir 1949: 185–86).

~~~

The Impact of the Second World War: Pan-Asianism and a New World Order

In the aftermath of the global depression of 1929–30, it appeared that a new world order would emerge from the ruins of the free-enterprise capitalist system and liberal parliamentary democracy. By 1938, it had become apparent that attempts in the mid-1930s to create 'popular fronts' in Europe between liberal-democratic, socialist and communist political forces, in order the block the advance of fascism and national socialism (Nazism), had failed, as had the half-hearted efforts by Britain and the United States to coordinate resistance to Japanese aggression in China. In 1939, the Soviet Union – and thereby in effect the global communist movement represented by the Comintern – concluded a 'non-aggression' deal with Nazi Germany. This pact indirectly enabled Nazi Germany and Fascist Italy to gain almost complete domination over western and central Europe. After the invasion of the Soviet Union in June 1941, it appeared that Hitler was also poised to achieve his major ideological goal: the expulsion of communism from Europe.

Emboldened by the defeat of France by Germany in the summer of 1940, Japan moved into Southeast Asia in the autumn of that same year. They began by forcing the French colonial authorities to permit the stationing of Japanese troops in northern Indochina. Then, in July 1941, in the aftermath of the German invasion of the Soviet Union, they extended this military agreement with the French to southern Indochina. Finally, in December 1941, Japan launched attacks on Malaya, the Philippines and the American naval base at Pearl Harbour in Hawaii. By mid 1942, Japan controlled the whole of Southeast Asia and the Asian rim of the Pacific, and had significantly tightened its stranglehold on nationalist China.

In the ensuing period, lasting from early 1942 to mid 1945, Southeast Asian reactions to the Japanese take-over varied. Those considered below include both independent Thailand's and those of the colonized regions.

THE THAI 'NATIONAL PHILOSOPHY'

For almost a century, the kingdom of Siam had lived under the shadow of regional colonial dominance by Britain and France. It could be argued that to a great degree Siam's survival as an independent state had depended on its ability, not only to adapt its policies to the interests of the colonial powers, but also to modernize its government along 'acceptable' European lines. The 1932 'Revolution', however, was ambiguous in ideological terms. On the one hand, in the adoption of a constitution based on 'popular sovereignty' and the creation of a constitutional monarchy, the language of liberal democracy was used. On the other, the notion that the administrative elite who had carried out the revolution should continue to exercise 'tutelage' over the population until such time as the latter were deemed fit to exercise their democratic rights, pointed in a more authoritarian direction. Much of the debate surrounding the objectives of the Revolution – including that over Pridi Panomyong's aborted plan in 1933 to nationalize land (see chapter 4) – centred on the issues of nationalist mobilization and economic self-sufficiency rather than on the more conventional issues of liberal democracy.

By the late 1930s, indeed, Siam's political system had moved in a distinctly more 'authoritarian-nationalist' direction – a direction that very much accorded with the international spirit of the times. This trend was confirmed in 1938 when Field Marshal Phibunsongkhram, in his joint position as leader of the People's Party that had dominated the political system since the Revolution, and as Prime Minister, established a virtual military dictatorship. On 24 June 1939, Siam was officially renamed *Prathet Thai*. the 'land of the Thais', or Thailand. After Japan had gained a military foothold in French Indochina in the autumn of 1940, the newly-named 'Thailand' pushed its claim for territories that the Thais had been forced to cede to France at the beginning of the century. With the help of Japan, Thailand reclaimed these lost territories in western Cambodia and Laos. After the Japanese invasion of Southeast Asia in December 1941, Thailand entered the war on the side of Japan, and subsequently regained territories in British Malaya and Burma. Although it is clear that Thailand had no option but to adapt itself to Japanese power in the region if it was to maintain its independence, it is equally clear that the new Japanese-dominated order in Southeast Asia provided the perfect basis for an ambitious programme of Thai national regeneration.

This regeneration was not simply to be a matter of territorial expansion: it was also to involve the development of what might be called a Thai national philosophy. A key figure in this ambitious ideological plan was Luang Wichit (or Vichitr) Wathakan, who, in his varied positions at this time as an academic, a minister of state, Director-General of the Department of Fine Arts, and Chairman of the Broadcasting Committee of Thailand, straddled the world of politics and culture. Between 1936 and 1939, Wichit had written a number of plays on patriotic themes. In 1941 he published a book entitled *Thailand's Case*, which sought to justify the territorial claims that Thailand was pursuing at that time, while at the same time attempting to define Thai identity and the main ingredients of the Thai national character (Vichitr/Wichit 1941).

Wichit's attempts to define Thai identity and character formed part of a general government effort to link race, nation and state. For Wichit, the first step was the replacement of the many and deep-rooted regional differences by a general sense of overall Thai racial affiliation embodied in the nation and the state (Thak 1978: 318). By 1941, however, his nationalist horizon, along with that of Thailand itself, had become more ambitious: he was concerned to provide a justification – on the basis of racial and linguistic affinity – for the expansion of the boundaries of the Thai state to include Thai-related ethnic groups lying outside its existing boundaries (Vichitr/ Wichit 1941: 124–30).

As a nationalist ideologist, Wichit was not content simply to define the *existence* of a Thai racial identity. He also sought to define what he considered to be the unique cultural characteristics of the Thai race. Principal among these, he wrote in *Thailand's Case*, was the concept of 'gratitude' – a notion that underpinned a Thai's relationship with his parents, his teachers, the state and indeed the natural world itself. Gratitude to the natural world that provided sustenance and shelter was particularly manifested in the pre-Buddhist Thai practice of paying respect to the spirits (*phi*) inhabiting trees (Vichitr/Wichit 1941: 133). Gratitude to the state was expressed by the fact that the Thais did not treat their 1932 constitution as 'merely a law', but as a 'sacred thing': Wichit noted that 'official copies of the Constitution distributed to various provinces are being worshipped next to the image of the Lord Buddha' (Vichitr/Wichit 1941: 134). It seems clear from the examples of 'gratefulness' cited by Wichit, that this cultural characteristic included strong elements of innate conservatism and deference, much favoured by authoritarian elites.

The traditional nature of the Thai values that Wichit chose to celebrate was superficially at odds with the stated aims of the nationalist project of the period, in which he played a central role – those of instilling a sense of national pride in the Thai people, while at the same time modernizing and changing Thai culture. The ideological objectives of this project, outlined in a series of *ratthaniyom* (literally, 'state-approved action') decrees issued between 1939 and 1941, were conveyed to the population in a number of radio broadcasts during 1941 and 1942 (Thak 1978: 245). In essence, the *ratthaniyom* decrees were a comprehensive attempt to complete the plan for national mobilization that had begun in 1932. The Thai elite were acutely aware of the weakness and vulnerability of Thailand in an increasingly uncertain international situation. They saw nationalism – rather than democracy, which was potentially destabilizing for the elite, and discredited by the ideological currents of the time – as the surest and safest way of achieving political mobilization. Unlike colonized countries, where nationalist sentiment was bound to emerge of its own accord as a main component in any anti-colonial movement, in Thailand a sense of national identity had to be 'invoked' by the political leadership, while at the same time its characteristics were to be closely defined by a *dirigiste* nationalist philosophy.

As in Kemal Ataturk's Turkey after the First World War, in Thailand nationalism and modernization went hand in hand. The installation of a sense of national identity was intended to expand the horizons of the Thai people beyond their narrow traditional world. The national 'family' would not replace the core unit of traditional life, the family; but it would supersede it as the object of primary loyalty (Thak 1978: 291–94). In defining the Thai nation, the *ratthaniyom* decrees explicitly linked race to language, echoing the prevalent view of many nationalist thinkers that language was the expression of the unique character of a particular race that had evolved through common historical experience (Thak 1978: 251–52). The Thai language was, in its turn, connected to the institution of the monarchy, and the fact that the Thai writing system could be traced back to an inscription outlining the duties of Buddhist kingship produced by King Ramkhamhaeng of the old Thai kingdom of Sukhothai was particularly emphasized. The link between race, monarchy and language was carried into the modern era by the citation of King Rama VI's translations of Shakespeare's plays as monuments of Thai literature. The Thai language was presented as a sacred inheritance to be nourished and kept pure by the Thai race (Thak 1978: 296–301).

Using this enhanced sense of racial and national identity, the *ratthaniyom* decrees were intended to bring about a complete revolution in the Thai world-view and way of life. National characteristics and culture were to be identified and preserved: they were also, however, to be substantially 'revised' to meet the challenges of the modern world (Thak 1978: 256). This concern radically to change the outlook and behaviour of the Thai people arose from the assumption that a people who behaved – as it was put – in a 'civilized' way, and were seen to be 'modern' both in their general social behaviour and in their political organization, would thereby earn the right to be treated as equals in the family of nations (Thak 1978: 257).

Just as Pham Quynh had advocated the adoption of a more 'systematic' approach to social and political thinking (*la méthode*) by Vietnamese intellectuals, so, in a sense, the *ratthaniyom* decrees tried to force the Thais to adopt a systematic approach to the conduct of their everyday lives and abandon the rhythms and customs of traditional life. A proper division of the day into defined periods of work, leisure and rest was prescribed; a dress code was imposed; the need to maintain public etiquette and order (for example queuing) was emphasized, as was the use of utensils for eating. The Thai people were urged to use their leisure productively, by reading, listening to the radio, growing vegetables, or playing sports (Thak 1978: 252–54). In some senses, the decrees advocated a 'Westernization' of everyday life. More generally, however, the encouragement of reading, listening to the radio, and engagement in cultural activity was not only designed to make people more 'civilized'; it was also a means of disseminating a centrally-approved version of the national language, culture and sense of identity (Thak 1978: 272).

It was hoped that a revolution in everyday behaviour would lay the groundwork for new behaviour in the economic, social and political spheres. The decrees and the accompanying radio dialogues highlighted the need to develop a sense of public service and public responsibility – an awareness that the state belonged to all Thais, and that all Thais therefore had an obligation to ensure its proper and efficient functioning (Thak 1978: 250). Greatest emphasis, however, was placed on the development of a modern work ethic, and the inculcation of a sense that hard work would bring wealth, and that wealth would not only improve the life of the individual concerned, but would benefit the nation in general. In particular, the intention of the *ratthaniyom* edicts was that the traditional patterns of work on the land should be transformed – that the old subsistence mentality should be replaced by an awareness of the advantages of saving, of using all the land available, and of seeking to increase efficiency and productivity. Once again, the benefits to the nation in general of such a change in peasant mentality were emphasized. In an age when free trade was associated with the colonial system, and at a time when the war had in any case dislocated the international market, the achievement of self-sufficiency was considered to be an urgent and laudable national objective (Thak 1978: 277–86).

This attempt to change the outlook and behaviour of a people may seem, in retrospect, to have been over-ambitious and utopian. At the time, however, it was viewed as a pragmatic attempt to mobilize and modernize a nation from the bottom up, and to try to attune the everyday behaviour and attitudes of a mainly isolated and rural people to the broader needs of the nation.

JAPAN AND THE PAN-ASIAN IDEAL IN SOUTH-EAST ASIA

When Japan conquered Southeast Asia in early to mid 1942, the region became part of what was essentially the Japanese Empire: the so-called 'Greater East Asia Co-Prosperity Sphere'. Japan, however, envisaged different political destinies for different parts of Southeast Asia, based on an appraisal of levels of political development, and strategic and economic considerations. Both Burma and the Philippines had in the course of the

1930s gained a substantial degree of internal autonomy, and both were in theory *en route* to full self-government when the war broke out. The Japanese at first intended giving full independence to these nations only after the war had been won. Fairly rapidly, however, they pushed their programme forward, and both Burma and the Philippines were granted independence in 1943 (Benda 1965: 51).

For a number of reasons – because they were strategically vital, because they contained essential raw materials, and because the areas were politically 'undeveloped' due to the failure of colonial powers to promote self-government – it was decided by the Japanese that the Malay States, Singapore, and the whole Netherlands East Indies region should remain under direct Japanese control (Benda 1965: 171–72, 204–6). However, although 'nationalism' and political activity directed to nationalist goals were not countenanced in these directly-controlled areas, there was an explicit plan to mobilize the populations behind the Japanese war effort. Indeed the people of Southeast Asia as whole were encouraged to rally behind Japan in the creation of a new pan-Asian order that would eradicate once and for all the old order of Western colonialism. This massive propaganda effort had a clear ideological underpinning: namely, the notion that Asian civilization was based on certain distinct values that had been buried in the Western colonial era, but that could now be resuscitated.

By characterizing the 'old' economic order of colonialism as part of a global 'Anglo-American-Jewish conspiracy', the Japanese were of course linking their ideological war aims to those of Nazi Germany (Benda 1965: 100). At the core of Hitler's thinking was the view that the Jews posed a mortal threat to European civilization, and that they had used both international communism and global capitalism – both of them 'rootless' cosmopolitan forces inimical to European values – as weapons to weaken the social stability of Europe and the integrity of European nations. As the war progressed, therefore, Hitler's war aims were described as an effort to save Europe from the communist arm of the Jewish conspiracy represented by the Soviet Union, and the international capitalist arm of the Jewish conspiracy represented by the essentially non-European 'Anglo-Saxon' world headed by the United States and Britain. This picture of a world-wide 'communist-capitalist-international' conspiracy coordinated by international Jewry fitted in well with Japan's own confrontation with White power in East and Southeast Asia. The whole colonial system was depicted as just part of an 'Anglo-Saxon' plot in which colonial powers like the Netherlands or France played a subsidiary role as lackeys (Benda 1965: 112).

The Japanese asserted that this 'Anglo-Saxon' colonialism had tried to create a world based on the values of individualism, liberalism, and free enterprise, stimulated by the profit motive. The diffusion of these values through Asia had encouraged a spirit of selfishness and competitiveness for individual gain, and had accordingly weakened the social fibre that had held Asian society together, demoralizing a population who had formerly depended on the values of cooperation and had placed public welfare above individual gain (Benda 1965: 112, 115).

The moral imperative facing Japan, therefore, was clear: to create a new Asian order, and bring about a spiritual regeneration of Asia under Japanese leadership. These objectives were publicly embodied in the term *hakko-ichiu*, which could be interpreted as 'all directions leading towards the centre', or, in other words, all parts of Asia united under the guidance of Japan (Benda 1965: 97). Japan's ideological objective was to resuscitate what it considered to be the common values underlying the whole of Asian civilization: the priority of the public good over individual rights, an emphasis on social discipline and self-sacrifice, and an economic philosophy based on cooperation rather than individual profit (Benda 1965: 98–99, 115). It was Japan's intention to harness these values to the war effort, and create an 'economic philosophy' of cooperation among the people of Southeast Asia to match Japan's 'military philosophy' of self-sacrifice (Benda 1965: 113). It was envisaged that the cooperative principle would merge with the sense of a common goal to create an economic environment where the spirit of emulation for the public good would replace profit-based competition, and a sense of the 'dignity and pleasure of work' would accordingly be restored (Benda 1965: 116–18). The various public order organizations established in Java, in particular, were based on this intrinsically Asian 'spirit of service' (Benda 1965: 147).

As Japan's military position steadily deteriorated from late 1942 onwards, its ambition to create this new Asian order increased. In a revealing analysis of the future direction of Japanese policy towards Java, the commander of the Sixteenth Army suggested that, as compensation for the fact that Japan had nothing to offer but hardship for the Javanese in the economic realm, they should take measures 'to gratify the desires of the natives in the spiritual realm' (Benda 1965: 237). In other words, the policy of what was called 'political co-determination', under which Java was only permitted to mobilize politically within the framework of continuing Japanese control, should be replaced by a policy of encouraging Javanese – and ultimately Indonesian – independence (Benda 1965: 243). Quite apart from the pragmatic considerations driving this policy, Japan was explicitly motivated by a desire to put in place a new Asian order that would be irreversible even if Japan were to be eventually defeated (Benda 1965: 242).

This Japanese desire to create a new Asian order had its clearest possible expression when an 'Assembly of Greater East Asian Nations' met in Tokyo under the leadership of Japan in November 1943. Apart from Japan itself, the nations present included the Japanese-created states of China and Manchukuo; Burma and the Philippines, which had been given independence by Japan in 1943; and Thailand, which had – as noted above –

aligned itself with the war effort of Japan. The two main themes highlighted by the conference were, first, respect for each other's independence, culture and political development; and, secondly, an attempt to define the principles underlying the new Asian order (Ba Maw 1968: 340–41). This balance between mutual acceptance of national entities on one hand, and joint purpose on the other, was encapsulated in the formula enunciated at the conference by President José Laurel of the Philippines: 'coexistence, cooperation and co-prosperity' (Ba Maw 1968: 341–42). These sentiments were to be echoed in almost exactly the same terms at the conference of 'non-aligned' nations that met in Bandung in 1955 (see chapter 9): in many senses the 1943 Tokyo conference was an ideological forerunner of the Bandung Conference, even though the latter met in very different international circumstances.

Dr. Ba Maw, *adipati* or 'supreme leader' of Burma, used the opportunity of the Tokyo Conference to develop the salient theme of his declaration of independence on the first of August 1943: namely – that of racial consciousness (Ba Maw 1943: 165–66). He made the point that Asian unity should not just be an intellectual and spiritual commitment; it required Asians to, as he put it, 'think with our blood' (Ba Maw 1968: 343). It was because Asians had lost this instinctive sense of affiliation, had drifted into their own separate worlds, that it had been so easy for European colonialism to dominate the Asian nations one by one. With the help of the new order created by Japan, however, Asians could once again 'discover' each other and realize that East Asia – for it was East Asia that was represented at the conference – formed a 'world in itself' that need never again be violated so long as that innate feeling of common identity remained (Ba Maw 1968: 343–44).

For the ideological underpinning of his newly independent state, however, Ba Maw relied just as much on European political models as on the development of a specifically Asian consciousness. In Burma's 'New Order Plan', published in September 1944, Ba Maw borrowed from Italian fascism the concept of what might be called the 'organic-dynamic' state; from German national-socialism he borrowed the 'leadership-principle'. At the root of this 'New Order Plan' was the notion that the state should no longer be regarded as a static phenomenon, but as a living organism entrusted with specific tasks: in the first instance, that of winning the war for Asia; and, more generally, that of bringing about a complete regeneration of society. The state and society would not be bound together by institutions, with their routine networks of rules and procedures, but by a constant collective exercise of dynamic will: to use the fascist image, the state would be an army on the march (Ba Maw 1944: 171, 174–75).

Such a state required a leader who would not so much hold an office as be entrusted with the fulfilling of 'a revolutionary task' (Ba Maw 1944: 171). This in its turn would require an absolute concentration of power in the hands of the revolutionary state, and the abandonment of democratic delays and constraints. Throughout the administration as a whole the bureaucratic culture of 'red-tapeism', delay and the sharing of responsibility for making (or rather, evading) decisions would be abandoned: administrators at all levels would have to make decisions *and* be responsible for their immediate execution. Likewise, in a revolutionary state entrusted with a revolutionary task, there could be no static concept of office hours; a new culture of work would demand that working hours be determined by the goals that had to be attained (Trager 1971: 180–81).

The 'New Order Plan' was designed to shake the Burmese population out of what Ba Maw considered to be its existing state of inertia. In economic terms, this inertia had been induced by the abundance of mineral wealth at Burma's disposal; in political terms, energy had been dissipated by the futile procedures of parliamentary politics introduced by British colonialism. In the new Burma, 'vote value' would be replaced by 'human value': the labour-power of Burma was to be mobilized for the task of national regeneration, and given 'value', not so much by education and training – as would be the case in modern economic thinking – but by the inculcation of national spirit and discipline. Mobilization of the society was to be total, including women and youth, and the sole criterion for reward or punishment was to be service to the state. As in the case of Thailand, this popular mobilization was to go hand in hand with the modernization and dissemination of the national language through a translation programme, and through the production of an official Burmese dictionary and encyclopedia (Ba Maw 1944: 173–75).

THE SPECIAL CASE OF THE PHILIPPINES

Japan's pan-Asian ideological mission faced its most acute test in the Philippines. After centuries of Spanish occupation, the population as a whole had converted to Catholicism, and an almost wholly Westernized Spanish-speaking elite dominated Filipino society. One effect of the substitution of American for Spanish colonial rule at the turn of the century had been the rapid replacement of Spanish by English as the language of the elite. In addition, a new political system had been introduced that had, by the mid-1930s, permitted this elite to run a virtually self-governing 'Philippine Commonwealth', with the prospect that the Philippines would achieve full independence in the mid-1940s. When Japan took over the Philippines in 1941–42, the top echelon of the leadership left with the Americans to form a government-in-exile, and there was considerable local resistance to Japanese rule.

The vast bulk of the Filipino governing class, however, had had no alternative but to remain in the Philippines, and it was the objective of the Japanese to induce this group to support the Japanese war effort, and use their considerable authority to persuade anti-Japanese guerrillas to abandon their activities. Before Japan was prepared to give this elite the ultimate political reward of an independent Filipino state, however, they required of the Filipinos, not just a change of sides based on pragmatic considerations, but a fundamental change of heart and what would have amounted to a change of identity. As the Japanese director-general of the military administration put it to the Filipino leadership, what was required was a commitment to 'work for the speedy reorientation of your people both spiritually and intellectually', and a reorganization of the 'social structure of the Philippines in strict accordance with the ideals and standards of Oriental peoples'. In short, what was required was that the Filipino elite and the Filipino people should regain their 'original Oriental souls' (Garcia 1965: 48).

The Philippine elite as a whole accepted this implicit bargain, and the 'Philippine Republic' was granted its independence in October 1943 under the leadership of President José Laurel. In its public statements, the leadership did indeed commit itself to creating a new Philippine society. As a document entitled 'The Filipinos' Credo' of 14 November 1943 put it: 'we must go home spiritually to the Orient' (Garcia 1965: facing 96). Both in this 'Credo', and in a 'Manifesto' produced on 13 February 1943 by the Philippine Council of State, an undertaking was made on behalf of the Filipino people to recapture their 'racial pride' and 'racial dignity', and to reconnect with the pre-colonial Malay civilization and culture that had been swamped in the long era of colonial rule (Garcia 1965: 65, facing 96). Only then would it be possible for the Filipinos, 'nurtured by the fiery consciousness of race', to abandon an alien colonial culture based on individual greed, and adopt the true Asian values of 'social discipline', 'cooperation' and 'unselfishness', and thus establish an 'economic independence' from the West (Garcia 1965: facing 96).

The high-flown pan-Asian rhetoric that accompanied independence bore little relationship, however, to the everyday reality of Filipino existence. The Japanese military continued to requisition food and to carry out arbitrary arrests, reprisals and collective punishments without reference to the Philippine authorities. In June 1944, the Philippine Foreign Minister, Claro M. Recto, wrote a famous letter of protest to the Japanese military authorities, accusing the Japanese of violating and undermining the very values they were supposedly promoting. Claro Recto pointed out that the arbitrary and brutal behaviour of the Japanese military was a direct negation of what was supposedly a central pillar of the new pan-Asian order: namely, the concept of 'racial equality and reciprocity' (Garcia 1965: 113). Moreover, he continued, while in the abstract one might accept that the collective interest should have priority over individual rights, in practice this 'Asian' principle had taken the form of whole villages being punished for the actions of a few individuals in collective reprisals (Garcia 1965: 116).

But the substance of Claro Recto's criticism of the Japanese was that they themselves had violated a principle that lay deep within Filipino culture: that of mutual obligation, reciprocity and gratitude. As Recto explained, this concept of mutual obligation was not based on 'abstract principle' but on the actual inter-relations of social and political life (Garcia 1965: 110). The Japanese, though they had granted full independence to the Philippines, had by their *actions* weakened the bonds of reciprocity and obligation. For, while the Filipino elite had lent their status and prestige to the Japanese war effort, the Japanese, by putting the elite in a position where they could not protect the population from the arbitrary behaviour of the Japanese military, had seriously undermined the prestige of the very political class that had offered to support them (Garcia 1965: 117, 119, 122). Recto's letter thus contained a subtle criticism of the notion of the existence of common Asian values (Garcia 1965: 109–24).

THE IDEOLOGICAL BASES OF THE VICHY REGIME IN FRENCH INDOCHINA, 1940–1945

After France was defeated by Germany in June 1940, Germany occupied the north of the country, and the 'Vichy' regime (named after the town where the government was installed) was established in the southern half of the country under the leadership of Marshal Pétain. After a brief hiatus, the colonial government of Indochina under Governor-General Decoux declared loyalty to this Vichy regime. This government was compelled by the Japanese in the autumn of 1940 to permit the stationing of their armed forces in the north of Indochina; in July 1941, this right was extended to the southern part of Indochina.

The Japanese and Vichy French, therefore, lived between late 1940 and March 1945 in an uneasy state of co-existence, in which the French continued to administer Indochina, but with a huge Japanese military presence looming over the colonial regime. The continued existence of French rule in Indochina stood in the way of Japan's declared intention of removing the Western colonial presence altogether and creating an 'Asia for the Asians'. However, the Vichy regime shared much of the world-view of Fascist Italy and Nazi Germany, and this world-view was – allowing for a fundamental but generally unspoken divergence over the issue of European colonialism and Asian rights – at least officially endorsed by Japan itself.

At the core of the Vichy world-view – and that of the French who collaborated from conviction with the Germans in occupied France – was the notion that European civilization was under threat. The main source of this threat was seen, as noted above, to be an 'international Jewry' that had used the general concept of 'internationalism' – whether it be 'international socialism' of the Marxist variety, or 'international capitalism' of the Rothschild variety – to undermine the structures and values of European society, and to set European nation against European nation (Christie 1998a: 132–37, 146–49). One task facing Europe, therefore, was that of defeating and pushing back into its proper Asian lair that embodiment of the global Jewish-communist conspiracy, the Soviet Union. On Europe's western flank, however, the epicentre of the Jewish-capitalist conspiracy – Anglo-Saxon civilization – was thought to pose as great a threat. It was a central axiom of Vichy ideology that, while France and Germany shared a common European affiliation, 'Anglo-Saxon' civilization, with its commercial and maritime orientation and its Jewish-dominated 'mongrel' popular culture (viz. Hollywood), was essentially extra-European. Internally, the objective of Vichy was to put an end to the parliamentary republican system of the Third Republic that had, in its eyes – again, with Jewish help – corrupted and weakened France both morally and politically. Vichy's solution was to replace the parliamentary principle with an authoritarian system that would restore the 'real' France.

Vichy's aims were encapsulated in the slogan 'national revolution'. This ambiguous term, however, masked a fundamental split within the ranks of those who worked with the Vichy regime and the Germans. On one side, the 'revolutionary right', far from planning to return to a traditional patriarchal France, wished to create a newly energized France – along the lines of Fascist Italy and Nazi Germany – in which a liberated but at the same time disciplined youth would play a key role in rejuvenating society. The 'revolutionary right' wished to created a dynamic France within a dynamic Europe, whose spirit could challenge and overcome the revolutionary impetus behind communism. On the other side of this divide, the 'conservative right' wished essentially to return to a pre-1789 France, in which the traditional values embodied in the Catholic church, the family and rural continuity could be reasserted, under the umbrella of a patriarchal leader who would exercise absolute but benevolent authority. In the short term, Marshal Pétain filled the 'conservative right's' leadership role admirably. Although both sides of this ideological divide wished to create an 'organic' state to replace what they saw as parliamentary anarchy, the 'revolutionary right' saw this French state – in the manner of Ba Maw in Burma – as a dynamic force, while the 'conservative right' saw it as a well-rooted tree that had been badly neglected.

Not surprisingly, the colonial outlook of the 'national revolution' was, in practice, almost entirely conservative. For Vichy, the first task was to undo the damage done in the colonial sphere by the Third Republic. At the very time that the great French 'proconsuls' had been enlarging and consolidating France's 'civilizing mission' in Africa and Asia, it was argued, the Third Republic at home had been disseminating to the empire such destructive ideologies as democracy, nationalism, and socialism, which had systematically undermined that civilizing mission (Leblond 1941: 155–56). This inrush of modern European ideologies had debilitated traditional societies and subverted the authority of the traditional political systems on which these societies depended. What was needed above all in the colonies, therefore, was the expulsion of the febrile ideologies of 'struggle', a restoration of traditional authority and, in general, the installation of a *régime de convalescence* (Leblond 1941: 158).

Admiral Decoux, Governor-General of Indochina, based his overall policy on the conservative Vichyist policies outlined above. What might be called the 'cult' of Marshal Pétain was encouraged by the colonial government, and evidence suggests that this venerable patriarchal figure did indeed appeal to traditional Vietnam (Decoux 1949: 360). The Pétainist slogan, *'travaille-famille-patrie'* ('work-family-country') was disseminated throughout the country, and Decoux in fact made the concept of 'patriotism' (*la patrie*) a cornerstone of his policy. Decoux defined 'patriotism' as a traditional virtue, embodied in the indigenous monarchies of Annam (Vietnam), Cambodia and Laos. He therefore attempted to strengthen 'patriotism', and at the same time eradicate the Western-imported and subversive ideology of 'nationalism' that threatened the position of both the monarchies and French colonial rule (Decoux 1949: 388–89). As part of this general policy, he set out to bolster the status and the symbolic patriotic significance of the indigenous monarchies. This involved, among other things, his personal attendance at important royal ceremonies, an increase in the civil list of the respective monarchies, and a programme of modernization and renovation of the royal palaces (Decoux 1949: 270). These cosmetic actions did not alter the fact that the monarchies had in practice been reduced to an almost exclusively ceremonial and ritual role; but they were designed to raise the prestige of the indigenous political systems among the populations as a whole.

The key to the rehabilitation of the monarchies, however, lay in the reform of the mandarinate. In this area, Decoux made substantial efforts to equalize the status and pay of indigenous and French civil servants throughout the Indochina administration. At the same time, he tried to restore the old ceremony and sense of occasion that had once surrounded the annual mandarin exams (Decoux 1949: 401). Further, the restoration of the principle of authority among both rulers and ruled required a fundamental change in educational policy. Accordingly, Decoux took steps to ensure that, once the war was over and international travel once again became possible, the education made available to Vietnamese students in France would be carefully monitored and controlled to ensure that its provisions strictly met Indochina's administrative and economic needs, and did not merely create a pool of revolutionary malcontents, as had hitherto been the case (Decoux 1949: 402).

If Decoux's policies reflected the conservative trend in Vichy's 'national revolution', the activities of his Commissioner-General for Youth and Sports, Maurice Ducoroy, had a distinctly 'revolutionary' tinge. In practical terms, the achievement of Ducoroy in making sports facilities available and in creating a 'sports-orientated' mentality among the youth of Indochina was considerable (Ducoroy 1949). More politically significant, however, were Ducoroy's attempts to reproduce in Indochina the cult of youth that was so striking a feature of fascism and national-socialism in Europe, and the distinctly fascist-style choreography and iconography of the parades and athletic displays that he supervised: for example, the festival of May 1944 celebrating Jeanne d'Arc, a potent ultra-nationalist and anglophobic symbol in the Vichy period (Ducoroy 1949: 93). This familiar emphasis on health, fitness and the open air was extended to the training of young recruits to the mandarinate, and was explicitly designed to inculcate the notion – unfamiliar to the traditional mandarinate – that physical endurance and bodily discipline were as important a training for leadership as purely intellectual activity (Le Van Tuan 1942: 98–102).

PHAM QUYNH AND CHARLES MAURRAS: A PHILOSOPHY OF ORDER

One of the most remarkable documents to emerge from this strange interlude in Vietnamese history was a talk given in 1942 by Pham Quynh, Minister of the Interior for the Emperor Bao Dai in the court of Hué, on the subject of the French political philosopher Charles Maurras (Pham Quynh 1942). In this talk, Pham Quynh addressed the question of whether there was in fact a fundamental divide between the values underlying Western and Asian civilizations.

In his earlier writings, Pham Quynh had been inclined to draw a distinction between the French (and thereby European) *méthode* – that is, systematic ways of thinking, which could be beneficially borrowed by Vietnamese intellectuals – and French *doctrine* – the end result of this organization of ideas (see chapter 5). It is evident that he had regarded the latter, particularly the political system deriving its legitimacy from presumed natural and individual rights, as inapplicable to essentially different Asian societies. But in the ideas of Maurras – who had, since the late nineteenth century, been a leading figure of the French conservative right, and whose reputation had been revived during the Vichy period – he discovered the basis for a reconciliation between European and Asian *doctrine*.

Of those aspects of Maurras' thought that Pham Quynh addressed in 1942, the first point to note is that Maurras' whole intellectual endeavour was based on a repudiation both of the 'republican' political principles that had formed the foundation of the French Revolution of 1789, and of the notion that the only legitimate governments were those that were based on the 'natural rights' of individuals – these 'natural rights' being discoverable through rational analysis of the intrinsic nature of man. Maurras argued that this political concept, which had formed the ideological basis for Republican France since 1789, was not, as claimed, founded on rational analysis. Rather, it emerged from a compound of the Protestant notion of individual conscience untrammelled by received dogma, and the, essentially Germanic, romantic idea of the individual free from society's constraints. Under the malignant influence of Jean-Jacques Rousseau – who could from his vantage-point in Geneva act as a conduit for the infiltration of these protestant-romantic concepts into France – an entire political system had been constructed on the basis of what was in fact a sentimental and irrational view of the inherently good and rational individual (McClelland 1970: 242–44).

The effect of this, continued Maurras, was to create a political system built upon the unstable foundation of 'rights' against the state. The whole political philosophy of individual rights had been based on an optimistic view of human nature, but at the same time, a wholly pessimistic view of human institutions as they had evolved over time (Pham Quynh 1942: 31–37). Since these 'human rights' were founded on a premiss that was in fact irrational and vague, a situation had been created where citizens were placed in a condition of permanent opposition to the state and society: a kind of institutionalized sedition (McClelland 1970: 248). This fundamentally destabilizing and destructive political system was then incorporated into France's 'civilizing mission' and disseminated to colonial regions. Instead of supporting and culturally enriching traditional systems and cultures, France had introduced the notion that *subversion* was the only legitimate form of 'civic energy' (McClelland 1970: 256).

Against the destructive and sentimental formulae of republicanism, Maurras sought to apply a pragmatic, history-based 'political reason' to discover the underlying laws governing society and the state (Pham Quynh 1942: 7–12). In an exact reversal of republican ideology, Maurras' political philosophy was founded on a pessimistic view of human nature, and an optimistic view of human institutions. Indeed, argued Maurras, the pattern of the development of social and political institutions through history was precisely determined by the recurrent and inherent defects of human nature. Since these defects were ineradicable, the task of political and social institutions was to act as a permanent control on human nature (Pham-Quynh 1942: 36–37). As Maurras put it, 'clear and tangible necessity dictated the construction of the pillars of order'; political and social institutions, as they have emerged over time, can therefore be understood as the living embodiment of cumulative political reason (McClelland 1970: 279). It followed, therefore, that the individual had only limited rights against the institutions of society, and that the relationship between the individual and these institutions was not 'equal' in any sense: any more than a baby had an 'equal' relationship with the parents who had given it life and guaranteed its continuing existence (McClelland 1970: 266–68). Any state or society constituted an organic growth of accumulated political and social experience through time, and the relationship of the individual to that organism was like the relationship of a leaf to the tree that nurtured it.

For Pham Quynh, Maurras' political philosophy almost exactly matched the world-view of Confucianism. Maurras, like Confucius, understood political reason as the ability to see things as they are, not as we would like them to be (Pham Quynh 1942: 12–15). Political institutions, therefore, should seek, not to change human nature by the construction of utopian political systems, but rather to control the effects of its irrational and anti-social tendencies (Pham Quynh 1942: 20–27). Above all, both philosophies stipulated the primacy of social and political institutions over the individual. Individuals inherited, as Pham Quynh put it, the accumulated 'capital' of the society into which they are born. But, as Chinese or Vietnamese history had shown, this accumulated capital could, in periods of disorder, be dissipated with frightening speed and ease (Pham Quynh 1942: 37–41). State and social institutions, therefore, were engaged in a permanent struggle to uphold *tri* ('order') against the ever-present tendencies to *loan* ('chaos, anarchy') (Pham Quynh 1942: 27–31).

Pham Quynh noted that the only major difference between Confucianism and the conservative Western world-view elucidated by Maurras, was the fact that in the West there was a clear divide between *political and social morality* – that is, practical codes of collective behaviour according to the precepts of political reason – and *religious morality* which, in Christianity, inhabited the separate world of individual conscience. In Confucianism, on the other hand, the religious and political worlds were united in an all-embracing moral order that linked heaven, society, and the individual, and that was sanctified by local and state rituals (Pham Quynh 1942: 27–28).

While Governor-General Decoux had drawn a distinction in Vietnam between the beneficent political force of 'patriotism' and the subversive political force of 'nationalism', Pham Quynh – in line with Maurras – viewed the relationship between patriotism and nationalism differently. Patriotism, Maurras had insisted, was a natural instinctive force: nationalism, however, was the application of conscious reason to that patriotic instinct. The concept of the 'nation' was the encapsulation of the cumulative social and political heritage of a particular people, and a nationalism that supported the survival of these accumulated values and institutions was the very embodiment of political reason in action (Pham Quynh 1942: 43–44). For Pham Quynh, as for Maurras, the nation was a rational entity – possibly the last redoubt that could safeguard *tri* ('order') in a world increasingly threatened by *loan* ('anarchy').

CHAPTER SEVEN

Revolution: 1945–1947

The victory of Japan in Southeast Asia dealt a decisive blow to European colonial rule in Southeast Asia. This victory appeared complete in March 1945, when they brought an end to French rule in Indochina by force; thus, in theory at least, enabling the monarchies of Vietnam, Cambodia and Laos/Luang Prabang to resume the independent status that they had had before the imposition of the French protectorates. However, the various political structures created by Japan began to disintegrate in the wake of Japan's military retreat in early to mid 1945, and the defeat of Japan in August 1945 put an end to its pan-Asian plans.

Following the comprehensive defeat of the fascist powers and their accompanying ideologies, both in Europe and in Asia, the United States and the Soviet Union dominated the world scene. The United States had considerable prestige among Southeast Asian populations at the end of the Second World War, not only because of the real power and influence it wielded in the region in the wake of the defeat of the colonial powers and Japan, but also because of its anti-colonial ethos, which was given substance by their willingness to grant independence to the Philippines in 1946. But it is important to note also the huge ideological influence exerted by the Soviet Union in Southeast Asia at this stage. From the time of the Russian Revolution of 1917 onwards, the Marxist-Leninist ideology of the Soviet Union had emphasized the intrinsic link between socialism and anti-colonialism. With the Soviet Union's historic victory over Nazi Germany at Stalingrad in 1943, it seemed as if the tide of world history had decisively turned in a socialist direction and – as the Burmese nationalist leader, Aung San, put it in 1946 – that the Soviet Union was marching 'in tune with the music of history' (Aung San 1946a: 101). The very fact that the Soviet Union was not directly involved in the region probably served to enhance its ideological status at the time.

In more immediate terms, however, ideological leadership of the communist movements of East and Southeast Asia had been taken over, in the critical decade between 1937 and 1947, by the Chinese Communist Party and its leader Mao Tse-tung. By the late 1930s the international ideological leadership of the Communist International had become compromised by its need to follow the twists and turns of Stalin's policy towards Nazi Germany. The ideological 'line' taken by Mao Tse-tung during this period, on the other hand, was more consistent, and had more relevance to Asian communism. In 1937, in the face of Japan's war for the conquest of China, the Chinese communists and nationalists had forged a patriotic alliance against Japan, thus halting a decade of bitter civil war between the Chinese Communist Party (CCP) and the Chinese Nationalist Party, the Kuomintang (KMT), although the communists retained their 'Red Base' in the remote north-western region of Yenan. In 1941, the 'anti-fascist' struggle of China against Japan merged with the general war of Britain and the United States against Japan in the Pacific and Southeast Asia. From Burma to the Philippines, and from Vietnam to Indonesia, Southeast Asian communists found themselves in the anomalous position of forming a de facto alliance with the Western colonial powers directed against Japanese and global 'fascism'.

Between 1937 and 1942, Mao Tse-tung wrote three essays – 'On Contradiction' (1937), 'On New Democracy' (1940), and 'Talks at the Yenan Forum on Arts and Literature' (1942) – that were to have a direct ideological influence on Vietnamese communism, and an indirect influence on Southeast Asian communism as a whole, during the revolutionary period of 1945 to 1947. Mao Tse-tung's overall objective in these essays was that of providing the Chinese Communist Party with a solid theoretical base for its policies, in a complex global situation in which the pursuit of a Marxist-Leninist strategy appropriate for China's internal conditions had to be balanced against an understanding of the trend of international developments.

In his essay, 'On Contradiction' (1937), Mao Tse-tung began with the fundamental Marxist tenet that all human historical development was based upon a 'dialectical' process: that is, the 'struggle', 'antagonism' or 'contradiction' between competing economic, social and political forces and systems, encapsulated in the general concept of the 'class struggle' (Mao Tse-tung 1937: 75). Mao then went on to argue that this dialectical process of confrontation between 'antagonistic' economic and social systems was not a stately, even process, in which feudalism was replaced by capitalism, and then capitalism by socialism, in a synchronized global progression. The reason, of course, was that different parts of the world were at different levels of economic development. The 'uneven' development of world history was made even more complex by the fact that classes dominating social systems at different levels of economic development might form temporary alliances of convenience. Thus, in the process of European colonial expansion, the bourgeois class dominating the capitalist system of industrialized Europe had often formed an alliance with feudal classes in the colonized regions. Conversely, in semi-capitalist, semi-feudal Tsarist Russia, the anti-capitalist force of the industrial proletariat had formed a revolutionary alliance with the anti-feudal force of the peasantry. The ensuing Russian Revolution had created the basis for a new world order that linked globally the socialist struggle against capitalism, the 'national-liberation' struggle against capitalist-based 'imperialism', *and* – in countries that had not yet reached the capitalist stage of industrialization – the so-called 'bourgeois-democratic' struggle against feudalism (Mao Tse-tung 1937: 83).

In this complex and 'uneven' historical situation, Mao Tse-tung continued, it was the task of the leadership of a communist party to assess the relationship, at any given time, between the contradictions that prevailed at the international level, and between those that prevailed at the national level; and then to assess, on that foundation, the general relationship between international and national contradictions as a whole. On the basis of this analysis – and always on the understanding that historical developments were in a state of continuous and often unpredictable flux – it was then the task of the party to distinguish between those 'contradictions' between classes (for example, between the bourgeoisie and the proletariat) that were in economic terms inherently at odds, but which could be, at a given historical stage, 'non-antagonistic'; and those contradictions that were, at the same historical stage, 'antagonistic'. It would then be possible, Mao argued, to identify what he called the 'principal contradiction' or historical fault-line – either at the national or international level – that divided 'progressive' economic and political forces pushing history along the dialectical path that would ultimately lead to socialism, and 'reactionary' forces that were at the same time trying to halt that process. For Mao Tse-tung, as for Lenin in his 1902 work, *What is to be Done?*, a communist party was far more than the protector and promoter of the interests of the working-class. Because of its ability to see beyond the complexities of political and economic developments to the fundamental 'contradictions' that drove those developments, it was able to manipulate and guide history in a 'progressive' direction (Mao Tse-tung 1937: 80, 84, 91–93). In effect, 'On Contradiction' amounted to a qualified opportunist's charter, adding a philosophical gloss to the doctrine that long-term ends justify short-term means. The central message was that the communist party, on behalf of the working class, could and should ally itself with any force or class whose energies could be channelled – even if unwittingly – in a 'progressive' historical direction.

Although China had never, unlike Southeast Asia, been fully colonized, its internal and international situation during this period was roughly similar to that of the Southeast Asian region. In international terms, China was waging a national-liberation struggle against imperialism – although, in China's case, the imperial power between 1937 and 1945 was Japanese rather than Western. The 'principal contradiction', therefore, pitted all 'progressive' forces confronting Japanese imperialism against 'reactionary' elements that collaborated with the Japanese. Internally, however, China was engaged in a 'bourgeois-democratic' struggle against feudalism. The complexity for China, therefore, as for Southeast Asia, lay in the fact that, while from the international perspective, capitalism in its imperialist guise was holding back China's progress, from the internal perspective, capitalism, in its bourgeois-democratic guise, was a progressive force helping to break down the structures of feudal society within China (Mao Tse-tung 1940: 154–57).

Precisely because capitalism's role in China was simultaneously reactionary and progressive, China's bourgeois class was itself divided between those elements that benefited from, and collaborated with, imperialism; and the 'national bourgeoisie', whose interests were stifled by imperialism, and who therefore sought to liberate China's economy from foreign control (Mao Tse-tung 1940: 159). Therefore, although China was technically in the 'bourgeois-democratic' phase, the weak and divided Chinese bourgeoisie were unable to play a leading role in the twin struggles against imperialism and feudalism. In the special circumstances facing China (and Asia), Mao Tse-tung argued, outright bourgeois political dominance would have to be replaced by an alliance of classes – national-bourgeois, peasant, petty-bourgeois and working-class – who had a common anti-imperialist and anti-feudal agenda, and whose class differences were therefore at this stage 'non-antagonistic'. This class alliance was described by Mao Tse-tung as 'New Democracy', and it was of course assumed by him that the communist party – in its role as 'trustee' of the nascent working-class, and as the long term 'progressor' of history – would play a guiding role, even though Chinese society had not yet reached the socialist stage of development (Mao Tse-tung 1940: 157–59).

The primary, 'historical' tasks of the New Democracy state would be to expedite measures against feudalism in the countryside, and to mobilize the people in the national struggle against imperialism. But also, Mao insisted, the communist party would have to use its leading position within New Democracy to push forward the 'dialectical process' by introducing socialist principles within this broad agenda. For example, cooperative systems of land reform should be introduced instead of encouraging peasant owner-ship, and, while small-scale capitalist industrial enterprises should be encouraged, he believed – like Tan Malaka before him – that the 'commanding heights' of the economy should come under state regulation and planning (Mao Tse-tung 1940: 162).

In his essay 'On Contradiction', Mao Tse-tung made the point that the 'uneven' development of history not only affected the relationships between classes, but also between the broad categories of politics, society and 'culture' – that is, the collective phenomena affecting the world-view of people in general within a society. He rejected the mechanical interpretation of Marxism which asserted that social and economic change would *automatically* bring about cultural change in its wake. Rather, the cultural norms of a particular social structure – for example, feudalism – could persist among the people in general long after its economic rationale and its political power base had been destroyed. In these circumstances, wrote Mao, 'culture' could become the principal block to the progress of a society; or, in Marxist-Leninist terms, it could become the principal 'antagonistic contradiction' within a society (Mao Tse-tung 1937: 87).

Mao Tse-tung believed that this was exactly the case in China, and that the vast majority of the Chinese people were deeply rooted in a feudal culture. One of the principal tasks of the CCP was, therefore, to create a 'New Culture' to match 'New Democracy'. In line with the objectives of 'New Democracy', this would involve building a world-view that would help the people understand the nature of imperialism, and thereby develop a patriotic consciousness and a will to resist the Japanese. Mao felt that while specifically national cultural *forms* should be retained, these traditional forms should, as he put it, be 'infused with new content' (Mao Tse-tung 1942: 193). Thus, the creation of a 'New Culture' meant the elimination of the old feudal mentality – bolstered as it was by Confucianism and religious ritual – through the use of appropriate folk-tales, literature, music and drama to encourage the rural peasantry to see the world in a new way. Above all, the Chinese Communist Party should strive to develop a 'scientific' outlook among the people (Mao Tse-tung 1940: 168–69). This involved the ability to organize one's thoughts clearly and systematically as a first step towards understanding, and thus changing, one's social and political environment. For Mao Tse-tung, the basis for such a 'scientific' world-view must be Marxism-Leninism.

Below, the ideological bases of three different revolutions in Southeast Asia are considered: those of Vietnam, Burma and Indonesia. These cases differed, in that, while Marxism-Leninism played a central role in the Vietnamese revolution, and was a major influence in the Burmese revolution, the range of ideological debate in the Indonesian revolution was more eclectic.

THE IDEOLOGICAL BASES OF THE VIETNAMESE REVOLUTION

In the summer of 1944, parts of France were beginning to be liberated from the German occupation. One immediate consequence of this was that the 'Vichy' regime that had collaborated with Germany disintegrated, and was replaced by a 'Free French' government headed by General De Gaulle, the leader of French resistance to Germany during the war. By this stage, the

Japanese position in the Pacific and in Southeast Asia had become increasingly precarious, and the Japanese military took the view that the continued existence of a French administration in Indochina constituted a threat to its security. Accordingly, in March 1945, the Japanese removed the French administration in Indochina, and – as has already been noted – invited the respective Indochinese monarchies to form independent governments freed from French control. Although this was clearly a historic moment and historic opportunity for the indigenous states of Indochina, Bao Dai, the then Emperor of Vietnam, admitted in his memoirs that the Hué mandarinate – weakened as it had been over the years by the steady expansion of French control – simply did not have the capacity to administer Vietnam (Bao Dai 1980: 113). The inevitable result was that, in the months following March 1945, Vietnam fell into a state of anarchy. It was in this vacuum of power that the Indochina Communist Party (ICP), headed by Nguyen Ai Quoc/Ho Chi Minh, was able to build up from the grass-roots an alternative government, and then, a few days after the surrender of Japan, to seize power in what has become known as the Vietnamese Revolution of August 1945.

The groundwork for this seizure of power was laid in May 1941, when the Indochina Communist Party set up a patriotic front, designed to include all elements of Vietnamese society willing to oppose French colonialism and Japanese 'fascism', and known colloquially as the Viet Minh. Between May 1941 and March 1945, its activities were mainly confined to the building up of a revolutionary nucleus in its remote base on the Sino-Vietnamese border, and establishing contacts across the border with Chinese nationalist leaders, American and Free French liaison officers, and other anti-Japanese Vietnamese nationalists. The Viet Minh seized the opportunity, presented by the removal of the French Indochina administration in March 1945, to spread out networks of 'liberation committees' from their northern base, and to build up an armed force. When the Japanese surrendered in August 1945, Ho Chi Minh judged the moment right to seize power openly, both at the local level – through the agency of the liberation committees – and at the central level – through the establishment, on 2 September 1945, of the ICP/Viet Minh-dominated Democratic Republic of Vietnam.

The ideological underpinnings of this revolutionary process can be elicited from the successive statements of policy issued by the Indochina Communist Party, the Viet Minh 'front', and by Ho Chi Minh himself between March 1945 and 1948, by which time the Vietnamese revolutionaries were engaged in an all-out war against the returning French. Although the Communist Party roughly followed the 'New Democracy' line outlined by Mao Tse-tung, there were significant 'indigenous' features of Vietnamese revolutionary strategy that should be noted. The experience of the 1930–31 revolts (see chapter 3) had shown the ICP the great dangers of alienating the wealthy peasantry and landlords by prematurely emphasizing class issues, and of alienating the peasantry generally by taking a 'dogmatic' attitude towards traditional culture. The Viet Minh front, therefore, was initially conceived as a purely national-liberation movement, *not* as a 'New Democracy' front fighting simultaneously for national-liberation and against feudalism (Rathausky 1963: 44).

The point that the revolutionary struggle at this stage was purely patriotic and had no class-based ingredient was given even greater force in November 1945, when the Indochina Communist Party was officially 'dissolved'. In practice, of course, the ICP continued secretly to dominate the Viet Minh. More than this, conscious of the need to compensate for 'breadth' of patriotic appeal by 'depth' of political education, if the ideological coherence of the revolution was to be preserved, the party pursued what might be called a policy of 'anti-feudalism by stealth' (Rathausky 1963: 9). This involved among other things a campaign for literacy, the introduction of 'universal elementary education', and a recognition of the 'equality of nationalities and the equality of sexes' (Rathausky 1963: 41, 46).

By mid August 1945, the goal of creating a 'new culture' was proclaimed by the National Congress called by the Viet Minh (Rathausky 1963: 50). But – always keeping in mind the lessons of 1930–31 – Ho Chi Minh was, in the ensuing years, most anxious that educational efforts in the countryside to create a new culture and new attitudes should not at that stage be couched in terms of 'class struggle'; and that peasant and minority superstitions and cultural traditions should be treated with respect. As he put it, educational cadres should go out of their way to understand and respect local customs in order to 'create an atmosphere of sympathy'; only on this basis should they then put forward new ideas and encourage the people 'to abate their superstitions' (Ho Chi Minh 1948: vol. 3, 146–47).

However, although the communists carefully played down class 'contradictions' within Vietnam at this stage, they provide an almost text-book example of the application of the criteria of 'antagonistic' and 'non-antagonistic' contradictions in the international sphere. For a small and vulnerable country like Vietnam, it was vitally important to identify international forces that were fundamentally hostile to the objectives of the Vietnamese Revolution – that is, where there was an inherent 'contradiction' between these forces and the Vietnamese Revolution – and at the same time to distinguish, at any given time, between those contradictions that were 'antagonistic' and those that were temporarily 'non-antagonistic'. This perspective was important for the conduct of foreign policy, since in practical terms it enabled the Vietnamese revolutionary government to build alliances and isolate particular enemies, while at the same time maintaining a proper Marxist historical perspective on the course of events. It was also important internally, since it gave local Viet Minh cadres a theoretical base on which to understand that today's friends could become tomorrow's enemies.

When the revolutionary era proper began in March 1945, the fault-line between 'antagonistic' and 'non-antagonistic' contradiction was placed between the Japanese and other world forces of fascism on the antagonistic side, and all 'anti-fascist' forces on the other. In the eyes of the communist leadership, therefore, while the Free French government fully intended to resume colonial control in Vietnam, and while there was an inherent 'contradiction' between Free France and revolutionary Vietnam in the long term, in the short term the Free French and Vietnamese revolutionaries had a common interest in ousting Japan from Indochina; therefore, their relationship at this stage was 'non-antagonistic' (Rathausky 1963: 5, 11). Once Japan surrendered, however, the axis of antagonistic and non-antagonistic contradiction shifted. The principle contradiction was now no longer that between global fascism and global anti-fascist democracy, but between colonialism and national-liberation: that is, between the French government and the Democratic Republic of Vietnam (DRV).

This change in the international situation after the defeat of Japan was signalled in the wording of the Declaration of Independence of the Democratic Republic of Vietnam, which was issued on 2 September 1945 (Ho Chi Minh 1945a: vol. 3, 17–20). By quoting from the American Declaration of Independence, with its quintessential statement of 'bourgeois-democratic' rights, including the right of national self-determination, the Vietnamese declaration was highlighting the 'contradiction' between French colonialism and American anti-colonialism. By then going on to quote from the French 'Declaration of the Rights of Man and the Citizen' that was issued at the beginning of the French Revolution in 1789, the Vietnamese declaration was drawing attention to the 'contradiction' between the stated 'bourgeois-democratic' values of the French Republic, and its colonial practice. The practical intention, of course, was to appeal to the better political instincts of the French people over the heads of their government (Ho Chi Minh 1945a: vol. 3, 17–19).

Although the Vietnamese Declaration of Independence is deliberately couched throughout in the language of bourgeois-democracy, it is, paradoxically, precisely for that reason that the declaration is a profoundly Marxist-Leninist document. Unlike other declarations of independence – for example, the Irish proclamation of independence of 1916 – it does not appeal to the 'inherent' values of the Vietnamese people, or invoke the idea that the Vietnamese nation had some kind of unchanging core identity or 'soul' that was being redeemed. Rather, the declaration reflects the fact that Ho Chi Minh saw independence as just part of a long-term dialectical process that had a vital international dimension, in which the declaration could play a pragmatic role.

In the event, the DRV effort to recruit sufficient international support to discourage any French attempt to reconquer Indochina failed, and by early 1947 French and Viet Minh forces were embroiled in a bitter guerrilla war that was to last till 1954. Already, by the summer of 1946, when the two sides were squaring up for what seemed inevitable conflict, the ideological focus of the Vietnamese revolutionary movement had begun to change, even though the Indochina Communist Party still theoretically remained 'dissolved'. Truong Chinh, who had been appointed General-Secretary of the ICP in 1941, wrote an influential essay in August 1946, entitled *The August Revolution*. In this, he argued that although the August 1945 Revolution had simply been a national revolution in its 'form', it had nevertheless been 'new democracy in its content' (Truong Chinh 1946: 47). In practice, in order to maintain the revolutionary momentum and general support of the population, it had proved to be necessary at the local level to begin the process of transforming the 'formal' rights of bourgeois-democracy into 'real' social and economic rights (Truong Chinh 1946: 56–57). Moreover, as Truong Chinh pointed out in a subsequent work, published in sections during 1947 and known collectively as *The Resistance Will Win*, the very fact of waging a guerrilla war – with the pressing need to create a war economy through centralized planning in order to ensure agricultural and industrial self-sufficiency – helped to develop at least the embryonic basis of a cooperative society and economy (Truong Chinh 1947: 125–32).

These two works of Truong Chinh produced in 1946 and 1947 – *The August Revolution* and *The Resistance Will Win* – contain the most comprehensive analysis of the theoretical basis of the Vietnamese revolution. Like Mao Tse-tung, Truong Chinh particularly emphasized the need to move beyond the introduction of social and economic reform, and to initiate a genuine cultural revolution in the Vietnamese countryside: a revolution, that is, in the minds of the Vietnamese peasantry. Truong Chinh cited three particular reasons why this task was an urgent priority. In the first place, while the French held the towns, the Viet Minh generally controlled the countryside; it was the peasantry, therefore, who held the key to success in the war effort (Truong Chinh 1947: 137). Secondly, it was clear that the war was going to be a long drawn out struggle, in which time would be on the side of the Revolution; it was therefore necessary that the mobilization of the peasantry should be deep-rooted and based, not simply on patriotic fervour, but on the notion that their lives would be entirely changed for the better (Truong Chinh 1947: 106). Finally, since all the 'objective' advantages in the war – in the shape of finance, weapons, and the apparatus that an industrial state could deploy – lay with the French, it was all the more vital that this should be offset by the decisive advantage that lay with the Vietnamese people: namely, the 'subjective' factor of the revolutionary will of the people as a whole (Truong Chinh 1947: 171).

Truong Chinh followed Mao Tse-tung in asserting that the campaign to create a 'New Culture' should retain and exploit old national 'forms': particularly those, like folk-song cycles, that were popular among the peasantry. The *content*, however, should introduce new 'scientific' ways of looking at the world, and help to eliminate all traces of the old feudal mentality (Truong Chinh 1947: 136–37). Above all, this cultural revolution of the countryside should change the traditional peasant notion that he was at the mercy of fate (Truong Chinh 1947: 171).

In his 'Talks at the Yenan Forum on Arts and Literature' of 1942, Mao Tse-tung had wrestled with a question that Truong Chinh also tried to tackle: What should be the precise method and approach of this New Culture? Mao insisted that there was no such thing as art or literature that *transcended* the class struggle. All art or literature served the interest of a particular class at a particular stage of historical development, and it therefore followed that the New Culture should consciously promote the social and political goals of New Democracy (Mao Tse-tung 1942: 193). More specifically, the literature should seek to tear aside the decorative frills of the feudal culture of the countryside that hid from the peasantry the real condition in which they lived; should then seek to demonstrate that these conditions were based on human injustice, not 'fate'; should show that these conditions were not immutable; and, finally, should inspire the peasantry to understand that they could change the world in which they lived (Mao Tse-tung 1942: 194).

Both in form and in content, the Chinese writer Lu Hsun (1881–1936) provided a model for this new literature, although Lu Hsun himself – writing as he did at a time when the feudal structures of the countryside were breaking down, but when a positive, alternative vision of a better life for the peasantry had not yet clearly emerged – was not an orthodox Marxist writer in the Maoist sense of prescribing through his literature the shape of the new world that the Chinese peasantry could create (Mao Tse-tung 1940: 163). If we consider examples of Vietnamese revolutionary literature written in the post-1945 period, the links with the Lu Hsun style are evident. Like Lu Hsun, the Vietnamese writers used a simple, vernacular language, and chose the short story as the ideal literary vehicle. Like Lu Hsun, they looked behind the idyllic picture of the countryside presented by the scholar-poets of the feudal era, and, when they depicted the real conditions of the peasantry, they concentrated on the petty tyrannies of the local henchmen of the feudal system that the peasantry would have experienced in their everyday life (Lu Hsun 1954: 55–65).

It is interesting to compare the role of the 'intellectual' in Lu Hsun's stories and in those of the Vietnamese Marxist writers of the revolutionary period. In Lu Hsun's stories, the local scholar-gentry had lost their traditional role as cultural transmitters between the Confucian state and the village; loafing in wine shops, teaching old Confucian precepts that had lost their meaning, or eking out a precarious living as 'advisers' to local warlords, they were Lu Hsun's central symbols of the disintegration of the feudal system (Lu Hsun 1954: 31–37, 119–33, 149–71). In the Vietnamese short-stories, the educated scholar was the pivotal figure in the confrontation between the old and the new culture. In his guise as a member of the local scholar-gentry, he was a bastion of reaction, sneering at the unsophisticated propaganda of the revolution (Anon. 1974: 24–41). In his (or her) new guise of 'revolutionary intellectual', however, the educated communist 'cadre' played the crucial role of showing the peasantry that their abject conditions were not the consequence of an unalterable fate. The stories, however, took care to ensure that such cadres were always sensitive to local customs, and did not behave – as Ho Chi Minh put it in 1945 – like 'mandarin revolutionaries' (Ho Chi Minh 1945b: vol. 3, 34).

The Vietnamese short stories illustrated all the varieties of hardships and injustices that the peasantry had to face: the artificial famine created by hoarding, the ill-treatment of women, the oppression of the minorities by their own chieftains, or the humiliation of a local acting troupe by village notables. But in each case, such people were shown standing up for themselves (sometimes with some timely prompting from a local cadre), taking control of their own lives, and, in effect, resisting rather than accepting fate. The famine-stricken villagers seize the granaries, and the other tales of oppression all had the same kind of *denouement*: the women, the minority family, and the actor whose wife had been casually raped and killed by the village chieftain, all end up joining the liberation forces (Anon. 1974: 9–23, 42–55, 103–11).

Clearly, the New Culture was not simply designed by the communists to 'democratize' the Vietnamese countryside and wipe out feudal attitudes; it was also designed to generate at the grass-roots level the beginnings of an irresistible momentum towards a socialist mentality and a socialist society.

THE WORLD-VIEW OF THE BURMESE REVOLUTION, 1945–1948

The Burmese road to independence between 1945 and 1948 has rarely been described as a 'revolution'. But it could in fact reasonably be called an 'averted revolution', and, although the guiding ideology of the nationalist leadership was not Marxist-Leninist in the orthodox communist sense, it was deeply influenced by the general world-view and analytical outlook of Marxism and Leninism.

When Ba Maw formed his independent government in August 1943 within the framework of the Japanese Co-Prosperity Sphere (see previous chapter), it is noticeable that many Burmese on the left of the political spectrum were prepared to join his administration: including Than Tun, who was later to lead the Burmese Communist Party (BCP), and Aung San himself (Silverstein 1993: 7). Political opportunism can only provide a partial explanation for this willingness of leftists to link with a government that was overtly fascist in character. As Aung San was later to explain, leftists throughout Southeast Asia were thoroughly ideologically confused during the war years (Aung San 1945: 82–87). As socialists, they saw Japan as a mortal 'fascist' enemy to world socialism, even more of a danger than Western colonialism itself. As nationalists, they felt that the destruction of European power in Southeast Asia gave Japan the status of liberator, whatever its ideological hue. In any case, Aung San was able to use his position as commander of the armed forces of newly independent Burma to build up the basis for an anti-colonial army that could be used against the British or the Japanese, as occasion demanded. In August 1944, the Anti-Fascist People's Freedom League (AFPFL) was secretly formed; this explicitly anti-Japanese movement linked Aung San – and, de facto, the army that he commanded – to the Communist Party of Burma in a general leftist coalition. On 27 March 1945, at the very moment that the Japanese army was about to be defeated by a British-led army invading from India, this movement launched a rebellion against the Japanese.

When the British reconquered Burma in early to mid 1945, they found themselves confronted by a mass movement – the AFPFL – that could claim that Burma had 'liberated itself', and that had at its disposal a mobilized force which may not have been well-trained or armed in conventional military terms, but which had been given an intensive political education designed to heighten its commitment and national consciousness (Tinker 1983: 297). The assessment of the AFPFL leaders in May 1945, however, was that, while it was true that a 'revolutionary' situation was developing, it was necessary – given the fact that Britain's position was militarily strong in the local sphere, even though it had become drastically weakened internationally – to pursue 'lawful' resistance to British rule, and in the meantime to continue to build up a mass base (Tinker 1983: 292–93).

The AFPFL's assessment that, while Britain was strong in the short-term, it was globally weak in the long-term, proved to be correct. By the summer of 1946, the mass political organizations created by Aung San and the Burmese communists had made Burma ungovernable by the British, except at a military and financial cost that they were no longer able to pay. When the AFPFL and Britain entered into negotiations for independence, however, and began in 1947 to put into place the preliminary political structures for an independent state, Aung San and the AFPFL leadership insisted that the political process in Burma was still 'revolutionary'; that, while the absence of British resistance meant that mass 'struggle' could be replaced by normal democratic procedures, the goal of the AFPFL was not simply that of self-government, but also that of bringing about a fundamental 'revolutionary' transformation of Burmese society (Aung San 1947a: 55–56).

Although their perspectives differed radically, neither the Burmese communists nor the British were inclined to take this revolutionary language seriously. In the course of 1946, two separate communist factions had broken away from the AFPFL, and the general communist line was that Aung San and the AFPFL had betrayed the revolution, had replaced a mass struggle by an elite deal with Britain that would protect Britain's interests in Burma and in return ensure British support for the AFPFL leadership. For their part, the British regarded Aung San as a pragmatist who used his radical rhetoric in order to keep up his mass support in Burma, but under whose aegis friendly British-Burmese relations could be maintained.

However, a study of Aung San's general ideological position from 1944 to the time of his assassination in July 1947 suggests that there was a considerable degree of consistency in his political thinking. Like most Asian nationalists of his age, Aung San made the link between colonialism and capitalism, and therefore between anti-colonialism and socialism. This sense of the inherently progressive nature of socialism was undoubtedly reinforced by the success of the Soviet Union since 1917, first, in building up a powerful modern state; and, secondly, in defeating the seemingly invincible power of world fascism.

An examination of the speeches that Aung San gave from 1945 shows that he took a Marxist view of the laws of historical development. Although he did occasionally compare the Marxist idea of the 'dialectical' progress of history, through the cumulative resolution of social and economic 'contradictions', with the Buddhist notion of *samsara*, or the cycle of desire and suffering that caused an inherent instability in human history, his political vision was in fact generally secular (Aung San 1946a: 97).

Aung San viewed pre-colonial Burma as a feudal society, but one in which the uglier manifestations of feudalism had at least been tempered by Buddhist values and the general availability of land (Aung San 1945: 78–79). In line with other nationalists of his time who were influenced by the Marxist schema, he saw British colonialism in Burma as a capitalist phenomenon that nevertheless enlisted the support of traditional feudal structures in Burma – particularly at the village level, and among the various feudal chieftains in the minority areas (Aung San 1945: 79–80). Following this general Marxist analysis, Aung San interpreted fascism as a last-ditch effort by capitalism in Europe to protect its economic interests. Fascism, however, had become what he called a 'Frankenstein monster' that threatened to destroy its creator; as a last resort, therefore, capitalism and its imperialist offshoots had been reluctantly compelled to align with global 'progressive forces' headed by the Soviet Union. Although this expedient had temporarily saved European imperialism from destruction, it had emerged from the Second World War gravely weakened; as a world force, imperialism was doomed, and would soon have to face what Aung San called 'the logical music of history' (Aung San 1946a: 98–99).

Aung San was clear, therefore, that the future lay inevitably with the socialist camp; following the same metaphor, Aung San asserted that the Soviet Union marched 'in tune with the music of history' (Aung San 1946a: 101). This, of course, left the awkward question of the historical role of the United States: a conundrum that puzzled other socialist-inclined Asian nationalists at this time. Aung San confined himself to the observation that the United States' 'international' and open version of capitalism – symbolized by such recently created institutions as the International Monetary Fund (IMF) and the World Bank – was inherently antagonistic to the economically exclusive European imperialist structures (Aung San 1946a: 98, 101). He noticeably did not pursue the issue of the relationship between this new version of world capitalism and the socialist camp headed by the Soviet Union. This was indeed an open question that was to confuse the world-view of Southeast Asian anti-colonialism in the ensuing decades.

Within the framework of this world-view, Aung San made clear that Burma was passing through the anti-imperialist and anti-feudal 'New Democracy' phase (Aung San 1946c: 145). Although the actual term fell into disuse after Aung San's break with the communists in late 1946, there can be no doubt that Aung San continued to pursue the broad outlines of a New Democracy strategy. However, regulation of the various 'non-antagonistic' but competing class interests, represented by different parties within the general framework of the AFPFL front, was to lie in the hands of Aung San and the overall AFPFL leadership, not – as in the case of orthodox Marxism-Leninism – in the hands of a communist party (Aung San 1946a: 112). The introduction of formal democratic structures in 1947 as part of the Burmese move to independence did not change the general New Democracy strategy; in fact, parliamentary democracy provided an ideal means of ensuring that competing class interests remained 'non-antagonistic' (Aung San 1947b: 153).

Aung San insisted, however, that formal democracy would not be enough in the revolutionary process that Burma was undergoing. Without the introduction of socialist principles, the abstract rights of bourgeois democracy would be incomplete. Likewise, without socialism, genuine national liberation from the economic power of global capitalism could not be achieved (Aung San 1946b: 132). The AFPFL, therefore, undertook to act as more than the mere 'regulator' of class interests: it would push forward the social and political agenda in a progressive, socialist direction, on behalf of those whom Aung San described as 'the poor masses' (Aung San 1947b: 155). More specifically, it became an explicit part of the AFPFL programme to create a socialist planned economy after independence, in which the main industries and services would be nationalized; to introduce measures for land reform that would at least move in the direction of the ultimate goal of the socialization of agriculture; and to take measures to regulate Burma's trading relationship with the outside world in order to protect the nation's autonomous economic development (Aung San 1947b: 154). The assassination of Aung San did not alter the basic ideological trend of AFPFL policy. Indeed, Aung San's successor, U Nu, explicitly stated in September 1947 that the goal of the AFPFL was ultimately to create a fully socialist society, in which natural resources and the means of production would come under common ownership, and in which the economy would be regulated on the general socialist principle of 'everybody contributing his share and getting his share' (U Nu 1947: 770).

Even in his consideration of the Burmese minority problem, Aung San was governed by the ideological framework provided by the Soviet Union. Given the fact that the minorities – although relatively small in number – dominated the whole peripheral area of Burma, and given the fact also that Britain had always administered these minority regions separately from Burma, the problem of integrating the minorities on a mutually-acceptable basis into an independent Burma was a matter of crucial importance for the Burmese political leaders. While it is true that in the detailed negotiations leading to independence, Aung San undoubtedly adopted a pragmatic policy on this matter, his broad perspective on the issue was directly influenced by the 'nationalities' policies of first Lenin and then Stalin. As a starting-point, he rejected the notion that national identity was based on 'inherent' qualities such as race, religion or language: rather, he argued, national identity emerged from 'the historic necessity of having to lead a common life' (Aung San 1946a: 104). In other words, the nation and nationalism were historically determined – not intrinsic – phenomena like any other human organization, and it therefore followed that national and minority rights should not be assessed in absolute terms, but relatively and 'dialectically' (Aung San 1947b: 157).

For Aung San, therefore, the essential question to be asked in handling the question of national and minority rights in Burma was the extent to which the granting or withholding of such rights would have a 'progressive' or 'reactionary' impact at any given historical moment. In general, he agreed with Lenin's and Stalin's view that the encouragement of cultural and linguistic rights of minorities, and even the granting of measures of autonomy, would have a 'progressive' impact. Such measures would be the most natural vehicle for social and educational progress, and would at the same time avert the risk of creating nationalist resentment on the part of the minorities against the mainstream ethnic Burmese. Following the 'nationalities' line taken (at least in theory) by Stalin in the Soviet Union, Aung San was even prepared to concede the right of complete self-determination to areas – like the Shan States – where the objective preconditions for full self-government could be said to exist (Aung San 1947b: 156–57). But Aung San insisted that the granting of such a right was not absolute, but dependent on existing historical circumstances. If, as in the case of the Shan States, self-determination would simply mean a transfer of power to the very feudal chieftains (*sawbwa*) who had been the local mainstay of colonial rule, then – in the dialectical relationship between *national* and *social* rights – the acquisition of national rights by the Shans would have an adverse effect on their democratic and social rights (Aung San 1946d: 104).

From one perspective, the transfer of power from Britain to an independent Burmese government may have the appearance of a purely pragmatic transaction. The speeches of the main Burmese leaders of the time indicate, however, that they intended to bring about a fundamental transformation of Burmese society along Marxist, indeed broadly Marxist-Leninist lines. This revolution was, however, to be guided by a supra-class leadership rather than an orthodox communist party.

THE IDEOLOGICAL BACKGROUND TO THE INDONESIAN REVOLUTION

By late 1944, the Japanese (see chapter 6) had decided that the granting of independence to Java, and possibly to the whole of Indonesia, would help increase local commitment to their war effort. In early 1945, therefore, they established a committee to prepare for independence. In August 1945, however, just as the Indonesian political leadership was poised to move to the final stages of what would have been a Japanese-conferred independence, Japan surrendered. In the period of the vacuum of power between the surrender of the Japanese and the arrival of the Allies – including the Dutch – this same leadership hurriedly declared the independence of Indonesia on 17 August 1945. In the ensuing days and weeks there followed a huge outburst of revolutionary activity at the local level, including assaults on the traditional regional authorities who had worked under the Dutch and the Japanese; the establishment of ad hoc substitute administrations backed by local militias; and, here and there, attacks on Japanese forces, and attempts to get hold of their arms.

The whole of Java and Sumatra were in ferment, and the leaders of the new Indonesian Republic in Jakarta did not have at hand any direct means of exerting their control. The returning Dutch were already gaining a firm foothold in the eastern islands of Indonesia, and – in the wake of the arrival from late September 1945 of British-led troops to administer the surrender of the Japanese – were able to establish bridgeheads in Java and Sumatra. In this perilous situation, Indonesian nationalist leaders had to maintain a delicate balance. They had to build a coherent state that would act in a unified manner against the Dutch; at the same time, they had to sustain the revolutionary momentum that had developed – albeit in a chaotic and diverse manner – in the regions; and they had to try to win international support as a responsible and functioning state with a legitimate claim for independence against the Dutch.

One of the key tasks, therefore, was to develop an ideological basis for the new state that would satisfy the revolutionary spirit that had been unleashed, and yet at the same time ensure unity between all the different cross-currents of political ideas and agendas that had emerged during the war period. In this context, Sukarno's speech to the 'Preparatory Body for Investigating Independence' in June 1945 was of central importance. In this speech, Sukarno analyzed and outlined the guiding principles that should be the foundation of an independent Indonesia (Sukarno 1945: 3–21).

This speech constituted a kind of 'crossroads' in Sukarno's political ideas, since it reiterated themes that Sukarno had been pursuing since the 1920s, and at the same time revealed the innate political instincts that were to dominate his approach to Indonesia's national problems for the rest of his political career. From 1933, Sukarno had argued that the political structure and ideological character of Indonesia should not be determined until Indonesia had actually achieved independence. Independence was the 'golden bridge' that had to be crossed by a unified, not ideologically-fractured, nationalist movement: only then could Indonesia have the real freedom to decide its own fate in its own way (Sukarno 1945: 4). On the other hand, he recognized that the momentum towards independence had to be driven by some kind of 'world-view' (*weltanschauung*) and guiding idea that would at the same time inspire and hold together the nationalist movement (Sukarno 1945: 8). This – in line with his overriding concern for the maintenance of the ideological and political unity of Indonesia – he identified as the spirit of *mufakat*, or consensus: the maintenance of unity within the context of debate. At the end of his speech, he alternatively described this quality as *gotong royong*, or the spirit of cooperation (Sukarno 1945: 9–10, 19).

On this fundamental basis, Sukarno – typically running away with himself, given his stated position that the principles of the state should not be defined before independence – outlined the five basic interlocking principles, or *pancasila* (*pantjasila* in the spelling of the time), that should be the foundation of an independent Indonesia. Briefly stated, these were nationalism, internationalism, democracy, social justice, and belief in God.

In his outline of the nationalist principle, Sukarno's position was in fact contradictory: on the one hand, he subscribed to the pragmatic view that a national entity emerged out of the common will of a people who had had a shared historical experience and a desire to be united; on the other, he asserted that Indonesia was, despite its diverse history and its multiplicity of pre-colonial states, defined by geography and by 'God Almighty' as essentially one nation. Whatever the expressed wishes of the different parts of the Indonesian archipelago, therefore, Indonesia was 'an already existing nation' whose predetermined destiny was to be a unified state (Sukarno 1945: 11–13). In his explanation of the principles of 'internationalism'

Sukarno warned against the adoption of a vapid 'cosmopolitanism'. The nation, he insisted, was the fundamental political unit of the modern world. But an independent Indonesia should avoid the inward-looking, race-orientated nationalism of Europe; it should be conscious of the broader international perspective, and thereby play a positive role in international affairs (Sukarno 1945: 14). This was to become a major, almost a dominating, aspect of Sukarno's thinking in the years to come.

However, at that time, the crucial linkages in Sukarno's elucidation of the five principles were those between nationalism, socialism and democracy. In line with general Asian thinking of this period, Sukarno regarded socialism as the essential linchpin connecting and perfecting democracy and nationalism. Without socialism, democracy was a mere conglomeration of abstract rights that had no effect whatever on the actual conditions in which people lived. Without socialism, national independence would remain incomplete, because the economy would still be at the mercy of international capitalism (Sukarno 1945: 16–19).

Sukarno urged that Indonesia should not follow the confrontational, party-based, 'winner-takes-all' democracy of the West. Rather, he advocated a traditionally-based, specifically Indonesian democracy in which, as he put it, the democratic process would involve 'unanimity (*mufakat*) arising out of deliberation (*permusyawaratan*) amongst representatives (*perwakilan*)' (Sukarno 1945: 15). The essential difference between Sukarno's *mufakat* and Marxism's 'non-antagonistic contradiction' lay in Sukarno's rejection of the notion that there were *inherent* differences of interest between classes within a nation, and that parties should represent and protect these separate interests.

It is, however, apparent from this key speech that Sukarno's vision of a political system based on conflict-avoidance clashed with his revolutionary temperament. While he clearly rejected the class analysis of Marxism, his political instincts accorded with the Marxist 'dialectic' – the view that the dynamic of history was driven by confrontation and struggle. In the peroration of his speech, he gave 'thanks to God' that Indonesia would not become independent 'under a clear sky', but rather 'with the sound of the drums of war'; and he warned the Indonesian people that, if they wanted independence, they would have to 'take a risk', and 'dare to dive for pearls into the depths of the ocean' (Sukarno 1945: 20–21). Earlier in the speech, he expressed the hope that the 'deliberation' (*permusyawaratan*) in the future legislative body should be a 'struggle of convictions' like 'the cauldron of Condrodimuko' (Sukarno 1945: 15). This image is significant, since Condrodimuko is the crater of a legendary Javanese volcano whose boiling water, if braved, would confer superhuman strength. Likewise, Sukarno saw the spirit of daring and relentless struggle as the vital means of enabling the Indonesian people to overcome their relative weakness, backwardness, and tendencies to disunity.

At this time, Sukarno's revolutionary instincts mirrored the actual social and cultural revolution that was taking place in the wider society. Between 1942 and 1945, a complete upheaval had taken place in Indonesia, particularly amongst its youth. The abrupt removal of Dutch colonial power had had the effect of removing the aura of prestige that had up to that time still surrounded the regional traditional elite on whom colonial authority had depended, and who had, conversely, depended on the maintenance of colonial power. Prompted by Japanese pan-Asian propaganda, Indonesian youth had trained and armed in the militia organizations that had been formed during the war years. Subsequently, in the course of 1945, these same youths joined the many local nationalist and revolutionary groups that sprang up throughout Java and Sumatra. This rise of local revolutionary and nationalist activity, coupled with the empowerment of youth, brought about not just a political, but also a profound cultural, transformation.

Such is the quality of the poetry of Chairil Anwar (1922–1949), that it would be quite unfair simply to pigeon-hole him as the spokesman for this new generation. It is, nevertheless, part of his literary genius that he put this cultural upheaval into words. Although Chairil Anwar's poetry was intensely personal, it did vividly describe the urban milieu of war-time and revolutionary Jakarta in which he lived and wrote. His poetry illuminated an uncompromisingly modern world: a world of anonymous individuals without relatives or social connections (Anwar 1974: 30–31). His poems describe the rootless urban world of the bus-stand, the cinema and the restaurant, and its symbols are ice-cream, coca-cola, American films, bicycles and the latest popular song playing on the radio (Anwar 1974: 104–5, 120–21). Chairil Anwar's 'romantic-individualist' themes reflected the influence of European lyric poetry of the nineteenth and early twentieth century. He depicted life as a permanent existential struggle that must ultimately be conducted alone: it is only by living life to the full, without compromise, that we can defy death and our own transience (Anwar 1974: 98–99, 60–61). Religion is no longer a refuge, but a permanent spiritual struggle between faith and scepticism; love is never stable, but an endless inner conflict between desire and entrapment (Anwar 1974: 52–53, 92–93, 96–97).

'This I write on a ship, in a nameless sea' (Anwar 1974: 96–97): such an unbending assertion of the individual might seem to be alien to political commitment. In fact, however, Chairil Anwar caught the mood of his time and wrote a number of patriotic poems about the war period, the revolution and the subsequent independence struggle against the Dutch. He infused this poetry with the same sense of struggle, the same romantic assertion of existence, this time against foreign power and traditional authority (Anwar 1974: 60–61). This attitude to politics – in which personal and national freedom (*merdeka*) were interlocked – was a natural basis for the 'revolutionary mentality', in the sense that revolution ceased to be so much the pursuit of a specific political objective, as a state of mind in which all that mattered was 'the storm of failure and victory' (Anwar 1974: 58–59). Even his straightforward patriotic poems implied that the marching in step mattered as much as the goal (Anwar 1974: 70–71). In other poems – suspended, as it were, between the personal and the political – the notion of struggle for its own sake was equally apparent: even if the cause was no longer clear, he wrote in one of his poems, 'the finger will not be removed from the trigger' (Anwar 1974: 108–9). One of his last poems suggested that what his generation of revolutionary sacrifice had given to the nation was an inspiration: it would be for future generations – after the ferment of struggle had passed – to 'give us meaning' (Anwar 1974: 128–31).

Such a state of mind may create great poetry, but it is also the breeding-ground for dangerous politics. While it would be quite unfair to associate Chairil Anwar with the political excesses of the revolutionary period, it is nevertheless the case that he claimed to speak for 'his' generation, and that the revolutionary mentality of this generation could breed nihilism and xenophobia. Such at least was the view of Soetan Sjahrir, who became the first prime minister of the Indonesian Republic in November 1945. At that time he published a political essay entitled *Perjuangan Kita* ('Our Struggle'), in which he tried to give a new and positive definition of the concepts of 'struggle' and 'revolution', and to indicate how these concepts should be put into practice in Indonesia.

Sjahrir argued that the overriding problem for the Indonesian Revolution was the general lack of political education, particularly among Indonesian youth. In consequence, a people who had not long before been locked in a feudal-patriarchal social and administrative system, and had not the remotest understanding of the concept or the workings of democracy, were being pitchforked *en masse* into the political arena. Worse still, in the new mass politics that had begun to emerge under the Japanese during the Second World War, the tone was fascistic, and the spirit that was encouraged was militaristic and xenophobic. As a result, in the wake of the Japanese surrender, a revolutionary movement had emerged that was dominated by fanatical youth, attached to a romantic psychology of action for its own sake, and endowed with what Sjahrir called a 'freedom or death' mentality (Sjahrir 1968: 20–21).

This combination of nihilistic undertones and xenophobic activity was not only intrinsically dangerous for Indonesia, Sjahrir argued, but also risked alienating the outside world upon which the success of Indonesia's war against the Dutch depended. Sjahrir – who, more than most of his nationalist colleagues could see Indonesia as Westerners might see it – knew full well that the West, after its harrowing experiences with Nazism and fascism, had had a belly-full of youth militancy in all its forms (Gellhorn

1967: 171–91). More to the point, perhaps, the assaults by nationalist groups on the local Dutch and Eurasians, and on Chinese and Ambonese communities that were traditionally loyal to the Dutch, gave credence to the Dutch claim that the Indonesian Revolution was driven by an ugly form of xenophobia, not the inclusive nationalism that Sukarno proclaimed (Sjahrir 1968: 17–19). Ad hoc seizures of foreign property and attacks on foreign economic interests, moreover, would help persuade others besides the Dutch that Indonesian society was in the grip of a political frenzy that combined extreme fascist and communist characteristics, and which the leadership could not control.

It was therefore vital that serious efforts should be made to educate politically the Indonesian people as a whole – ideally by creating what Sjahrir called a 'democratic revolutionary party' that could supervise this education and push forward the social and democratic revolution internally (Sjahrir 1968: 29–30, 36). Like other Asian nationalists of his time, Sjahrir was absolutely committed to the idea that democracy was incomplete without an accompanying social revolution (Sjahrir 1968: 27). But the key to his thinking at this time was his belief that, while the 'democratic socialist' war against feudalism and colonialism was vital, it was equally important to wage a democratic 'struggle' against the fascist and xenophobic tendencies that had infected Indonesian nationalism, particularly under the Japanese. The immediate task, therefore, was that of introducing the democratic principle, through the creation of a network of local and regional assemblies that would run on a democratic basis. The practical exercise of real local democracy – under central guidance at this stage – would in itself be the best possible form of political education. This would channel political energies in a positive direction, and at the same time harness those energies to a unified and responsible political goal (Sjahrir 1968: 29–34).

But it was Sjahrir's contention that the character and the pace of the Indonesian Revolution – with its national, democratic and socialist objectives – was dependent on international circumstances. And Sjahrir's world-view at this time was in many ways radically different from other political thinkers in Southeast Asia. Unlike Aung San, he dismissed the idea that there was any inherent 'contradiction' between the 'colonial capitalism' of Britain and the 'international capitalism' of the United States. Britain, he argued, had in effect fallen in line behind the United States, and, in the wake of the war, it was the United States that had become the regional arbiter. Whether it liked it or not, therefore, Indonesia lay within what he called 'the Anglo-Saxon capitalist and imperialist ambience' (Sjahrir 1968: 24–25). While he accepted that socialist and capitalist principles were engaged in a global struggle, he did not, unlike those who generally adopted the Marxist world-view, assert the historical inevitability of the ultimate victory of the socialist principle (Sjahrir 1968: 24).

Sjahrir agreed with the radical anti-colonialists that Indonesia's independence was only absolute in theory, not in practice. The implication of his position, however, was that the achievement of Indonesia's national, democratic and socialist goals could not depend simply on an exercise of revolutionary will-power or on the application of radical anti-imperialist policies. Ultimately Indonesia's ambitions would have to be tempered by international realities, particularly the reality of the international power of the United States.

CHAPTER EIGHT

Anti-Revolutionary Nationalism

It is a generally accepted notion that the Second World War precipitated a complete political transformation in Southeast Asia. Although the Japanese occupation of the region was temporary, it had a devastating effect on the hitherto impregnable edifice of colonial power: not only were the colonial regimes destroyed, but – perhaps more importantly – the mystique of White 'prestige' that underpinned these regimes was irretrievably lost. Furthermore, the United States' rise to regional pre-eminence in the post-war period, and the parallel decline of the European powers, ensured the creation of a new world order in which the principle of the right to self-determination was expanded globally to include the former colonial regimes. 'Decolonization', in the sense of conceding the ultimate right to self-government, was now accepted even by the colonial powers as an inevitable process. International disputes over the issue now centred on the pace and the character of this process.

When France, Britain and the Netherlands attempted to return to their respective colonial possessions in Indochina, Burma and Indonesia, therefore, they were not so much disputing the right to self-determination, as asserting their right to control the framework and the timetable within which this process should take place. The problem for the colonial powers was that, while they themselves were pursuing complex and blurred political goals, they were confronting single-minded and ideologically-mobilized revolutionary forces. Moreover, this mass mobilization by the new anti-colonial regimes made Vietnam, Burma and Indonesia ungovernable by the returning powers. In effect, revolutionary nationalist polities had been created in these countries in 1945 that could not subsequently be uprooted.

The situation was entirely different, however, in the Philippines, Malaya, Cambodia and Laos. Although the events of the war – particularly the willingness of the elites of these countries to collaborate with the Japanese –

temporarily disrupted the relationship between the colonial powers and these elites, the fact remains that there was a considerable degree of continuity between the colonial regimes and the independence regimes that emerged after the war. In the case of the Philippines, the pre-war timetable for independence was adhered to, but at the same time the independent Philippine state remained firmly within the United States' regional security framework. Likewise, when Cambodia, Laos and Malaya gained their independence, they too retained close economic, cultural and security links with the former colonial powers. The old colonial powers and the traditional elites were bound by a common fear of communism, revolution and political disorder during and after the transition to independence. The dominating ethos of these independence regimes, therefore, was essentially conservative and anti-revolutionary. Independence was achieved by negotiation rather than revolutionary struggle, and the indigenous elites of the colonial period continued to dominate the post-independence political structures.

In order to grant independence to a state, however, it is first of all necessary for that state to exist. Before the Second World War, the British had not created a united Malayan state, and the French had not created a united Laotian state – a defect in colonial policy of which certain members of the indigenous elites of both the Malayan and Laotian regions were acutely conscious. It was not until the war period that the British and French colonial administrations seriously began to address themselves to the task of creating a united Malayan state, and a united Laotian state. This involved defining the national identities that would form the ballast of the two states; creating an ideological base that would encompass the core values binding together their citizens; and putting in place appropriate constitutional structures. In other words, what the colonial powers were trying to create during the war and immediate post-war period – pushed along by the respective indigenous political elites – were not just new states, but comprehensive 'polities' that could survive the dangerous international situation that faced Southeast Asia after the Second World War.

LAOS: THE CREATION OF AN INDIGENOUS POLITY

At the end of the nineteenth and beginning of the twentieth centuries, France had gained control of the Laotian principalities on the eastern side of the Mekong river, and – on the western side – the Sayaboury region of the kingdom of Luang Prabang and the southern Lao kingdom of Champassak. These Lao regions had been incorporated into French Indochina, but they were not administered as a single unit. While France maintained a protectorate over the northern Lao kingdom of Luang Prabang, the remainder of French Laotian territory, including the former kingdom of Champassak, was directly administered as a colony, and the local indigenous rulers were coopted into the administration. A French *résident-supérieur* exercised general control over these disparate administrations (Katay don Sasorith 1953: 49–53).

In the inter-war years, a tiny Western-educated stratum emerged within the indigenous elite. Its main political concern was that French colonial policy was endangering, not just Lao unity, but Lao identity itself. In a study of the political status of Laos written in 1938, Katay don Sasorith (1904–1954) pointed out that Lao history had since the fourteenth century been one of steady decline and political disunity. In the eighteenth century, the kingdom of Lan Xang, which had once unified the Lao people, had split into separate states along the course of the Mekong river. A further blow to Lao unity had been dealt by the incorporation, in the period 1893–1907, of one half of the Lao people into the kingdom of Siam, and the other half into French Indochina (Katay don Sasorith 1953: 141–42). Katay argued that, although the French had justified their take-over of Lao territory as a means of protecting the Lao people from the threat of complete absorption by Siam, their own policy of maintaining different administrations in different parts of Laos had, if anything, deepened the crisis of Lao identity. By basing their policy towards the Lao on regional dynastic identities, moreover, the French were undermining the deep-rooted sense of unity among the Lao, symbolized by their collective historical memory of the kingdom of Lan Xang.

At the same time, similar concerns about French policy towards the Lao were being expressed by French members of the colonial administration in Laos. In 1935, a group of 'old colonial hands' in Paris formed a *Société des Amis du Laos*, and in July 1937 the first number of the *Bulletin des 'Amis du Laos'* was published in Hanoi. Their concern was that the French, tending as they did to regard Lao culture as the exotic remnant of a dead civilization, had made no systematic attempt to preserve, retrieve or make sense of the remaining fragments of this culture, and reconnect it to modern-day Laos (Eutrope 1937: x-xi). This failure had political implications. It was the duty of France as the protectorate power to enable the Lao people to survive in the modern world and at the same time to preserve their identity. Instead, it had allowed the roots of Lao culture and society to rot away. The danger for France was that future generations of Lao would have to face the modern world, and all its dangerous ideological temptations, cut off from their cultural roots, and deprived of the sure foundations of a sense of identity (Tullié 1937: 4, 6–9).

The aspirations of the 'Amis du Laos' merged cultural, archaeological and historical goals. The primary archaeological and historical tasks were to restore the crumbling monuments of Lao civilization, to place them in a historical and cultural context, and to connect this civilization to the modern Lao world (Tullié 1937: 9–10). This could help form the foundation for a secure sense of Lao identity – a recapturing in cultural terms of the ideal of Lao unity – and a framework of ideas on which Lao culture and identity was based (Tullié 1937: 10–11).

This cultural-political project was not interrupted, but accelerated by the events of the Second World War. In the winter of 1940–41 the nationalist regime in Thailand took advantage of the weakness of France and – with the timely help of Japan – forced French Indochina to cede to it the southern territory of Champassak and, in the north, the Sayaboury region of the Luang Prabang kingdom. In order the compensate the Luang Prabang monarchy for this dismemberment of the kingdom, Governor-General Decoux concluded in August 1941 a new protectorate agreement that, in effect, ceded all of northern Laos to Luang Prabang (Decoux 1949: 296–97).

Decoux's policy towards Laos, however, was not confined to the mere juggling of territory. It was the intention of Decoux that – under the framework of paternal French control exercised at the overall Indochina level – what he called a *politique indigène* should be developed in the constituent monarchies of Indochina (Decoux 1949: 395–96). As noted in chapter 6, this development of a *politique indigène* involved the careful restoration of the prestige of the respective monarchies, the boosting of the pay and status of the indigenous administrative elites, the revival of traditional culture, and the tight monitoring of the Indochina education system so as to ensure that it supported rather than undermined traditional political structures and values (Decoux 1949: 389, 395–401).

In Laos, however, there were special circumstances that made the creation of a *politique indigène* a matter of urgency. The strong position of Thailand during the war as an ally of Japan, and the weak position of France, opened up the very real possibility that the Lao political elite might be tempted to gravitate into the Thai orbit. In an age of the rediscovery of identities, this possibility was strengthened by the fact that the Lao and the Thai came from the same ethnic roots, followed the same religion, and had very similar languages and writing-systems. This stimulated the French to encourage the development of a specifically Lao national identity, and at the same time push forward a rapid modernization of Lao society. Upgrading the School of Administration in Vientiane and rapidly increasing the number of schools and health clinics formed part of Decoux's effort to 'orient' the Lao towards the French and the modern world (Decoux 1949: 408). Much more radical, given his naturally conservative instincts, was Decoux's support for the creation of a Lao movement – the 'Lao Renovation Movement' – which was formed in 1941 by young Lao patriots, and was the first genuinely nationalist organization in Laos (Decoux 1949: 409).

It was Charles Rochet, the Director of Public Education in Laos during the crucial war years, who played the major role in pushing through these changes. Rochet, in his semi-fictional book, *Pays Lao: Le Laos dans la*

Tourmente, 1939–1945, published in 1946, outlined his diagnosis of the condition of the Lao people under colonial rule, the measures needed to rejuvenate the Lao nation, and the steps that he had taken to implement these measures (Rochet 1946). That Rochet had a profound influence on the first generation of Lao nationalists was affirmed subsequently by members of that generation.

In his book, Rochet acknowledged that French colonial rule had brought 'tranquillity' to Laos. Even during the Second World War – at least, up to the time of the Japanese take-over of March 1945 – France had been able to shield Laos from the turmoil and bloodshed surrounding Indochina (Rochet 1946: 45–48). But this 'French peace' had carried a heavy price tag: Lao cultural cohesion had disintegrated; the Buddhist religion, the mainstay of Lao culture and identity, had lost all its vitality; and no serious attempt had been made to educate more than a tiny fraction of the people. Echoing the 'Amis du Lao', Rochet accused French colonialism, not simply of neglecting the Lao, but of creating among them a vacuum of values and culture: a condition he described as 'moral anarchy' (Rochet 1946: 41, 61–62).

Rochet, therefore, viewed his task as that of encouraging the beginnings of a cultural revolution in Laos. Indeed, developments in Laos during the war period were not unlike the elite cultural revolutions in other parts of Southeast Asia at the beginning of the twentieth century. The first step in this cultural revolution was the creation of a cadre of young educated Lao who could act as a spearhead and an inspiration. To this end, regular meetings were organized and a journal was set up (Rochet 1946: 42, 66–69, 85–88). Among the priorities of this reform movement were the encouragement of general literacy, the education of women, the standardization of the writing system of the Lao language, the resuscitation of traditional Lao literature and literary forms, and the development of a new literature that would connect with Lao tradition, and yet be relevant to the modern world (Rochet 1946: 72–78).

Nhouy Abhay (1909–1963), one of the founders of this reform movement, shared with Rochet the view that the key to national renovation was the Buddhist religion. Both agreed that Buddhism lay at the core of Lao identity. In the golden age of Lan Xang, the Buddhist *sangha* (monastic organization) had formed a vital centre of learning based on the Pali texts. This *sangha* had provided education at all levels, and presided over the ceremonies that had regulated and harmonized the everyday life of the Lao people. Lao society was thereby permeated by the values of a living religion. Both Rochet and Nhouy Abhay were only too conscious, however, of Buddhism's sad decline in Laos: ceremonies were carried out in a perfunctory manner, and monks mouthed the words of texts they no longer understood. Rochet and Nhouy Abhay were certain that the key to the rebirth of Laos lay in the drastic reform of Buddhism. They believed that unless Buddhist learning could be revived, and the *sangha* revitalized,

Laos would remain culturally rootless (Rochet 1946: 122–30; Nhouy Abhay 1959: 254–56).

In his programmes, it could be said that Rochet was faithfully following the lines of France's wartime Indochina policy. But he was aware that this cultural revolution and national awakening could not simply be imposed from above by a paternal French administration. The development of a genuine *politique indigène*, or Lao polity, he felt, must depend on the aspirations and the anxieties on the Lao themselves, not on the French political perspective. In his book, Rochet makes it perfectly clear that politically aware Lao, and sympathetic local French officials, believed that the main threat to Lao identity and culture came, not from Thailand, but from the very Indochina entity created by the French. The installation of an Indochina-wide administration had allowed the more numerous and better-educated Vietnamese to monopolize low-level civil service jobs in Laos; and the attempt to forge an Indochina-wide economy allowed the Vietnamese and Chinese to dominate the trading networks of Laos. On top of this, Vietnamese immigration had been encouraged to supply labour for the plantations and mines, and to fill the 'empty' spaces of Laos. Furthermore, such development as had taken place under the French had not been directed towards the advancement of the Lao and their networks of riverine villages, but rather towards the building of a road system designed to strengthen and facilitate Indochina links (Rochet 1946: 54–60, 103–20, 147). In consequence, the infrastructure of the modern economy in Laos was almost entirely non-Lao. The Lao people, Rochet insisted, were being steadily turned into aborigines in their own land, and he foresaw a real danger that a coherent Lao identity would eventually disappear altogether (Rochet 1946: 16–17, 64).

It was thus the belief of Rochet and of the reform movement that ultimately the creation of a genuine *politique indigène* for Laos could only be achieved at the expense of the 'Indochina polity' that the French had created. The ambiguity of Lao nationalist attitudes towards France and French Indochina came out into the open after March 1945, when the Japanese removed the French administration in Laos and cajoled the king in Luang Prabang to declare the end of the French protectorate regime. The Lao political elite divided between those who supported the view of the monarchy in Luang Prabang that France offered the best long-term protection for Laos in an uncertain future, and those – including some key figures in the reform movement – who were prepared to take advantage of the situation to create an independent and unified Lao nation-state. What united the Lao nationalists, however, was a fear that Laos would become embroiled in the revolutionary upheaval that broke out in Vietnam in the summer of 1945: their fears were confirmed by the fact that, during this period, Vietnamese nationalists in Laos behaved as if Laos was a mere annex to Vietnam. At least partly stimulated by this very real danger, the monarchy

in Luang Prabang and the anti-French Provisional Government in Vientiane reached agreement in April 1946 on the creation of a unified constitutional monarchy, in which the monarch of Luang Prabang would become the king of the whole of former French Laos (Katay don Sasorith 1953: 58–62).

At first, it seemed as if this whole carefully constructed political edifice – a genuine *politique indigène* – would collapse when the French returned to Laos in 1946, and the Provisional Government fled *en bloc* to Thailand. However, despite the policy declarations of the new 'Free French' regime, reasserting the primacy of an 'Indochina polity' over the rights of the constituent parts of Indochina, the political reality was very different (Cole 1956: 5–6). De Gaulle himself, the leader of the Free French, had argued that the only acceptable path to political progress in Indochina was the creation of self-governing states that were, as he put it, 'with us, not against us'; and that this would require a direct political accommodation with the 'solid dynasties' of Laos and Cambodia (De Gaulle 1960: 210, 226). In subsequent years, although France still officially clung to the Indochina concept, the fact that it was unable to reassert its political will in Vietnam – the linchpin of the Indochina structure – meant that the structure became more and more of a hollow shell.

Between 1946 and 1949, the French and the Lao were able to construct through negotiation a political framework that commanded the support of the vast majority of the Lao political leadership (Katay don Sasorith 1953: 65). Although equal citizenship status was afforded to all the races of Laos, including the Vietnamese, Chinese, and the dispersed minority groups living in the uplands, the key symbols of Lao identity – the monarchy and Buddhism – were given a special and linked status in the 1949 constitution (Laos 1949: 1–4). With the re-confirmation of the unity of Laos that had originally been declared by Lao nationalists in September 1945 – after the Japanese surrender and before the return of the French – a credible, if attenuated, version of Lan Xang had been re-created. But this essentially conservative, anti-revolutionary Lao polity needed protection in the political turmoil and anarchy of post-war Southeast Asia. In this context, the Lao nationalists regarded the maintenance of the link with France – particularly in the areas of defence, foreign policy and economic development – as a security for, not an abridgement of, their independence. As Phoui Sananikone, Minister of the Interior and Foreign Affairs of the Royal Lao Government (RLG), put it in a speech on 9 June 1954, the link with France '... merely safeguards and strengthens our independence in a world where absolute autonomy can only lead immediately to the worst forms of enslavement' (Phoui Sananikone 1954: 19).

It is at least possible to argue that the 'Lao polity' created in the years 1937–1949 could have provided the basis for a stable and prosperous future. As it was, it was destroyed in subsequent years by the impact of the Cold War and the Vietnam War.

MALAYA: TAN CHENG LOCK AND THE CONCEPT OF THE MULTI-RACIAL NATION

The 'Lao polity' was ultimately based on the concept of a homogeneous Lao identity, history and culture, oriented away from Indochina and towards its natural region of affiliation to the west of the Mekong river (Katay don Sasorith 1953: 92–93). The underlying concept of the 'Malaya polity' that Tan Cheng Lock (1883–1960) sketched out in the period of the 1920s to the 1940s could not have been more different. Tan Cheng Lock's central thesis was that, although the creation of a united Malayan nation was absolutely necessary, the multi-racial nature of Malayan society meant that this could not be achieved by any attempt to forge a homogeneous Malayan identity united in language and culture. Instead, he argued, a nation would have to be constructed in which politics and culture were separated, and in which a unified 'civic' political affiliation could live harmoniously side by side with diverse cultural affiliations.

The colonial Malaya into which Tan Cheng Lock was born had no unified political structure – or at least was only unified by a British-manned civil service that had authority over the disparate political units of the region. The Straits Settlements of Singapore, Penang and Malacca formed a British colony directly administered by Britain; the Malayan peninsula itself was divided into Malay sultanates, each of which had a separate protectorate agreement with Britain, although four of these Malay states had in 1896 formed a loose federation under British supervision. Within this diverse system, mass Chinese and Indian immigration had facilitated the creation of a modern Malaya-wide economy. This created an anomalous situation where political legitimacy lay in the hands of Malay sultans presiding over traditional Malay culture and society, while the economy was dominated by outside business interests and immigrant communities.

In the years between the First and Second World Wars, the British made attempts to negotiate some kind of political structure that could harmonize existing Malay rights embodied in the sultanates with the pressure from business interests to create a more unified political structure that would facilitate economic development in the peninsula. However, Britain's commitment to the concept of prior 'Malay rights', and the effective division thereby between what might be called a 'Malay polity' and an immigrant – particularly Chinese – economy, made it difficult for Britain to construct any plan for political progress that would not offend either the indigenous or the immigrant communities, and consequently generate racial tension. Britain's solution, therefore, was effectively to maintain the imperial system, where British administrators coordinated policy between the traditional Malay political sphere on one side, and the modern immigrant economic sphere on the other. The consequence was that the immigrant communities remained de-politicized.

Pressure against this policy came primarily from the Straits Chinese elite, whose political views have already been analyzed in chapter 2, and of whom Tan Cheng Lock was a prominent member. The revolution in cultural and social awareness among the Straits Chinese in the late nineteenth and early twentieth centuries gave them a sense of their identity and their role within Britain's imperial polity. The Straits Chinese had their own clear sense of what this imperial polity should be: they saw it, rather along the lines of the Roman Empire, as a structure in which British citizenship should be open to all races within the British Empire who owed their first loyalty to the empire and had the necessary education to play a proper civic role; in which there should be civic equality between such citizens, irrespective of race; and in which educational advancement should be linked to a commitment to broaden the base of multiracial civic participation in imperial responsibilities (Song Ong Siang 1967: 548–49).

However, with the growing debate in the inter-war years over the political structure of Malaya, the attention of the Straits Chinese shifted from imperial rights towards Malaya itself (Cheah Inn Kiong 1938: 13). It was during this period that Tan Cheng Lock emerged as an informal leader of the Chinese community, not only in the Straits Settlements, but in Malaya as a whole. In the 1920s and 1930s, Tan Cheng Lock urged Britain to begin the process of creating a unified Malayan state comprising the Malay States and the Straits Settlements. While he conceded that this state might have to have a federal structure, he also insisted that it should be a fundamentally unified state with as much self-government as would be compatible with the overall imperial system (Tan Cheng Lock 1926: 90; 1932: 80–81). The political core of any such state would be a legislative council and an executive council in which the principle of democratic representation, although restricted, would be gradually enlarged (Tan Cheng Lock 1932: 83–88).

Before considering Tan Cheng Lock's elaborations on his basic notion of a unified, self-governing Malaya, it is important to outline the premises on which this political outlook was based. Since there was a considerable degree of continuity between Tan Cheng Lock's pre-war, wartime, and post-war political thinking, his 'world-view', and what might be called his 'Malaya-view', can be assessed as a whole.

Tan Cheng Lock noted that the fundamental political ideal of the British Empire had, from the early twentieth century, been the creation of a world-wide network of self-governing nations, sharing the same civic values, and linked in a mutually beneficial partnership (Tan Cheng Lock 1944: 57; 1945: 63). He accepted that the British Empire had provided a framework within which its subjects had enjoyed civil liberties: such as freedom under the law or the freedom of religious belief. The climate of the time, however – particularly at the end of the Second World War – now made it imperative that Britain should move to the next stage and confer 'political freedom'

(Tan Cheng Lock 1946a: 125). Tan Cheng Lock pointed out that the right to such political freedom and 'self-determination' was not just a British Empire obligation, but an intrinsic part of the Allied plan for the post-war world order. He added that another of the international principles announced at this time – the ending of racial discrimination and the right to racial equality – had a particular relevance for Malaya (Tan Cheng Lock 1943: 42; 1945: 61–62).

So far as Malaya itself was concerned, Tan Cheng Lock's central point was that the Chinese community in Malaya had, over the generations, established a permanent home there. Moreover, the Chinese had earned their right to be treated as equal citizens of Malaya, both because of the crucial role they had played in building up the Malayan economy, and because of the aid their community had given the British in the war effort against the Japanese. They had fought and suffered for what had become their homeland (Tan Cheng Lock 1943: 10–15). Before the Second World War, the political focus of the Chinese community as a whole – excluding the Straits Chinese – had largely been concentrated on what they had still considered to be 'their' Chinese homeland. The events of the war had irrevocably directed their 'political consciousness' towards Malaya (Tan Cheng Lock 1946a: 128). Unless, Tan Cheng Lock warned, the interests and the rights of the Chinese and other non-Malay communities were addressed, communism and subversion would gain a substantial foothold among those communities (Tan Cheng Lock 1943: 27–36).

From the early 1920s onwards, Tan Cheng Lock urged that the solution to the political dilemma of Malaya and its multi-racial society was the creation of a 'United Malaya'. This would require first of all the 'fostering and creating of a true Malayan spirit and consciousness', and, at the same time, 'the complete elimination of racial or communal feeling' (Tan Cheng Lock 1926: 90). The key to the generation of such a 'Malayan spirit and consciousness' was the conferring of a 'common citizenship' giving equal political rights to all those who, as Tan Cheng Lock put it in 1934, owed 'undivided loyalty to this country and the British Crown' (Tan Cheng Lock 1934: 97, 107–8). In the more nationalist climate of 1946, he narrowed the definition to those who 'regard Malaya as their homeland and the object of their single-minded devotion and loyalty' (Tan Cheng Lock 1946b: 7).

But, in his definition of Malayan identity, Tan Cheng Lock was always most anxious to draw a distinction between political or civic *unity*, and cultural *diversity*. In 1934, he argued that the objective in Malaya should be to enable each community to preserve its 'racial individuality' within the context of a common citizenship: he absolutely rejected any notion of creating a 'homogeneous amalgamation of the component races', or even such lesser measures as that of making Malay the official common language of all the races of Malaya (Tan Cheng Lock 1934: 96–97). Each community, he suggested, should be permitted – indeed encouraged – to maintain contact with their cultural roots and what he described as their fundamental 'ethos' (Tan Cheng Lock 1934: 105). In essence, Tan Cheng Lock was asserting something that has since become a central tenet of 'multi-culturalism': that it was possible for a nation to be 'politically united', even though the different communities within it maintained 'their own intellectual, cultural and spiritual life' (1946b: 6).

In the years before the Second World War, for Tan Cheng Lock, the solution to the dilemma of reconciling loyalty to a common political entity and loyalty to separate racial communities was provided by the British Empire and the English language. Not only did the English language enable what might be called 'neutral' inter-racial communication; it was also the key to progress and engagement with the modern world (Tan Cheng Lock 1934: 103). It could in addition form the basis for building a 'community of allegiance' to the British Empire and Malaya, and help to foster common civic values: what Tan Cheng Lock called 'a unity of outlook and [a] community of ideas and sentiments' (Tan Cheng Lock 1934: 101, 107–8). In many ways, it could be said that Tan Cheng Lock saw the English language as the binding force in Malaya that would in the end enable the gradual removal of the exercise of direct British administrative authority.

One of Tan Cheng Lock's stated aspirations was the 'elimination of communalism from political life' in Malaya (Tan Cheng Lock 1946c: 134). However, this objective of making an absolute distinction between the political realm and the extra-political world of socio-cultural diversity would appear to be at variance with his other repeatedly stated idea that there should be a 'balanced representation of the various communities' in the future government of a united Malaya. On the face of it, such a plan actually institutionalized communalism within the workings of the political system itself. Tan Cheng Lock's objective, however, was to 'ensure that no one community' would be 'in a position to dominate or out-vote all the others put together' (Tan Cheng Lock 1945: 64). As such, it was designed, not so much to entrench as to neutralize the workings of communalism within the political sphere.

In sum, what Tan Cheng Lock aspired to was a united Malaya, in which ultimately the right to equal citizenship would be available to all inhabitants who were loyal to Malaya; in which the state itself would not 'belong' to any particular racial group, would have in-built mechanisms to protect the interests of all its communities, and could move rapidly to self-government under the umbrella of what had become the British Commonwealth.

After the to-ings and fro-ings of British policy following the Second World War, however, the only parts of Tan Cheng Lock's concept that were substantially realized were the creation of a united Malaya and the commitment to eventual self-government. The political structure that became the basis for moving to Malayan independence was the 'Federation of Malaya' that the British set up in 1948. This Federation, which excluded the Chinese city of Singapore, was essentially a federated Malay kingdom: its component parts were the Malay sultanates, its head of state was chosen from among the sultans, Malay was elevated to the level of the national language, and a special status was conferred on its Malay inhabitants, along with an automatic access to citizenship. The Federation of Malaya was a confirmation of the notion that Malaya was *tanah Melayu*, the land of the Malays.

Even before the establishment of the Federation of Malaya, Tan Cheng Lock had urged that the best guarantee for the protection of the rights of the Chinese community was the creation of what he called a 'Pan-Malayan Chinese Association'. Such an organization would, he hoped, unify politically the Chinese community, help promote its welfare and interests, and at the same time operate as a powerful pressure group within the political system (Tan Cheng Lock 1946b: 5–6). Moreover – in the absence of guarantees that there would be any in-built protection for community rights within the constitutional structure – such a Chinese association would act as a spring-board for the creation of a 'United Front of Malayan peoples based on inter-communal concord and joint action' (Tan Cheng Lock 1946b: 7). In other words, since guarantees for inter-communal political harmony did not exist in the structures of the state, they would have to be created by the political organizations that would compete for power in the self-governing state.

Ultimately, Tan Cheng Lock's concept of the nation accorded with the pragmatic-historical view – elucidated most clearly in Ernest Renan's lecture, 'What is a Nation?', in 1882 – that nations are formed by a people's 'common suffering and common rejoicing' in the past, and a common 'will to live together' in the present. In the end, Tan Cheng Lock believed, the peoples of Malaya had no alternative but to 'make the best of ... [an] inheritance shared jointly' (Tan Cheng Lock 1946d: 119). Whatever the constitutional formulae, a united Malayan national identity, he implied, was gradually being forged by the attrition of time and the day-by-day experience of sharing a common space and solving common problems. Whether this optimistic view was – or is – true of the population of Malaya as a whole, it was certainly true in the post-war years of the Malayan political elite – the leaders, that is, of the different communities in Malaya. From late 1948 onwards, this political elite – which of course included Tan Cheng Lock – came to the realization that they had an overriding common interest in the political, economic and social stability of Malaya. It was on the basis of this fundamental perception that an elite-arranged alliance was forged between the main mass organizations, representing the Malay, Chinese and Indian communities. After half a century, this elite alliance still dominates Malayan politics.

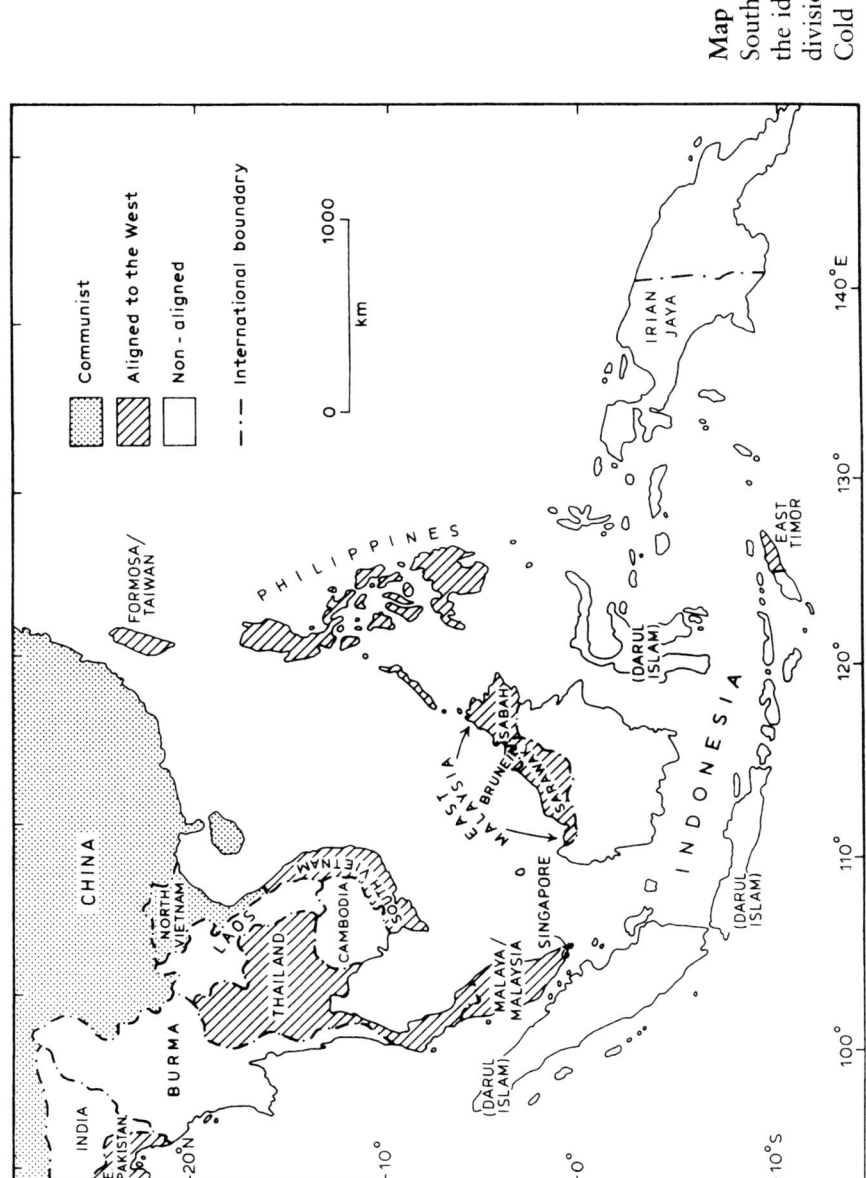

Map 2
Southeast Asia:
the ideological
divisions of the
Cold War period

CHAPTER NINE

The Cold War and the Ideological Foundations of Non-Alignment

Just as Southeast Asia was decolonizing, and independent states were beginning to emerge, the global ideological confrontation between the West and communism, known generally as the 'Cold War', intruded into the region. By the 1950s, moreover, Southeast Asia had become the focal point of that global confrontation. It is not surprising, therefore, that the contest of world-views embodied in the Cold War had a profound impact on political thinking in Southeast Asia at the time. Consequently, it is necessary to clarify the respective ideological positions of the Cold War opponents, before considering local reactions – in particular, the phenomenon of 'non-alignment'.

THE COMMUNIST WORLD-VIEW AND THE COLD WAR

Between 1941 and 1945, the Soviet Union under Stalin had been completely absorbed in the struggle for survival against Nazi Germany, whose avowed goal was the eradication of communism from Europe. The abrupt twists and turns of Soviet policy in the period immediately before the German invasion of the Soviet Union in 1941 made it increasingly difficult for the Comintern to coordinate a credible revolutionary strategy, and the organization effectively dissolved itself in 1943.

In the summer of 1945, however, the Soviet Union emerged from the war as one of the two major world powers, with its boundaries enlarged, and with *de facto* control over the whole of eastern Europe. More than this, as noted in chapter 6, the global prestige of the Soviet Union was considerably enhanced by its defeat of Nazi Germany. This victory was seen by many in the colonized world – and indeed in the West itself – as not just the victory of one power over another power, but as a verdict of history attesting to the superiority of the socialist system over capitalism, and what were seen as capitalism's offshoots, fascism and Nazism.

Very quickly after the end of the war, a new confrontation began to take shape in Europe between the Soviet Union and the Western democracies, headed by the United States, Britain and France. By 1947, the tensions between the Western and communist 'camps' had become acute, particularly in the Balkan region, and, in March of that year, the United States committed itself to the protection of European states against communist 'coercion' or 'political infiltration' (Truman 1947: 411–15). It was in this context that A. A. Zhdanov, the chief 'ideologist' of the Communist Party of the Soviet Union, outlined in September 1947 the Soviet Union's new global strategy in the changed circumstances of the post-war world (Zhdanov 1947).

In this report Zhdanov outlined what has become known as the 'Zhdanov' or 'Two Camps' doctrine. In fact, as Zhdanov pointed out, two opposing camps representing opposed world systems had existed ever since the Russian Revolution of 1917: on the one side, the socialist or 'progressive' camp headed by the Soviet Union; and on the other, the capitalist or 'reactionary' camp, encompassing Europe, North America and the whole of the colonized or semi-colonized world of Asia, Africa and Latin America. What had changed as a consequence of the Second World War was the relative strength of these two camps. Ranged on the 'progressive' side headed by the Soviet Union were the 'People's Democracies' – that is, class-coalition governments dominated by communist parties – that were in the process of establishing themselves in eastern Europe; the various national-liberation movements that were confronting colonialism, particularly in Asia; the new or rejuvenated communist movements that were emerging world-wide; and groups within the West itself who saw the Soviet Union and its system as having the future on its side (Zhdanov 1947: 11). Even though some of the above elements, including many of the national-liberation movements, were not Marxist-Leninist, and therefore not socialist in the orthodox sense, insofar as they were committed to the defeat of colonialism, they were weakening a major prop of world capitalism, and therefore to that extent were in the 'progressive' camp.

The course of history had, according to Zhdanov, dramatically turned towards the progressive camp headed by socialism, while the world capitalist camp was emphatically in retreat. As a consequence of the economic crisis of the inter-war period, capitalism had proceeded to tear itself apart in a civil war between the branch of capitalism that had followed the fascist road, and the 'open-market' branch of capitalism headed by the United States (Zhdanov 1947: 3–4). European capitalism, already severely weakened by the defeat of fascism, was now in a terminal decline brought about by the world-wide challenge to colonialism (Zhdanov 1947: 5). This vacuum of power in the capitalist camp, however, had been filled during the war years by the United States. Zhdanov acknowledged that the United States was a formidable enemy, driven by the same ideological mission to destroy communism as the fascist states before it (Zhdanov 1947: 8). He argued, however, that the United States was faced by an economic crisis, caused fundamentally by the destruction of the global market system during the Second World War. The United States' response to this threat, continued Zhdanov, was the same as capitalism's had always been when confronted by a threat to its existence: it had dropped its ideological mask of 'democracy', had bolstered authoritarian regimes, and would certainly resort to war as a last expedient to save itself from the complete collapse of its economic system (Zhdanov 1947: 15–17).

Zhdanov outlined two fundamental tasks that the socialist camp had to address in order to face this American threat. The first was for the Soviet Union to show sufficient strength and firmness to convince the capitalist camp that a resort to war could not succeed (Zhdanov 1947: 26). Defended by this solid wall of Soviet strength, it would then be the duty of communist parties within the national-liberation movements in the colonial world to ensure that the nationalist leadership remained firmly in the 'progressive' camp, and did not seek to make some sort of accommodation with the colonial powers, thus effectively returning to the capitalist fold (Zhdanov 1947: 26).

Inevitably, perhaps, the unintended consequence of this last injunction was the creation of serious splits within the liberation movements of Southeast Asia. Even before the enunciation of the Zhdanov Doctrine, the communist parties of Burma, Malaya, Indonesia and the Philippines were aware that, in one way or another, they were being sidelined in the negotiations between the respective nationalist leaderships and the colonial powers. The Zhdanov Doctrine provided them with the ideological justification for accusing these nationalist leaderships of 'betraying' national interests by negotiating forms of independence that would leave colonial economic interests intact. In the course of 1948, communist rebellions – either directed against the still-existing colonial government, or the leaderships of the newly-independent states – broke out in Malaya, Burma, Indonesia and the Philippines. (See the next chapter on the role of the Zhdanov Doctrine in determining communist policy in Burma during 1947 and 1948.)

By the time of Stalin's death in 1953, however, the international situation had changed dramatically. In 1949, the Chinese Communist Party achieved victory in the renewed civil war with the nationalists, and established a communist state; and it was apparent by 1953 that the French had lost heart in their war in Vietnam against the communist-dominated Viet Minh. On the other hand, the United States had responded vigorously when, in June 1950, communist North Korea had directly assaulted non-communist South Korea, and subsequently gave every indication that they would defend the East and Southeast Asian regions against any further communist advance. Moreover, the effects of the Zhdanov Doctrine, and the speed and aggression of the communist advance in East Asia clearly alarmed and alienated Asian nationalist opinion in equal measure.

In these changed circumstances, the new Soviet leadership did not so much abandon the essential features of the Zhdanov Doctrine as change its emphasis. The primary point made was that the socialist camp – bolstered by the victory in China and the possession of nuclear weapons – was stronger than ever and therefore able, as the new Soviet leader Nikita Krushchov put it, 'to compel the imperialists to renounce war' as an instrument of policy (Krushchov 1961: 8–9). The Soviet leadership accepted Lenin's position that capitalism would never renounce power voluntarily, and they pointed to the creation of 'aggressive military blocs' like NATO (the North Atlantic Treaty Organization, formed in 1949) as an example of the capitalist camp's readiness to prepare for and threaten war (Krushchov 1961: 10). But if the socialist camp was sufficiently strong, and global public opinion in favour of peace sufficiently influential, capitalism would have no alternative but to let the process of historical evolution take its natural course (Krushchov 1961: 12–14). The two assertions – that the socialist and progressive camp was powerful enough to deter any resort to military force by capitalism; and that there had now developed an irresistible global momentum towards the socialist system – enabled the Soviet leadership to square the circle between the fundamental Leninist dictum that socialism could not be achieved by 'evolutionary' and peaceful means, and the fact that modern technology had made war so destructive that it could no longer be used as a rational instrument for pursuing political goals.

There was, however, a danger that the new Soviet doctrine of 'Peaceful Coexistence', as it was called – with its central notion that normal state-to-state relations could be conducted between the two 'camps', while the ideological contest between the opposing communist and capitalist 'systems' would be gradually resolved by peaceful competition (Krushchov 1961: 77–96) – could lead to an ideological *stasis* that might enable capitalism to recoup its position. It was from this perspective that the national-liberation movements of Asia and Africa assumed such importance in the ideological stance of the Soviet leaders. Indeed, a statement of a world conference of communist parties held in November 1960 described the general phenomenon of national liberation as 'ranking second in historic importance only to the formation of the world socialist system' (Carrère d'Encausse 1969: 307). In this era of decolonization, the opposing capitalist and socialist systems were competing for the allegiance of the nationalist movements and newly independent governments of the former colonial regions. If the socialist camp could triumph in this competition, it would help bring about a decisive global momentum towards socialism (Zhukov 1956: 290).

The Soviet leadership argued that their camp had an inherent advantage in this ideological competition. In the first place, whereas in previous decades newly independent states would have had no other alternative than to fit into the globally dominant capitalist system, there now existed an alternative global system to which such states could turn for economic support (Zhukov 1956: 289). In the second place, national-liberation movements tended to link capitalism to colonialism. It was, therefore, generally accepted that complete independence involved, not just self-government in the political sense, but a complete break from the economic networks of capitalism. Sometimes – as in North Vietnam after the partition of Vietnam in 1954 – this break took the form of building an orthodox socialist system; more often, however, the newly independent states would 'nationalize' the 'commanding heights' of the economy, and adopt a system based on state regulation and at least a measure of economic self-sufficiency. Although these latter economic policies were not fully socialist in the Marxist-Leninist sense, they were anti-capitalist, and they therefore had the effect of weakening the links in the chain of the economic system of capitalism. As such, even national-liberation movements and national governments that were 'subjectively' only semi-socialist deserved full support from the socialist camp, since their policies were 'objectively' progressive, to the extent that they weakened capitalism and thereby strengthened the world position of socialism (Zhukov 1956: 289).

THE WESTERN WORLD-VIEW AND THE COLD WAR

In many ways, the Western and American perspective on the communist threat was a mirror-image of the Soviet view of the West. The United States saw the Cold War between the West and the Soviet Union, not as a traditional contest between big powers, but as a global confrontation between two absolutely opposing world-views and political systems, between which any accommodation could only be a temporary stand-off, and in which any advance anywhere in the world by communism meant a commensurate retreat for the West. While the Soviet Union viewed this confrontation as one between socialism and capitalism, from the United States' perspective it was a global collision between democracy and totalitarianism (Truman 1947: 413–14). The United States saw communism as an ideology driven by an inherently aggressive dynamic, always seeking to expand its sphere of control, either by the direct use of force, or by subversion and the exploitation of economic weakness or political instability. The dire condition of post-Second World War Europe offered a perfect target for communism, and the 'Truman Doctrine' of March 1947 was basically an affirmation of America's commitment to 'contain' the communist advance in Europe through the provision of military and economic aid and advice (Truman 1947: 415). This initial commitment to containment was subsequently backed up, in June 1947, by the Marshall Aid Plan, which provided a secure basis for the economic rehabilitation of non-communist Europe; and then, in 1949, by the creation of a military pact – NATO – that could give collective security to non-communist Europe against military threats from the Soviet bloc.

After China 'went communist' in 1949, and the Russian-backed communist regime of North Korea invaded South Korea in 1950, East and Southeast Asia became the main theatre of the Cold War. The United States responded to this perceived communist threat by consolidating its military position in Japan, introducing troops into Korea, and establishing a close military link with the Nationalist Chinese government in Taiwan. From 1950 on, the United States' attention was also extended to the situation in Southeast Asia, where there appeared to be a real danger that the communist-led Viet Minh would force France to leave Vietnam and even Indochina as a whole. The American fear was that a communist victory in Vietnam would create a 'knock-on' effect in a region passing through a period of political turbulence and economic weakness, enabling local communist parties to seize power throughout Southeast Asia (NSC 1952: 28). The United States' reaction to this threat was similar to its anti-communist strategy in Europe a few years earlier: the provision of military advice and aid, and economic and technical assistance; the encouragement of a trading network that would link Southeast Asia to the potential regional economic 'dynamo', Japan; and the diffusion of pro-Western propaganda (NSC 1952: 29). This strategy for the containment of the communist threat in Southeast Asia culminated in the creation of a collective security pact, the Southeast Asian Treaty Organization (SEATO) in 1954, which included amongst its local members Thailand and the Philippines.

In a most important analysis of the Cold War situation in the colonized world, Walt Rostow – one of the principal advisers to President Kennedy – warned in 1961 that Asia and Africa had become the key targets for global communist expansion (Rostow 1961: 108–15). Thwarted by the formation of NATO in Europe, and by the clear evidence provided by the Korean War that the West would resist outright military aggression, the Soviet leadership had – under the ideological cloak of 'Peaceful Co-existence' – turned their attention to political *subversion* of the nations of the decolonizing world of Asia and Africa (Rostow 1961: 108–9). This subversion could take many forms, from economic sabotage to assassination, but its overall goal was the destabilization of newly independent states from within. Rostow noted that the newly independent governments of Asia and Africa were peculiarly vulnerable to this kind of covert action. In many cases, they had engaged in a debilitating anti-colonial struggle; were grappling with the problems of trying to create effective administrations in the wake of the departure of the colonial powers; or were faced with the problem of trying to create modern economies as fast as possible, in order to satisfy the natural aspirations of their populations for a better life. In general, they had to contend with the deep-rooted political and social conflicts that such a period of fundamental change would naturally bring in its wake (Rostow 1961: 110).

In this general situation of vulnerability and turbulence, local communist movements – backed by the Soviet Union and China – had a golden 'window of opportunity' that would be closed once these nations achieved political and administrative stability, and had built the foundations for economic progress. In negative terms, covert communist actions could sabotage political and administrative structures; in positive terms, Rostow had to admit that communism's resolute anti-colonialism, along with its model of forced-pace economic change under tight state control was attractive to many Asian nationalists (Rostow 1961: 110).

Ultimately, according to Rostow, the real advantage for the communists lay in the fact that the West and the regimes it supported were in the uncomfortable position of defending an extremely shaky status quo. While the communists could promise a golden age of prosperity and social justice in the future, the Americans – whatever their claims that they too were supporting a modernizing social revolution based on democracy and economic freedom – were associated with the colonialism of the past, and the poverty, injustice and corruption of post-war Asia. What the Americans and the West were discovering, in fact, was the reality that it was far easier to subvert weak states than to protect them (Rostow 1961: 110–14).

In a notable phrase, Rostow saw the world communist movement as the 'scavengers of the modernization process', and communism as 'a disease of the transition to modernization' (Rostow 1961: 110). As such, the primary ideological struggle was not in Europe, but in the 'whole creative process of modernization' in Asia and Africa (Rostow 1961: 115). It is possible to detect, in Rostow's 1961 speech and in another seminal analysis, written in 1947 by George Kennan, an eminent State Department official and academic, an underlying tone of pessimism over the West's and the United States' capacity to sustain and win complex and long-term struggles of this kind. As Kennan had observed in 1947, democracies had, by their very nature, a short attention span and an 'instant gratification' demand for quick results from foreign policy measures; the communist leaderships, on the other hand, were not only inclined by their innate Leninist approach to take the long-term view, but also did not have to cope with democratic dissent in the conduct of their policy (Kennan 1947: 421–22). Kennan and Rostow were agreed that the real advantage for the communist camp lay in its ability to pursue a long-term strategy, making gradual, step-by-step gains that created the sense of an inevitable global momentum towards communism. This in its turn generated a 'bandwagon' effect – a growing conviction, even among those who were not sympathetic to communism, that the ultimate victory of the communist camp was in some way historically inevitable (Kennan 1947: 426–27).

Kennan argued, however, that the greatest apparent strength of communism – its one-party state structure, and thereby its ability to conduct a global policy without the obstacles of democratic constraint – was also its fundamental weakness. The Soviet Union, Kennan observed, had huge structural, economic, social and national weaknesses ticking away like a time-bomb within its system. But the Soviet Communist Party, whose legitimacy depended on its assertion that it was the ultimate and infallible guarantor of social and political progress, lacked either the mechanisms or the will to reform itself or undertake a fundamental change of policy if circumstances required. In the end, Kennan argued, time was on the side of the West. If the latter could maintain a position that was open to negotiation but firm on the essentials, the communist bloc would find its room for manoeuvre and its ability to maintain a global revolutionary momentum gradually curtailed. Over time, the internal problems would accumulate, and the sclerotic machinery of party and state would eventually grind to a halt (Kennan 1947: 425–27).

While, therefore, both camps were agreed that the main threat to the West lay at the periphery, in Asia and Africa, from an early stage more astute Western observers believed that the main vulnerability of the communist camp lay at the very heart of its system.

THE BANDUNG CONFERENCE: PAN-ASIANISM AND NON-ALIGNMENT

The opposing communist and Western camps were agreed, therefore, that Asia was *the* crucial region where the outcome of the contest between their two ideological systems might finally be resolved. Consequently, Asia found itself in the 1950s and 1960s at the very centre of international relations. It was in this context that the Indonesian Republic, in 1955, called a conference in Bandung of all independent states in Asia and Africa. The conference had three principal objectives: to build a sense of Asian-African solidarity; to institute generally agreed principles that would govern relations between the states of the region, and ensure that disputes were resolved peacefully; and to state a common resolve to end racism and colonialism (Kahin 1956: 3).

In his opening speech on 18 April 1955, President Sukarno of Indonesia described the conference as 'the first intercontinental conference of coloured peoples in the history of mankind' (Kahin 1956: 39). In reality, since most of the African states – including north Africa – had yet to achieve independence, Asian states dominated the conference. From this perspective, the conference could be seen as the 'pan-Asian' successor to the 'Assembly of Greater East Asian Nations' held in Tokyo in November 1943. At the Bandung

Conference, however, there was no ideological uniformity: communist, pro-Western and neutral nations were all represented. Indeed the 'five principles of co-existence' agreed at the Conference, were precisely designed to ensure that ideological differences between states should not become a source of conflict in the region. These principles also stipulated that all the states of the region should respect each other's 'sovereignty and territorial integrity', undertake not to interfere in the internal affairs of other states, and treat each other on a basis of equality (Kahin 1956: 8).

The participants at the Conference also agreed on their opposition to all continuing manifestations of colonialism, ranging from French colonialism in North and West Africa to continuing Dutch control of West New Guinea, an area that the Indonesians regarded as an intrinsic part of their nation (Kahin 1956: 82). It naturally followed that the Conference also supported the right of self-determination of all 'peoples and nations', and the Final Communiqué added that such a right to self-determination was a 'pre-requisite of the full enjoyment of all fundamental Human Rights'. The Conference also deplored all forms of racism and racial segregation (Kahin 1956: 80–81).

This apparent consensus, however, glossed over very considerable ideological differences that emerged in the course of the Conference. There was, for example, a dispute over the definition of 'colonialism'. Ceylon/Sri Lanka, at that time a pro-Western state, suggested that the Soviet Union should be categorized as a colonial entity – a line that Nehru of India strongly opposed (Kahin 1956: 18–21, 31). While Sukarno pronounced *laissez-faire* liberalism to be 'obsolete', Carlos Romulo of the pro-Western Philippines spoke up for the traditional liberal values of political democracy, free speech and the 'open society'. He also suggested that racism was not an unknown phenomenon in Asian societies, and that the Conference's condemnation of racism was somewhat hypocritical (Kahin 1956: 48; Bandung 1955: 115–16). While on the one side Chou En-lai of China and Nehru of India condemned the military pacts that the West had created in Europe and Asia, the Thai Minister for Foreign Affairs, Wan Waithayakom, asserted that, since communist China's stated support for the principles of 'co-existence' had had no effect on its covert campaign to destabilize Thailand, Thailand had every right to protect its national security by joining the American-dominated Southeast Asian Treaty Organization (SEATO) (Bandung 1955: 131–32).

VARIETIES OF 'NON-ALIGNMENT': SUKARNO AND NEO-COLONIALISM

Despite the fact that states of all ideological variety attended the Bandung Conference, there can be no doubt that the concept of 'non-alignment' – the notion, that is, that Asian and African states should hold themselves aloof from either ideological camp – exerted a considerable attraction then and thereafter. The proponents of non-alignment, however, did not interpret their stance as mere neutralism, or what would effectively amount to a refusal to get involved in international issues. Rather, non-alignment was seen as a way of enabling the decolonized world to play an independent role and exert a positive 'moral' force on international affairs (Kahin 1956: 45–46, 66–67). Through the late 1950s and the early 1960s, President Sukarno took this idea to its natural conclusion in arguing that the European-dominated international order should be re-shaped to take into account the political values of the decolonized world.

The most comprehensive outline of Sukarno's world-view was contained in his speech to the General Assembly of the United Nations, on 30 September 1960; but earlier speeches of the 1950s give an indication of the trajectory of his thinking (Sukarno 1960b: 122–47). In general, Sukarno asserted that decolonization and decolonization's natural corollary, national independence, were not just the fulfilment of basic human rights, but a fundamental guarantee of world peace. Colonialism was an extension of capitalism – and two enduring features of capitalism were, first, its dependence on a dynamic of conflict and competition; and second, a limited notion of human rights that accepted the outer form of political freedom, but denied the one human right that might make a reality of political freedom, namely social justice. A world that had rid itself of colonialism would be a world in which capitalism would necessarily be in global retreat, and in which a genuinely new world order based on freedom *and* social justice could be built (Sukarno 1960b: 133–34).

Unfortunately, Sukarno's basic argument continued, the mere acquisition of independence was not enough. This was because the old threat of colonialism had been replaced by the new and more insidious threat of 'neo-colonialism'. In the new global system created by neo-colonialism, old and new colonial powers conceded the principle of national self-government, but ensured that the economic structures of these 'independent' states remained locked into the international capitalist economy. Therefore, although capitalism was historically doomed, neo-colonialism had given it a new lease of life. It was therefore a central part of Sukarno's thesis that a new and more complex form of anti-colonial struggle would have to be fought – one in which the individual national struggles of former decades would have to be replaced by a combined struggle of anti-colonial forces throughout Asia and Africa (Sukarno 1960b: 129).

In order to equip themselves for this struggle, continued Sukarno, it was necessary for Asia and Africa to see the world through their *own* eyes, not through the prism of Western ideology. Ultimately, the body of Western ideas – whether they leaned, as he put it, to 'Jefferson' or 'Marx' – reflected Western experience, Western values and Western interests. The temptation for Asia and Africa, he suggested, was to try and create some kind of 'synthesis' out of Western ideology that would suit local political values, traditions and cultures. (Indeed, it could be said that this was a marked feature of Sukarno's own thinking.) But, Sukarno asked, had the time not come for the people of Asia and Africa to 'turn towards each other for guidance and inspiration' and look for 'the experience and accumulated wisdom of our own nations?' (Sukarno 1960b: 136).

Sukarno pointed to the *pancasila* principles that he had enunciated in 1945 (see chapter 7) as a suitable foundation of core values that could serve, not just an independent Indonesia, but a post-colonial world order. In *pancasila*, the concept of the 'nation' had been detached from its fundamentally aggressive, capitalist moorings, and the limited capitalist notion of 'democracy' had been inextricably linked to what Sukarno called *pancasila*'s 'ultimate pillar', social democracy (Sukarno 1960b: 139). Moreover, the principle that encapsulated the whole *pancasila* concept, which could be summed up as consensus rather than competition in the conduct of public life, not only naturally accorded with the traditional values that had governed Asia and Africa, but could form an ideal basis for global co-existence in the future (Sukarno 1960b: 142).

Sukarno pointed out that the post-Second World War world order had been created by the West, both in terms of its structure and its guiding ideals. The Charter of the United Nations, he suggested, 'reflects the political and power constellation of the time of its origin'. The existing world order was, as he put it, 'a product of the Western state system', and, given the fact that 'imperialism and colonialism were offspring of that system', it had not only failed to accommodate Asian and African aspirations; it was in many senses a reactionary force holding back the evolution to a new world order based on the principle of consensus and social justice (Sukarno 1960b: 144–46).

VARIETIES OF 'NON-ALIGNMENT': SIHANOUK AND THE SURVIVAL OF HIS 'CAMBODIA POLITY'

Cambodia gained its independence under King Sihanouk in 1953–54, and the process was somewhat similar to the Laotian evolution to independence between 1945 and 1954. As part of its take-over of Indochina in the last half of the nineteenth century, France had established a 'protectorate' over the Cambodian monarchy and its political system. At the end of the Second World War, it was a key objective of French policy to establish a self-governing Cambodia that remained closely linked to France. This involved a gradual transfer of power to the 'reliable' Cambodian monarchy then headed by Sihanouk, and the maintenance of a stable, essentially patriarchal political structure, within which the principle of democracy would only be introduced gradually (Sihanouk 1955: 14).

In many senses, this view of the key role that the monarchy should play in Cambodian politics accorded with Sihanouk's own political outlook. In a survey of the recent history of Cambodia that he published in 1958, Sihanouk argued that his ancestors had always been acutely conscious of Cambodia's vulnerability to her immediate neighbours, Vietnam and Thailand, and had seen the monarchy's key responsibility as that of maintaining a policy that linked internal stability to external security. It was with the objective of ensuring security from outside threats that the monarchy had accepted the French protectorate. However, what had originally been conceived as an *alliance* with France had rapidly degenerated into a dependent status in which the monarchy lost its freedom of action (Armstrong 1964: 33–36). Moreover, though the French protectorate warded off the threat from the Siamese kingdom, the 'Indochina' structure that France had created constituted in itself an insidious threat to Cambodia's survival as an independent entity. As in the case of Laos, Cambodia had become an adjunct of Vietnam: Vietnamese and other immigrants dominated the networks of the modern economy that had been created, while the Khmers remained marooned in their traditional, mainly rural world (Armstrong 1964: 37–38).

At the end of the Second World War, a consistent outlook based on a clear view of the long-term responsibility of the monarchy underlay what appeared at the time to be the unpredictable zig-zags of Sihanouk's policy. In this outlook, the internal and external factors affecting Cambodia were intertwined. From Sihanouk's viewpoint, the internal situation in Cambodia was potentially extremely unstable. On the one side, a small but vociferous educated or semi-educated elite had become politically conscious during the war years, particularly in the crucial last months of the war after the Japanese had removed the French administration. This political elite had shown itself to be factious, and vulnerable, both to the revolutionary turbulence of the time, and to the blandishments of foreign powers seeking covertly to extend their influence within Cambodia. The vast mass of the population, on the other hand, – *les humbles*, or the 'poor folk', as Sihanouk called them – was still cocooned in the traditional world of deference and political apathy. In the decade between 1945 and 1955, Sihanouk tried to raise these people out of their somnolence by giving them a sense that the destiny of the country lay in their hands, while at the same time maintaining and indeed tightening the traditional links that bound monarchy and people (Sihanouk 1955: 4, 11). In essence, Sihanouk sought to strengthen his control over Cambodia by converting a traditional patriarchal polity into a modern populist polity; a process that was completed in 1955, when he abdicated the monarchy, but maintained – even increased – his absolute control over the political system (Armstrong 1964: 45–46, 50–51).

For Sihanouk, it was politically vital, not only that he should regain the complete sovereignty of Cambodia, but also that in his foreign policy he should have a free hand to protect Cambodian national interests. It was the hope of the French – and initially of the Americans – that the states of Indochina, while being given independence, would remain under a French security umbrella: the French wished to retain influence; the Americans wanted a building block in an anti-communist collective security network. Sihanouk's perspective was entirely different. His position was – as stated in a Royal Declaration of September 1953 – that if the Cambodian people were sure that they were clearly defending Cambodian national interests, they would rally round the monarchy to drive out the threat of communist infiltration. If, however, Cambodia was drawn into a *general* anti-communist pact, its security, far from being enhanced, would be greatly imperilled (Sihanouk 1955: 86). This remained his consistent position during the ensuing years. 'Alignment', he argued in 1958, 'would expose Cambodia not only to retaliation from the rejected bloc, it would also divide Cambodia internally and encourage its citizens to become tools of one bloc or another' (Sihanouk 1959: 104).

Ultimately, therefore, Sihanouk's 'non-alignment' stance was pragmatic: it was dictated by his sense of Cambodia's geopolitical vulnerability, and his fear that the immature and unstable political establishment of Cambodia could easily be manipulated by foreign interests and seduced by ideological formulae. Sihanouk was under no illusion as to the threat that communism posed to his country. Moreover, he saw the communism of the Vietnamese revolutionaries as nothing more than an ideological mask to conceal Vietnam's age-old ambition to gain control of Cambodia and Laos, and re-create Indochina, this time under Vietnamese rather than French control (Sihanouk 1959: 105, 110). Sihanouk, however, could not escape from his certainty that, in the long run, the communists would triumph in Asia and Africa. He felt the West was trapped by its colonial heritage, and by the fact that it inevitably found itself in the position of defending the status quo. Not only this, but the West – particularly what he called the 'Anglo-Saxons' – made a bad position worse by their inept attempts at 'nation-building'. This normally began with the undermining of the traditional political status quo, which at least had some basis of support, and ended with the propping up of military regimes that had no 'roots among the people', and that, 'lacking popular consent, are reduced to maintaining themselves by the protection and subsidies of foreign powers' (Sihanouk 1959: 137–38).

In the end, what Sihanouk described as 'the superiority of the world position of communism' could be explained by 'the extreme susceptibility of the underdeveloped masses of Asia toward it' (Sihanouk 1959: 121, 139). His non-aligned strategy for the survival of Cambodia's independence and identity, however, depended on a distinction being drawn between the immediate threat to Cambodia – which Sihanouk succinctly summarized as

Vietnamese-inspired communist infiltration and propagandizing among Cambodia's youth – and the overall and long-term strategies of the Asian communist powers (Sihanouk 1959: 116–18). His gamble was that if Cambodia maintained a strict non-aligned stance, and even 'leaned towards' the communist side, the main Asian communist powers, China and North Vietnam, would calculate that it would be counter-productive to destabilize Cambodia, and therefore restrain activity directed to that end. A policy of non-alignment, therefore, would give Cambodia at least a breathing-space and some room for manoeuvre in the short term – the most that a country in its position could reasonably hope for.

Sihanouk, however, avoided the discretion and self-effacement that is normally associated with the pursuit of a neutralist policy driven by prudence. On the contrary, he very deliberately turned the issue of Cambodia's independent survival into a long-running drama played out on the international stage. His hope was that this ploy would make it more difficult for either side to threaten Cambodia's independence, either covertly or overtly. Sihanouk's Cambodia could perhaps be described as a modern version of a 'theatre-state', with the whole world forming the audience.

CHAPTER TEN

Ideological Crises of the Independence Regimes: Burma, South Vietnam and Laos

In the late 1940s and early 1950s, independent regimes were set up in Burma, Laos, Cambodia, South Vietnam, and Indonesia. In the following years, these weak and unstable regimes experienced prolonged political crises, which prompted reassessments of their ideological bases. Although all of the states of mainland Southeast Asia engaged in this ideological soul-searching, perhaps the most significant debates occurred in Burma, South Vietnam and Laos. Indonesia's internal debate was, as usual, more complex, and will be treated separately in the next chapter.

BURMA: FROM 'DEMOCRATIC' SOCIALISM TO 'BURMESE' SOCIALISM

When the British Government effectively began to reverse its post-war policy towards Burma in mid 1946 (see chapter 7), and brought the Anti-Fascist People's Freedom League (AFPFL) leadership into the negotiating process for an accelerated move towards independence, the communists within the AFPFL found themselves increasingly isolated. In October 1946, differences came to a head when the Communist Party of Burma (CPB) was expelled from the AFPFL. In March 1947 the CPB began a tentative rapprochement with the AFPFL – who by then were well on the way to securing independence on their own terms – and, as a result of the crisis brought about by the assassination of Aung San in July 1947, they supported the AFPFL against what seemed to many Burmese to be a last-minute imperialist plot to cripple the Burmese nationalist movement on the very threshold of independence (Fleischmann 1989: 44–45). When Aung San's successor, U Nu, concluded the details of an independence agreement with Britain in the autumn of 1947, however, the CPB moved into outright opposition to the AFPFL. In March 1948, a few months after the AFPFL leadership had formed the first government of an independent

Burma, the CPB 'White Flag' began an armed rebellion (Fleischmann 1989: 41–42).

The justification for this communist rebellion was provided by an analysis – known thereafter as the 'Goshal Thesis' – written by the leading ideologist of the Communist Party of Burma, Ba Tin Goshal. The Goshal Thesis is of particular interest, since it was the clearest attempt to apply the principles of the 'Zhdanov Doctrine' in Southeast Asia (Ba Tin 1948). According to the Thesis, the root cause of the mistakes made by the CPB after the war was that it had been insufficiently Leninist. In the first place, it had completely failed to appreciate the relationship between class, power and the state. During the months of negotiation with the British before independence, the AFPFL had not created a new nationalist state, but had simply inherited the colonial state and used it to protect and promote its interests. The vague Burmese communist aspiration to infiltrate and gradually 'take over' the newly independent state from within had, therefore, been fundamentally flawed, because it ignored the fact that no class or section of a class (such as the AFPFL leadership) would voluntarily concede the core of its power: namely, the state machinery that it controlled. 'We totally forgot', wrote Ba Tin Goshal, 'the Leninist principle that the imperialist bureaucracy and state machine cannot be taken over and run in the interest of the people; on the contrary, it has to be smashed' (Ba Tin 1948: 86).

The Goshal Thesis provided the ideological justification for a communist guerrilla war directed against the Burmese government, which, along with a number of separate ethnic rebellions, plunged Burma into a state of semi-permanent civil war that has never truly ended. Burma, in fact, presented a text-book example of the kind of newly independent state that Walt Rostow described in his lecture of 1960 (see previous chapter). It was a fundamentally weak and unstable state, with a small and poorly trained administrative cadre, a tenuous control over outlying regions, and a relatively undeveloped economic base; at the same time, however, it was a state in which the population had been 'politicized' and promised a better future. Burma was, in other words, a state that was difficult to defend and easy to subvert.

During the course of the 1950s, the first prime minister of independent Burma, U Nu, tried to discover the root causes for Burma's unending political turbulence and the state of civil war that developed during this period. These causes, U Nu realized soon after independence, lay far deeper than conflict over ideology and political programmes. There was, after all, a considerable degree of consensus among communists and non-communists alike in favour of the creation of a socialist economy and society run on the basis of state planning, nationalization of key industries, strict control of trading relations with the international economy, and a land-reform programme that would lead to the ultimate goal of the social ownership and use of land (U Nu 1953a: 80–89).

The reasons for Burma's political instability, argued U Nu, lay deep in Burma's history. While it was true that the survival and even legitimacy of all regimes depended ultimately on the ability to exert or threaten overwhelming force, it was a peculiar feature of successive Burmese pre-colonial dynasties that their legitimacy had been based on military power alone. Dynastic succession, therefore, and even the succession from one monarch to the next within a ruling family, had taken the form of a series of *coups d'état* in which the state and its outlying dependencies had had to be reconquered, and then held in a constant state of military alert (U Nu 1953a: 51). The natural consequence had been permanent political and social instability: even if the founder of a dynasty combined military prowess and statesmanship, there had thereafter been a natural tendency for that dynasty to degenerate into a bleak alternation between civil war and pure tyranny (U Nu 1953b: 5).

Such a political system, argued U Nu, not only depoliticized the people – a common enough situation, after all, in traditional states – but, much more significantly, 'demoralized' them. A state founded on the basis of pure power could offer no moral guidance to its subjects. If, as in the reign of King Thibaw just before the British take-over, it also combined extreme tyranny with abject weakness, the 'moral decay' of the nation would be complete (U Nu 1953a: 8). It was precisely this state of demoralization that the British were able to exploit, both for their take-over of power, and for their subsequent maintenance of colonial rule (U Nu 1953a: 33–34).

The nationalist struggle against British colonial rule had indeed politicized the Burmese people. But U Nu felt that this political mobilization, despite the often utopian revolutionary rhetoric, was essentially negative in its objectives. Quite naturally, it was directed to the destruction of the colonial system and, even after the British had conceded a degree of political responsibility to Burmese politicians before the Second World War, the organizations of Burmese nationalism continued to exist in a state of permanent dissidence against the colonial adminis-tration. The very nature of anti-colonialism, in fact, made it inevitable that Burmese nationalists would pursue what U Nu called 'destructive politics' (U Nu 1953a: 1). This was the essence of the Burmese political dilemma: now that Burma had complete responsibility for its own destiny, it had to unlearn the habits of destructive politics, and learn the entirely new statecraft of the 'constructive stage' (U Nu 1953a: 76).

Unfortunately for Burma, U Nu pointed out, Burmese communism had proved to be master of the art of exploiting Burma's inherited 'destructive' political habits. Reverting to the pre-colonial political tradition, it had abandoned democratic politics immediately after independence and had set about seizing power by armed force. In effect, therefore, success for the communists would have involved once again the 'depoliticization' of the population (U Nu 1953b: 4–6). This reality, however, was masked by the fact that the communists manipulated to the full the 'anti-authority' instincts that had prevailed in the politics of the nationalist period, and the language of 'revolution' and 'struggle' that had exerted such a strong influence over the youth of that era (U Nu 1953a: 38–39). U Nu was well aware that the politics of hyperbole, with its extravagant rhetoric and utopian promises, could have a considerable impact on a population that had become used to an anti-colonial style of politics involving permanent opposition to the status quo, and that had only very recently been introduced to the idea of politics as a form of responsibility (U Nu 1957: 100–6).

If the above formed the basis of U Nu's diagnosis of Burma's deep-rooted political ills, what was his solution? In U Nu's eyes, the primary task was the inculcation of a sense of political responsibility among the Burmese people. As he put it to the Burmese in a speech he delivered in August 1952: 'it is your own new era to be created by yourself' (U Nu 1953a: 107). He was quite clear, however, that this new era of the politics of responsibility required, above all, a firm moral foundation – the 're-moralization' of Burmese society after the cumulative 'demoralization' of the pre-colonial and colonial eras (U Nu 1958: 10). In this overall plan for moral rehabilitation, the three essential pillars were to be socialism, democracy and Buddhist moral values.

U Nu viewed the creation of a socialist society as the essential first step. Insofar as U Nu's thinking was influenced by Marxism, it was the socialism of Marx the moral philosopher that attracted him, not the socialism of Marx the historian and social scientist. Like Marx the moral philosopher, U Nu believed that men and women could not begin to lead a full human existence, and thereby become morally responsible human beings, if their lives were completely absorbed by the animal struggle of day-to-day existence. The primary task of a socialist programme, therefore, was to provide food, shelter, the necessities of life, the basis for a healthy existence, sufficient leisure to live beyond the world of work, and sufficient education to use that leisure fruitfully. As U Nu put it: 'If a nation cannot have a decent standard of living, it cannot uphold moral principles' (U Nu 1958: 67).

A socialist programme would only have validity, however, if it was linked to genuine democracy. In the first place, democracy resolved the conundrum of the need to balance stability and continuity on one side, and the impetus for change and renewal within a political system on the other. In particular, it would put an end to the politics of violence and adjudication by force that had so disfigured Burmese history (U Nu 1953a: 52). Principally, however, U Nu saw democracy as the crucial means of linking political action to the fundamental Theravada Buddhist precept of individual moral responsibility, and therefore as the key to the development of a political morality. Democracy put responsibility for the nation's future squarely on the people of Burma themselves (U Nu 1953a: 48–50). More than this, the very act of operating democracy was itself a day-by-day political education. U Nu did not see democracy as some kind of crude expression of the 'will of the masses'; rather the reverse. Democracy in its true sense required an acceptance of the legitimacy of political differences, and an acceptance of the 'decision of the majority', even if – the most painful and difficult part of the development of a political morality – that decision did not accord with one's own views (U Nu 1953a: 54).

However, despite U Nu's aspirations to create a moral basis for a democratic socialist society, the reality was that Burma, in the course of the 1950s, sank into a state of ever-deepening political turbulence and corruption, while the communist rebellions continued unabated, and separatist movements threatened to break up the country. It was in these threatening circumstances that the Burmese army under General Ne Win seized power in 1962 and set about creating an entirely new political system.

The stated objectives of this regime were: the re-establishment of unified state power; the maintenance by the state of complete sovereignty in the conduct of its internal affairs; the creation of a socialist system that encompassed the entire society and was directed by the state; the creation of a specifically 'Burmese' political ideology that could to a degree absorb the ideologies that had up till then divided Burmese nationalism; and the creation of a single party that could, step by step, educate the entire population in the new consolidated ideology, and thereby mobilize society into a unified political system. Thereafter, state and party would merge, and the whole society would govern itself on the basis of 'democratic centralism' – that is, issues would be debated within the party of the whole people, and the democratically arrived-at decision would be implemented by the party and nation as a whole. This political plan was set out in three key documents: the policy declaration of the governing 'Revolutionary Council' entitled *The Burmese Way to Socialism* (30 April 1962); the Constitution of the Burma Socialist Programme Party (BSPP) 'for the transitional period of its construction' (4 July 1962); and the Burma Socialist Programme Party's ideological outline, entitled *The System of Correlation of Man and His Environment: The Philosophy of the Burma Socialist Programme Party* (17 January 1963).

The first step in the realization of its political programme was for the military leadership to engross under its supreme authority all the institutions of state power, and abolish all other sources of political legitimacy. The objective of this new leadership was, however, not merely the seizure of power for its own sake, but the fulfilment of a revolutionary task. It was for this reason that the military junta described itself as 'The Revolutionary Council'. As it explained, the Revolutionary Council, 'forged' as it had been by 'peculiar and powerful historical forces', may have worn 'the outward garb of a military council', but it was 'revolutionary in essence' (BSPP 1962: 57).

In its founding statement, *The Burmese Way to Socialism*, the Revolutionary Council outlined the basic political principles and objectives which formed the boundaries within which political debate thenceforth had to be confined. The first and fundamental step was to be the creation of a socialist economy that would end exploitation and ensure the welfare of the whole population. This socialist system, however, would not be dominated by a particular class, but would satisfy the 'material, spiritual and cultural needs of the whole nation'. All aspects of the economy would be run on socialist principles and would operate within the framework of 'socialist national planning controlled by the state' (Revolutionary Council 1962: 45). The institutions of the state – including the bureaucracy and the armed forces – were no longer to see themselves as ideologically neutral, but were to become instruments for the creation and defence of a socialist society (Revolutionary Council 1962: 47–48).

It was the opinion of the Revolutionary Council that the parliamentary democratic structure set up at the time of independence had failed because Burma lacked what it called 'a mature public opinion' (Revolutionary Council 1962: 47). In consequence, the paths of socialism and democracy had drifted apart. The first step in the rebuilding of the socialist democracy that Aung San himself, the father of the nation, had aspired to create, would therefore be a massive campaign for the political and social education of the people as a whole. The objective of this education programme would be the general inculcation of 'socialistic moral values' (Revolutionary Council 1962: 50).

The Revolutionary Council entrusted this task to what was to become the single legitimate party of the nation, the Burma Socialist Programme Party (BSPP). Under the overall direction of the Revolutionary Council, this party would, through an undefined 'transitional period', politically educate and at the same time mobilize the entire population of Burma (Revolutionary Council 1962: 51). The party itself would initially comprise a carefully chosen cadre who had to be educated in, and committed to, the ideals of the regime, and who had to be prepared to live by a spartan and self-sacrificing 'socialist' code of behaviour that would provide an example to the rest of the population (BSPP 1962: 74). Gradually, however, as the people were mobilized and inculcated with proper socialist principles, the cadre party would transform itself into a 'party of the entire nation' (BSPP 1962: 58). By a natural process of osmosis, therefore, party democracy would form the basis for a 'socialist democracy' that would encompass the whole population (BSPP 1962: 66).

It was the task of the Burma Socialist Programme Party to elaborate a complete political philosophy that would be ideologically inclusive, in the sense that it would harmonize Buddhist and Marxist world-views within a framework that could point the way to a specifically 'Burmese road to socialism'. In this respect the BSPP's attempt to fit the Marxist philosophy of history within a much broader – and vaguer – Buddhist cosmology harked back to Aung San's political thinking, particularly his speech, 'Problems for Burma's Freedom', of January 1946 (Aung San 1946a: 94–112).

Unlike classic Marxism, which saw material conditions and the conflict between social classes for control of material resources as the fundamental determinant in the development of human societies, the BSPP described history as a constant interaction between 'matter' and 'consciousness'. Human states of consciousness, therefore, were not determined solely by material factors existing at any given time: rather, mind and matter coexisted in what was called a 'dialectical correlation' (BSPP 1963: 4). In other words, the BSPP sought to weld together in a 'dialectical' relationship the Buddhist view of history as a history of morality, and the Marxist materialist interpretation of history. The 'correlative' relationship, however, was not static: 'mind' and 'matter' interacted in a relationship of 'inherent instability', and it was this disequilibrium that accounted for change and development in history in an 'ever-turning wheel of change' (BSPP 1963: 4–5). Just as there was a fundamental 'dialectic' between mind and matter, so human nature itself had selfish and social impulses that were contradictory and at the same time 'correlative'. The basic instinct of man is 'the fulfilment of his material and spiritual needs'. While this instinct might at times put the individual in an antagonistic relationship with society, at other times, because man is also inherently a social being, he 'serves social interests in order to serve his own'. This constant interaction between inextricable 'egotistical and social desires' was another driving force for disequilibrium and change in human society (BSPP 1963: 7).

Turning to the contemporary situation of mankind, the BSPP argued that the capitalist system represented an extreme form of disequilibrium, both between 'matter' and 'mind', and between man's individual and social instincts. Based as it was on a pitiless calculation of profit and loss at the expense of broader human considerations, its motive force was entirely materialistic; it also exalted, in the most extreme way, the interests of the individual as against those of society as a whole (BSPP 1963: 12). Such an intense form of disequilibrium must eventually create a social and spiritual crisis that would lead to a qualitative change in the system that could take the form of either a violent or peaceful revolutionary process (BSPP 1963: 17).

This revolution would culminate in the creation of a socialist economy and society in which material and spiritual needs, and the relationship between the individual and society, would be brought into a proper correlation through the creation of an economic system that would benefit society as a whole (BSPP 1963: 21–23). The BSPP did not, however, see this revolution in the same terms as the essentially materialist Marxist concept of a class struggle for the resources of the economy. Rather, the BSPP argued that the socialist society should be created by, and in the interests of, all 'working people' in general: that is, all those who, by their manual or mental contribution, were 'serving the interests of the society' (BSPP 1963: 12).

Like Aung San, the BSPP were anxious to keep Buddhism and the *sangha* out of the political arena, not least because they saw that its impact would be entirely unpredictable and to a degree uncontrollable. In a sense, this made it all the more important to incorporate elements of a Buddhist world-view into their political philosophy. By this means, it was possible to argue that socialism, by satisfying the basic human needs of the whole society, would help contain instincts of greed and self-interest, and could thereby encourage the Buddhist spiritual virtue of 'non-attachment' as much as it could the civic virtue of social altruism (BSPP 1963: 31–33).

IDEOLOGICAL BASIS OF THE REGIME OF NGO DINH DIEM IN THE REPUBLIC OF VIETNAM (SOUTH VIETNAM)

At the end of the Second World War, the French were determined to reassert their authority in Vietnam as well as in Laos and Cambodia (see chapters 7 and 8). Ultimately, this would have involved the destruction of the Democratic Republic of Vietnam (DRV) established by the Vietnamese communist leadership in September 1945. At first, the French tried to weaken the authority and legitimacy of the DRV by encouraging the establishment of autonomous entities among the T'ai groups in the north, the 'Montagnard' minorities of the central region, and the 'Cochinchinese' of south Vietnam. By early 1947, however, by which time it had become apparent that this strategy was alienating Vietnamese nationalism in general, the French belatedly set about creating a nationalist but anti-communist Vietnamese state with which they could negotiate an acceptable independence agreement, thereby sidelining the DRV, and mobilizing all Vietnamese anti-communists to the French side.

For a number of reasons, however, this 'State of Vietnam' – which was gradually put in place between 1947 and 1949 – lacked the nationalist credibility that would have made it effective for French purposes: first, because the French were reluctant to cede it genuine independent powers; secondly, because the head of state of this new Vietnamese entity was none other than the former emperor, Bao Dai. Even the most fervently anti-communist Vietnamese could not avoid concluding that the old protectorate was being resurrected in a new guise, and that the State of Vietnam was indeed – as communist propaganda repeatedly stated – nothing more than a 'puppet' of French colonialism. Furthermore, as a member of the 'French Union', the State of Vietnam had no control over overall military and economic policy in Vietnam, and the French tended to conduct the war against the communists as if Bao Dai and his state did not exist. Equally damaging for this State of Vietnam was the fact that it had no effective authority over many of the war-torn provinces of Vietnam. In these provinces the French largely depended on local warlords, who were given a free hand internally in return for suppressing communist activity.

After 1950, the French gradually lost the will to continue a war that was becoming more and more remote from their genuine national interest. Had it not been for the intrusion of the Cold War into the region, it is quite likely that France would have struck a deal conceding independence to the Democratic Republic of Vietnam, and abandoned the ramshackle State of Vietnam to its fate. That this did not happen was due principally to the fact that the United States had, by 1950, come to see Vietnam as a front line of the Free World that must be defended from communism at all costs. Even if France had been willing to continue the war against the Vietnamese communists, it became increasingly clear to the Americans that the former colonial power would be unsuitable for the role of the local bulwark against communist aggression. In the years 1950 to 1954, the United States put its weight behind the anti-communist State of Vietnam that the French had created, and in effect increasingly took over the war against Vietnamese communism from the French.

The Geneva Agreement of 1954, which was designed to put an end to the Vietnam conflict and enable France to withdraw from Indochina, was therefore little more than a stand-off in a continuing struggle. Vietnam was divided between two administrations – the communist DRV in North Vietnam, and the anti-communist State of Vietnam in the South – and it was envisaged in the terms of the agreement that a unified Vietnam would be created in 1956 by means of free and fair Vietnam-wide elections.

It was precisely during the Geneva Conference that Bao Dai appointed Ngo Dinh Diem (1901–1963) as prime minister of the State of Vietnam. Diem came from a family that formed part of the mandarin elite of central Vietnam, and he himself had served in the highest ranks of the imperial government during the protectorate period. Unlike his ministerial colleague of the time, Pham Quynh, however, he had retired from government when it became apparent to him that the French were not prepared to grant the Vietnamese imperial government any freedom of political action. Although Ngo Dinh Diem's family belonged to the mandarin elite, they, like many others of the same social rank, were Roman Catholics. Diem's outlook and education were, therefore, what might seem a strange compound of Confucian and European. Unlike his brother Ngo Dinh Nhu, however, Diem had not been educated in France, and his world-view was in consequence more firmly rooted in the classical Confucian tradition (Phuc Thien 1956: 14–15). It was possibly through his younger and French-educated brother that he became acquainted with the Catholic-influenced social and political philosophy known as 'Personalism', and with the ideas of the main articulator of Personalism, Emmanuel Mounier. A close examination of Diem's public statements – particularly during the period 1954–1956 when he was in effect trying to create a new state – reveals the extent of Mounier's influence on his political outlook.

In the very broadest terms, the Personalist philosophy of Mounier could be described as an attempt to link the liberal notion of the free individual as the core of any acceptable political or social system; the Christian notion of the individual conscience as the basis of the moral order; and the broad socialist concept that society itself was a moral entity that not only had to balance the right of the individual against the welfare of the whole society, but had to take positive steps to ensure that individuals increasingly behaved as social beings (Mounier 1952, 1956). Put more simply, it was an attempt to protect the 'spiritual personality' of the individual human being in an age of mass politics. In its right-wing aspect, manifested in Christian Democracy, it accepted the role of the socialist idea in modern society, but tried to preserve an inviolable space for the role and responsibility of the individual; in its left-wing aspect, manifested in Christian or Catholic Socialism, it tried to inject the idea of individual moral responsibility and rights into socialist thinking.

Like so many other European intellectual movements of the post-First World War period, Personalism accepted the basic socialist premiss that capitalism and the social and political phenomena connected with capitalism – including liberalism – had had their day (Mounier 1952: 98). In any case, the pure capitalist ideal of the acquisitive, self-interested individual, struggling for survival in a world governed by an abstract economic law of profit and loss, scarcely provided a context in which spiritual values and the idea of moral responsibility could flourish (Mounier 1952: 103–4).

The great fear of Personalist thinkers, however, was that the apparent substitutes for liberal capitalism – whether they be the fascist concept of the organic state and the collective will, or the Marxist concept of the 'great moving forces of history, which are super-personal in character' (as Trotsky put it in his analysis of the Russian Revolution) – offered no defence whatever for the notion of man as a spiritual being with moral rights and responsibilities. Human beings, who had been atomized by capitalism, would now be swallowed up in the collective. Mounier acknowledged the value of socialist principles, since he viewed social responsibility as an intrinsic part of each individual's full humanity. But he saw that, in an exact reverse of capitalism's exaltation of the individual and profound mistrust of the state, the tendency of socialism was to repose excessive confidence in the virtue of the state, but mistrust the moral integrity and capacity of the individual (Mounier 1952: 112).

While Personalism saw social responsibility and social values as an inextricable part of the individual's 'spiritual personality', it also sought to protect the individual's freedom of action as a moral entity from the tendency of the state – particularly a state influenced by the socialist idea – to engross all social, moral and sometimes even political responsibility (Mounier 1952: 99, 104–5). The first task, therefore, in the retrieval of man's spiritual being was the creation or strengthening of institutions that could protect him from the abstract power of market forces on one side and the impersonal state on the other. These institutions should be designed to uphold the fundamental premiss that 'the state is meant for man, not man for the state', and, by extension, that the economy was meant for man, not man for the economy (Mounier 1952: 112).

In this search for 'state-limiting' institutions and structures, the Personalists naturally placed their faith in 'constitutional democracy', with its checks and balances, rather than in democracy conceived as a facilitator of the 'general will'. A federal system that devolved substantial power to regions was also recognized as a means of diffusing political responsibility and at the same time checking the central power of the state (Mounier 1952: 113). Mounier also saw in the concept of the 'nation' – that is, a state that has assumed an independent and unique national 'personality' as well as independent power – a valid means of ensuring that the state could never become an entirely abstract force 'above' society, but would always ultimately 'belong' to its inhabitants. A state whose 'personality' as a nation emanated from the identity of its inhabitants could also form a natural defence against 'cosmopolitan economic interests' (Mounier 1952: 110).

Within society itself, the Personalists emphasized the importance of social organizations that could mediate and hold the balance between the spheres of private interest and social responsibility, and could at the same time have sufficient autonomous authority to resist over-encroachment by the state. In this respect, trade unions and other organizations that emerged independently from within society and operated on democratic lines were seen as essential means of enlarging the principles of democracy in the economic realm (Mounier 1952: 115). The family likewise was seen as a vital institution which, although it had evident faults, nevertheless mediated between the individual and society – introducing the social principle into private life, while at the same time protecting the sanctity of the private world within society (Mounier 1952: 107).

That the ideas of Personalism had a major impact on Ngo Dinh Diem is evident from a careful reading of his speeches on matters of policy. There was, however, a vast difference between the world facing the European Personalists, and that facing Ngo Dinh Diem. Even after the destruction of the Second World War, the European state was a powerful institution; it therefore made sense for the Personalists to seek means of limiting and diffusing its power. Ngo Dinh Diem, on the other hand, presided in June 1954 – when he was appointed Prime Minister – over a state that barely existed, lacked nationalist credentials, and was about to be abandoned by its colonial patron.

In Diem's own eyes, the problems he faced were far more deep-rooted than the weakness of the State of Vietnam. The period of the Vietnamese monarchy's collusion with the colonial French in the protectorate system had in his view completely discredited the traditional political system in Vietnam, and indeed the Confucian values that underpinned it (Phuc Thien 1956: 9). The natural consequence was not just a contempt for the traditional administrative elite, but a complete loss of respect for authority in general; which, since it had been exercised by French administrators, was seen as inherently illegitimate. The links of affiliation between peasant and state had been cut, and the natural inclination of the peasantry in a feudal society to avoid all contact with authority had been exacerbated by the colonial experience.

This condition of moral, political and social decay was made worse, asserted Diem, by the prolonged conflict between the French and the Vietnamese communists from 1945 to 1954. Instead of allowing the State of Vietnam to become a strong and independent entity – the only way it could have gained nationalist legitimacy – the French had relied in practice on a network of local provincial warlords who by-passed the Vietnamese state and maintained a direct patron-client relationship with the French (Ngo Dinh Diem 1955c: 8). Even worse, perhaps, the endless depredations and dangers of a war conducted over their fields and villages had confirmed the peasantry in their traditional 'trouble-avoiding mentality', and deepened their apathy and resentment against all forms of authority (Diem 1956b: 34).

This, then, was the underlying condition of a state that, through the partition of 1954, had been separated from northern Vietnam, which was seen by Diem as the cradle of Vietnamese identity and culture (Ngo Dinh Diem 1955a: 210–11). Vietnam as a whole was confronted by a communist movement that posed a deadly threat to all that Vietnamese tradition held dear: 'religion, fatherland and family' (Ngo Dinh Diem 1955d: 18). Vietnamese communists were, moreover, seen by Diem as merely the puppets of a new and at the same time ancient imperialist enemy, China, which was now cloaking its aggression in communist ideology (Ngo Dinh Diem 1955a: 213–14).

In these dire circumstances, Diem saw it as his first task to revive the legitimacy of the state, re-establish 'unity' and 'order', and thereby restore 'the national characteristics of our people' (Ngo Dinh Diem 1955a: 214; 1955b: 216). The elimination of the colonial and 'warlord' political structures created by the French was an essential precondition for ending the demoralization of society as a whole, and breaking down the feudal mentality of the peasantry. Once a sense of national sovereignty and purpose could be reasserted, the foundations of political and economic democracy – the necessary preconditions for the development of the full spiritual life of the individual – could be established.

Accordingly, in the period 1954 to 1956, Ngo Dinh Diem systematically destroyed the power of the provincial warlords, established a national army and a new administrative structure, put an end to the constitutional relationship with the French, and – finally – used a referendum to oust Bao Dai as head of state, replacing the 'State of Vietnam' with a new 'Republic of Vietnam' with himself as President. This process of resuscitating Vietnam's independent national 'personality' was consolidated in the ensuing years, particularly through the introduction in 1958 of a new educational curriculum that emphasized Vietnamese language and literature at the expense of French (Donnell 1961: 53).

An essential part of Ngo Dinh Diem's political plan was to prevent the creation a mirror-image of the communist totalitarian state, in which an ideologically-based political party engrossed all the powers of the state, and the individual had no scope whatever for a truly independent existence (Ngo Dinh Diem 1956a: 25). The new Republic of Vietnam was therefore based on a system of constitutional democracy, in which – in theory at least – a balance would be ensured between the executive powers of the presidency and the legislative powers of the new National Assembly, and the integrity of the law would be maintained by an independent judicial system (Ngo Dinh Diem 1956a: 28). Following the lines of Personalist thinking, Diem did not see democracy merely as a static 'right', but rather as a 'permanent effort to find the right political means for assuring to all citizens the right of free development and of maximum initiative, responsibility and spiritual life' (Ngo Dinh Diem 1956a: 27). Democracy was, in other words, a continuing education in the complexities of political and social existence, in the interplay of rights and duties, and the balance between self-interest and the needs of the community: as such, it required 'much more effort of understanding and imagination than any other regime' (Phuc Thien 1956: 10).

But if Diem rejected the communist totalitarian model, so he aspired to transcend the traditional Western liberal model of the state, in which, although 'positive' freedoms were confirmed, they were not matched by measures to ensure social justice. It was the duty of the new Vietnamese state, therefore, to engage in 'dialectical efforts' to 'smooth the conflict between social justice and liberty, for the sake of the private person' (Ngo Dinh Diem 1956a: 25–6). It was a fundamental objective of Diem's Personalist approach to ensure that a careful balance be maintained between society and the promotion of social welfare on one side, and the survival – indeed flourishing – of the institutions that protected private existence on the other. Diem saw the restoration of Confucian values as a key to the reassertion of the status of the family. Although Diem and his family were Catholic, this did not in any way conflict with his view that a

Catholic by faith could subscribe to the general *social* values of a civilization whose 'personality' was Confucian.

Another obvious 'private sphere' was that of private property. As in the case of democracy, Diem saw private property, not as a good in itself, but as a means of realizing a 'harmonious and complete progress of the people in every domain, material as well as spiritual' (Ngo Dinh Diem 1955a: 212). The broad objective of the land reform programme that he initiated in 1955–56, therefore, was to eliminate the feudal 'rentier' system of land ownership, along with the mentality that such a system perpetuated, and to redistribute to peasant families 'sufficient individual property to assume a dignified and free life' (Ngo Dinh Diem 1956a: 27). Diem's hope, of course, was that the acquisition of self-sufficient units of land would end the 'state-avoiding' feudal mentality of the peasantry, while at the same time preventing the development of a socialist style 'state-dependence'. Land redistribution would ensure that the peasantry had a stake in, and responsibility towards, society as a whole.

The sphere of private economic activity was viewed through the same moral prism. Diem made it clear that private ownership and foreign investment would not be discouraged. On the other hand, government policy would be geared to the promotion of genuinely productive industrial activity that would strengthen the national economy, not the speculation and profiteering that had marked the colonial era and the 1945–54 war period (Ngo Dinh Diem 1955d: 16–17). In the same way, Diem saw trade union organizations, not just as means of facilitating 'economic democracy', and of mediating between private and public interests, but as a moral force that could help 'the laboring class to clearly understand its rights as well as it main duties to society, [and] to guide the workers toward participating in the management and direction of the economic machine of the nation' (Ngo Dinh Diem 1955a: 212).

It could be said that none of these ideological objectives of Ngo Dinh Diem were achieved in practice. Ultimately, the problem remained that, while the main objective of the European Personalists was to restrain the power of the state so as to preserve a space for the individual and private life generally, Diem, throughout the period of his power, was entirely absorbed in an increasingly unsuccessful attempt to sustain the power and legitimacy of his state. Despite all Diem's efforts, the Republic of Vietnam could never escape from its colonial origins, and could never seriously challenge the communist Democratic Republic of Vietnam as a genuinely nationalist entity. From 1955 onwards, local communist resistance to the Diem family gradually increased, and by 1958–59 this resistance had reached the stage of a full-scale insurgency. A semi-permanent condition of emergency strengthened Diem's natural authoritarian instincts and – despite the elaborate checks and balances of the constitutional system – the presidency steadily absorbed all political authority, and institutions that had been designed to promote society and the private realm against the power of the state simply became propaganda tools and instruments of the regime.

Perhaps the most telling criticism of the gap between the political ideals of Ngo Dinh Diem and the political reality over which he presided is contained in the 'Manifesto of the Eighteen', produced on 26 April 1960 by a group of non-communist politicians, academics, lawyers, clerics and others, protesting against the tyrannical nature of his regime, and demanding that it practise the democratic principles that it professed. The Manifesto pointed out that Diem had never really allowed for – and perhaps never understood – the fact that the surest guarantee for a healthy democracy was the existence of an opposition that was prepared to operate within the democratic structure and to accept its rules exclusively. For Diem, all forms of opposition – communist or non-communist, undemocratic or democratic – constituted a threat to the state itself (Fall 1967: 435–41). In this respect, his outlook on democracy was radically different from that of U Nu of Burma. U Nu's primary objective was the incorporation within a democratic structure of all those groups that challenged the legitimacy of the Burmese state. For U Nu, the value of democracy, therefore, lay in the fact that it allowed for political contest and debate, and at the same time ensured a framework for peaceful political change.

LAOS: BONG SOUVANNOUVONG AND THE CONCEPT OF BUDDHIST DEMOCRACY

By the end of 1960, Laos – in contrast to Cambodia – had become completely enmeshed in the Cold War (see chapter 9). A rightist government, backed by the United States and Thailand, controlled Vientiane and the southern 'pan-handle'; the communist Pathet Lao movement controlled the provinces bordering Vietnam; and a neutralist faction dominated the region to the north of Vientiane. It was in this context that Bong Souvannouvong (bn. 1906), an educationalist by training who had had a chequered career in politics in the post-war period, outlined his plan for peace in Laos, and indeed for the creation of a new political system based on Buddhist precepts (Bong Souvannouvong 1961).

Although Bong Souvannouvong described the body of his philosophical and political principles as *Socialisme Dhammique*, socialist principles and anti-colonialism as such did not dominate his thinking. In this respect, his was different from other currents of Buddhist thinking of his time, most of which tried to create some kind of synthesis between Buddhism and socialism. Bong Souvannouvong was one of the few Buddhist thinkers, aside from U Nu in Burma, who concentrated on the relationship between Buddhism and *democracy*.

Bong Souvannouvong argued that if Lao Buddhism was ever to become an effective and relevant force in the modern world, it would have to shake off the superstitious detritus that had accumulated around the spiritually liberating core of its ideas (see chapter 8). At best, Buddhism had degenerated into a religious faith in which belief had superseded intellectual clarity and effort; at its worst, it had become an incoherent jumble of ritual and superstition (Bong Souvannouvong 1961: 21–22, 84–85). In either case, it had generated a mentality of apathy and fatalism about the human condition and the state of the world.

Any return to the real principles of Buddhism, argued Bong Souvannouvong, must begin with Buddha's central discovery: that all phenomena, including human beings, were governed by the law of cause and effect. Since this fundamental law dictated the operation of the universe, it could not be diverted or mitigated by 'divine intervention'. As he put it, a cause cannot be separated from an effect any more than a human being can be separated from his shadow (Bong Souvannouvong 1961: 13–14). From the discovery of this first principle, Buddha had then – by a process of unbending intellectual effort and spiritual insight – discerned a moral law (*dhamma*) that emerged from the principle of cause and effect. This was that 'selfish' or 'amoral' actions and thoughts led, through the operation of cause and effect, to a condition of spiritual suffering or discontent (*dukkha*); whilst actions and thoughts that are governed by selflessness or morality led to a condition of increasing spiritual freedom (Bong Souvannouvong 1961: 24). The next Buddhist tenet that had to be rediscovered was that of *anatta*, or the non-existence of the soul. The individual soul was not 'born' and 'reborn' through different bodies. Just as a candle passed on its flame to another candle, so what passed through the chain of cause and effect was not our souls, but the accumulated effects – tending either to spiritual suffering or spiritual freedom – of our actions (Bong Souvannouvong 1961: 94). This could be described as a form of moral evolution, but one that was governed by an unchanging moral law, or *dhamma*.

The human individual, therefore, should be understood, not as the possessor of a soul, but as what might be called a '*dhamma*-vehicle' – the basic unit, in human society, for the operation of the moral law. But, since humanity naturally lived in collective units, these units too – whether they be described as society, states or nations – were also '*dhamma*-vehicles' (Bong Souvannouvong 1961: 22). Bong Souvannouvong emphasized that cause and effect and the *dhamma* operated *through* the actual workings of the world – in the natural world, and the everyday world of human contact. It therefore followed that the notion that seclusion from the world would cut the chain of cause and effect and lead to spiritual freedom was yet another of the illusions that had attached themselves to Buddhism – one that had contributed to social and political apathy. He pointed to the obvious fact that the Buddha, although he had fled from the court, had subsequently rejected the life of a hermit, and created a religious community, or *sangha* (Bong Souvannouvong 1961: 69–70).

In terms of the *dhamma*, therefore, the individual and society were interlocked. Individuals lived, not in a vacuum, but within society; and the overall character of a society depended on the actions of each and every one of the individuals that composed it. Since it is an unavoidable consequence of the law of cause and effect that no individual can assume the moral burden of another individual, the first essential step on the road to individual spiritual freedom is the assumption of individual moral responsibility. The collective moral 'condition' of a society depends, therefore, on the extent to which each of its members is able to assume individual responsibility for his or her actions, and the extent to which that freedom then leads of spiritual freedom or selfish enslavement. In the same way a nation – and Bong Souvannouvong saw this as the most significant collectivity in the modern world – must achieve independence before it can assume moral responsibility for its actions. Independence, therefore, was not an end in itself, but an essential precondition for the collective achievement of what Bong Souvannouvong described as 'moral sovereignty' (Bong Souvannouvong 1961: 22, 58–59, 98).

Bong Souvannouvong – like U Nu – concluded that if the moral condition of a society depended on the collective effect of the moral condition of each of its constituent members, then it followed that the only political system that could enable this was democracy (Bong Souvannouvong 1961: 60–61). An authoritarian system – even if it was directed to the welfare of the people as a whole – curtailed the freedom of its individuals to assume moral responsibility for their actions. Democracy was, therefore, not a good in itself; it was simply the only way of linking the individual to the collective in the quest for 'moral sovereignty'. The more individuals within a democracy were morally defective, the more that democracy would be morally defective; but all attempts by self-appointed groups within society to prescribe morality for its members negated the fundamental precept of cause and effect, that no being could carry the moral responsibility for another being (Bong Souvannouvong 1961: 56–59).

Democracy, like independence, was a 'moral facilitator', and its ultimate objective should be to create what Bong Souvannouvong called *dhamma-solidarité*, which he defined as 'the concretization of the sovereignty of the people animated by the same ideal to do good' (Bong Souvannouvong 1961: 74). The model for what might be called this 'Buddhist democracy' (though Bong Souvannouvong did not use this term) was Buddha's own monastic community, or *sangha*. And just as one of the greatest sins of traditional Buddhism was action that led to the breaking up of the *sangha* (*bheda-sangha*), so the fomenting of civil strife leading to the break up of a democratic system was a mortal threat to the achievement of a nation's moral sovereignty (Bong Souvannouvong 1961: 64). This observation had particular relevance for Laos at the time that Bong Souvannouvong wrote his book.

The core of Buddhist morality – the guidelines to action that would help put one on the road to spiritual freedom – was the *panca-sila*, or the five chief rules of conduct for Buddhists. (Although they bore the same name, these were quite distinct from the *pancasila* of Sukarno.) In traditional form, these were a simple guide to the proper conduct of everyday life: the avoidance of killing, stealing, adultery, lying and intoxication (Rhys-Davids 1972: 712). Bong Souvannouvong argued, however, that if one looked beyond the basic precepts themselves, one could discern underlying principles that constituted a code to cover all areas of social and political action. To take just two examples, the injunction against stealing could be extended to the area of corruption, or tax evasion; 'intoxication' could mean intoxication with ideologies that would lead to civil conflict (Bong Souvannouvong 1961: 41–42, 47).

The fundamental objective of this code, Bong Souvannouvong asserted, was the achievement of a genuine economic and political self-sufficiency, which was the necessary precondition for *moral* self-sufficiency, and the ultimate goal, moral sovereignty. Before a nation could engage fruitfully with the rest of the world, it had to build itself from within; it had to accept complete responsibility for its own destiny (Bong Souvannouvong 1961: 92–93). 'Good' actions were therefore judged by the extent to which they helped to achieve this goal. The amassing of wealth, for example, was not good or bad in itself. If that wealth contributed to the strengthening of the economy and the general welfare of society, it was beneficial; if it was used to fund subversion, or was spirited out of the country for private use, its effect was harmful both to the society and the individual responsible (Bong Souvannouvong 1961: 98). Good actions were those that were motivated by altruism towards one's fellow citizens: this could be summed up as a concern for the rights of others, and an acceptance of civic responsibility (Bong Souvannouvong 1961: 93).

It is clear, therefore, that this aim of achieving economic and political self-sufficiency was not, in Bong Souvannouvong's thinking, based on economic or ideological imperatives. Like independence, economic self-reliance was not seen as a good in itself; nor was it part of any ulterior scheme directed either against the capitalist or socialist systems as such. Its *point d'appui* was moral. And, just as a nation could only begin to achieve its moral goals if it was composed of individuals who had control over their own moral destiny – whether for good or ill – so a global society of nations required its components to be morally self-sufficient. Once this had been achieved, a genuine world community – the ultimate '*dhamma*-vehicle' of humanity – could come into existence, and strive to create a global *dhamma-solidarité* (Bong Souvannouvong 1961: 17–18).

The Laotian civil war came to an end in 1975 with the withdrawal of the United States from Indochina and the complete victory of the Lao communist movement. Bong Souvannouvong spoke out against the new communist regime, particularly because of its treatment of Buddhism. He was arrested in October 1975 and sent to a 're-education' camp. He died in captivity shortly thereafter (Stuart-Fox 1992: 14).

〜〜〜

CHAPTER ELEVEN

Ideological Crises of the Independence Regimes: Indonesia

After a confused period of alternating negotiation and conflict that had lasted from August 1945 to the end of 1949, the Netherlands ceded independence to Indonesia (see chapter 7). There then followed a decade and a half of what might justifiably be described as ideological civil war, in which political forces competed, not just for power, but for control over the ideological framework that would form the basis of the independent Indonesian state.

The first major debate within the nationalist leadership, after it declared independence in August 1945, concerned the question of whether the provisional constitutional system should be 'presidential' or 'parliamentary' in form: that is, whether the *locus* of power should reside in the *ad hoc* 'National Committee' formed by the leading members of the nationalist parties, or in the hands of President Sukarno himself. In November 1945, the party-parliamentary system prevailed – with the understanding that an elected body would replace the current *ad hoc* system once conditions permitted – and the struggle against the Dutch between 1945 and 1949 was orchestrated by governments formed from parties within the 'National Committee'.

Throughout the 1945–49 period, there were considerable tensions between the parties over policy towards the Dutch – particularly between those who argued that the inherent weakness of the Republic of Indonesia necessitated a policy of negotiation combined with an attempt to win over international opinion, and those who argued for an all-out armed struggle. It was the natural inclination of the Partai Komunis Indonesia (PKI), or Communist Party of Indonesia, to take a radical stance on this issue. This tendency was strengthened in 1948 by the general communist 'line' announced by Zhdanov in late 1947, which at least implied that communist parties should act as a distinct and, where possible, leading force in the struggle for national-liberation. From this perspective, as in the case of

Burma (see chapter 10), the willingness of the 'national-bourgeois' leadership of the Republic of Indonesia to negotiate and compromise with the Dutch could easily be interpreted as a 'betrayal' of the struggle for genuine independence. Accordingly, the communist uprising in East Java in September 1948 was not directed against the Republic of Indonesia itself, but was designed to ensure 'proletarian hegemony' in the struggle against the Dutch. This revolt was decisively crushed by the newly formed Indonesian armed forces.

In 1948, however, the Republic began to face an even more fundamental challenge to its legitimacy, when the leadership of an Islamic militia organization in southwest Java declared the creation of a Negara Islam Indonesia (NII) or 'Indonesian Islamic State'. This so-called Darul Islam ('House of Islam') movement in effect sought to replace the apparently half-hearted struggle that the Republic of Indonesia had conducted against the Dutch with a *jihad* or 'holy war' directed by the Indonesian Islamic State against the Dutch *kafir* ('unbelievers'). The Darul Islam movement, unlike the PKI, did not seek merely to take over the leadership of the Indonesian Republic: rather, it sought to replace the Republic by a new state based on Islamic principles. This Darul Islam movement subsequently spread to other parts of Indonesia, and continued its armed challenge against the Republic until the early 1960s.

In 1950, after independence had been negotiated, a new provisional constitution entrenched the 'party-parliamentary' system, and preparations were eventually made for the election of a Constituent Assembly that would work out a permanent constitutional structure. The leadership of the armed forces, however, was never reconciled to a parliamentary system that deprived them of the political power that they had exercised on an *ad hoc* basis during the period of conflict against the Dutch. In particular, the armed forces looked back nostalgically to the last year of that conflict, when the civilian political leadership of the Republic of Indonesia had fallen into Dutch hands, and the army had taken over political as well as military leadership of the independence war against the Dutch, and had at the same time beaten off the challenge to the Republic posed by factions such as Darul Islam. The notion that the armed forces were the ultimate guarantor and saviour of the Indonesian Republic, and that in order to fulfil this task they had to play a central political and administrative, as well as security role, was to persist throughout the ensuing period of turbulence (Nasution nd.: 97–99, 105–7).

In 1953, Islamic resentment against what was seen as an essentially secular and overly leftward-leaning Republic – combined with regional resentment against the Republic's centralizing tendencies – finally pushed the political leadership in the province of Aceh in northwest Sumatra to join the Darul Islam revolt. Nation-wide elections held in 1955 merely deepened the political instability of the Republic, since – among other things – the results sharpened the divide between a generally leftist domination of Java and a mainly Islamic and essentially rightist domination of the outer islands. After 1955, a sense that the political system favoured Javanese interests and 'populist-leftist' policies led to a series of regional revolts – particularly in Sumatra in the 1956–60 period. It should be noted, however, that these revolts did not have separatist objectives; they were designed to assert the rights of the regions, and at the same time compel a change of policy at the centre.

Each of these ideological strands – Sukarnoist, communist and Islamic – contributed to the increasing turmoil in Indonesia during its most volatile period.

SUKARNO: FROM 'GUIDED DEMOCRACY' TO REVOLUTIONARY ANTI-COLONIALISM

It was in this context of accelerating political instability that Sukarno, after years of criticizing the inherent infirmity of the party-parliamentary system, took steps in 1959 to reinstate by degrees the old presidential system of government that had prevailed in the early months after the 1945 Revolution. In this new 'Guided Democracy' regime, as it was called, sovereign authority reverted to President Sukarno, while the re-shaped representative bodies became mainly 'advisory'. The ultimate guarantors of state power – particularly in the regions – were the armed forces, who welcomed this chance once again to play a politico-administrative as well as military role. But if the armed forces provided the essential ballast of centralized authority for 'Guided Democracy', it was Sukarno who directed the broad outlines of policy, and gave the new system its ideological vision. Certain general themes in Sukarno's political thinking remained consistent throughout his political career, and these have already been explored in chapters 4, 7 and 9. His fundamental vision led him, perhaps inexorably, towards a stance that became more, not less, revolutionary once independence from the Dutch had been negotiated in 1949. This ideological vision was increasingly to coincide with that of the well-organized and powerful Indonesian Communist Party (PKI) that had rapidly recovered from its setback in the rebellion of 1948. It should be noted that the Partai Nasional Indonesia (PNI) – a party that was ideologically eclectic in the years after its formation in 1945 – also moved decisively to a leftist orientation during the Guided Democracy period.

Sukarno had always taken the position that independence was a goal over which ultimately there could be no compromise or negotiation. Like Padraic Pearse and the Irish Republicans, he saw the nation in almost mystical terms as an organic whole, a living entity (Sukarno 1959: 52). It therefore followed that no concession on national identity or essential national rights could be considered as legitimate, and that a nation could not claim to be free unless it was free in all respects (Sukarno 1960a: 109). Along with the vast majority of the anti-colonial nationalists of his time, Sukarno also believed that political freedom of itself could not be described as true independence: economic independence needed to be achieved along with political independence. On this issue as well, Sukarno took what might be called a 'maximalist' position, and asserted that Indonesia's independence required the removal of 'even the slightest trace of colonialism' in the economic sphere (Sukarno 1952: 78).

As has already been noted in earlier chapters, it had also been a consistent part of Surkarno's political thinking that the Indonesian nationalist movement and the subsequent independent Indonesian state should be rooted in the values and traditional political systems of indigenous society. Foremost among these traditional systems were *gotong royong*, or the tradition of mutual aid within a community, and *musyawarah*, or general consultation and consensus in the reaching of community decisions. He also argued that the Western class categories of Marxism were inappropriate to Indonesian society, since Dutch colonialism had 'equalized' through impoverishment the status of the vast bulk of the population, and levelled the distinctions between peasant, worker, petty-bourgeois and other categories. Sukarno borrowed the name of a chance-met Javanese peasant, Marhaèn, to describe this mass of humanity that shared a virtually undifferentiated existence of poverty and oppression (Sukarno 1957b: 7). It is important to note, however, that this invocation by Sukarno of traditional values and categories that sprang from Indonesia's own historical experience was the reverse of 'conservative' in its political implications. Sukarno insisted that *gotong royong* and *musyawarah* should operate 'dynamically' as a form of constant political debate, not as some form of static conflict avoidance (Sukarno 1959: 69). Likewise, it was precisely because the *marhaèn* of Indonesia lived in absolute poverty, and therefore lacked any form of economic or political leverage, that the only form of anti-colonial weapon they had at their disposal was mass revolutionary activity (Sukarno 1957b: 14–18).

Given this basic political viewpoint, it was natural that Sukarno should regard the independence settlement agreed in 1949 as wholly inadequate, and the 'national revolution' as incomplete. The agreement had permitted the Dutch to retain control of Dutch New Guinea, which Sukarno, and indeed the Indonesian nationalist movement as a whole, regarded as an intrinsic part of Indonesia. It had, moreover, safeguarded Dutch colonial economic interests in Indonesia itself. The Indonesian entity had, therefore, been truncated, and the essential networks of the colonial economy remained intact.

Sukarno was also dissatisfied with the political system in 'independent' Indonesia itself. The parliamentary system, based as it was on the precepts of Western liberal democracy, was not, as Sukarno put it, a form of democracy that was 'in harmony with our spirit' or 'our personality' (Sukarno 1957a: 84). In his eyes, this was precisely reflected in the fact that the system had failed to bring unity, coherence or a sense of purpose to the new Indonesian nation. The parliamentary-party system had vacillated and betrayed the national revolution in 1949–50, and left Indonesia in its semi-colonial, semi-independent condition (Sukarno 1959: 42).

Sukarno's alternative political 'conception', which he advocated throughout the 1950s, and finally put in place in 1959, involved a complete redefinition of the concept of representation. The major political parties that reflected different strands of political thinking were to have their views 'represented' in a so-called *gotong-royong* cabinet appointed by Sukarno: but only on an advisory basis, and on the condition that they contributed positively – on the basis on consensus – to the fundamental goal of completing the national revolution. Those political elements that could not accept either the structure or the aims of 'Guided Democracy' were to be excluded from the political system (Sukarno 1959: 61–62). This representation of varieties of political opinion was to be matched by a body, later known as the Supreme Advisory Council, that was to reflect all the different 'functional groups' within society as a whole: the peasantry, the military, intelligentsia, youth, womens' groups and so forth. As such, it would be, as Sukarno put it, 'a compressed form of the living society' (Sukarno 1957a: 88).

The ultimate goal of this new political structure was, of course, the completion of the national revolution. This involved a continuation of the struggle to end the colonial grip on Indonesia's economy, and the 'liberation' of Dutch New Guinea, or Irian Jaya, as it was called by the Indonesians. National unity was to be re-emphasized, and all 'counter-revolutionary' and 'imperialist' attempts to disintegrate national unity and purpose by the promotion of federal schemes were to be resolutely resisted (Sukarno 1959: 52). Likewise, in order to lay the groundwork for the creation of a 'just and prosperous society' based on socialist principles, policy would be directed towards progressive state control of the economy in general, particularly in the main areas of production and distribution (Sukarno 1959: 55–56). Although foreign and therefore 'colonial' ownership of land was to be ended, Sukarno was most anxious not to destroy unity of purpose among the *marhaènis* masses by igniting what he saw as an unnecessary class war over the issue of land ownership. Traditional property rights were in general to be guaranteed, but Sukarno was clear that the state, as the embodiment of society, had the right to regulate property matters, and ultimately to redistribute land on the basis of socially agreed 'maximums' and 'minimums'; and that property rights in general were therefore subservient to the interests of society as a whole (Sukarno 1960a: 103).

Finally, the general objectives of Guided Democracy were to be underpinned by what Sukarno called the comprehensive 'retooling' of the main institutions of state and society (Sukarno 1959: 56). Fundamentally, this involved the elimination of the Western liberal notion that the instruments of the state such as the armed forces and the bureaucracy were politically 'neutral': *all* public bodies were to be politicized and mobilized for the tasks of the national revolution. The key objective here was the effecting of a psychological transformation, which would involve the instilling of a revolutionary mentality, the 'rooting out' of 'the spirit of individualism', and its replacement by a 'spirit of mutual cooperation' (Sukarno 1959: 59).

For Sukarno the revolution that had begun in August 1945 was not merely about a transfer of power between colonial and nationalist leaderships. What had begun in 1945 had been a genuine revolution: that is, a fundamental upheaval throughout Indonesian society that was directed towards a complete transformation of the social as well as the political organization of that society. The revolution, in fact, was nothing less than the irresistible expression of the national will, and it was therefore his duty as leader of the nation to articulate that national will and ensure that it achieved all of its objectives (Sukarno 1951: 60–62). As he put it in his Independence Day speech of August 1959, the will of the nation had 'burst forth in a historically revolutionary way', and would have to be realized 'by revolutionary means' (Feith 1970: 105).

In fact, Sukarno increasingly saw revolution, not simply as a means to achieve national ends, but as an end in itself. As he proclaimed in August 1960, 'I belong to the group of people who are bound in spiritual longing by the Romanticism of Revolution' (Sukarno 1960a: 83). Sukarno believed that the manifold weaknesses of the Indonesian Republic – its administrative and institutional weakness, its tendency to fragmentation, its ideological dissension, and, above all, its desperate state of economic backwardness – could only be overcome by a colossal and united effort of national will. Only revolution, it seemed, could mobilize the masses behind this common purpose. More than this, Sukarno – for whom, as for others of his generation, the Russian Revolution must have seemed the decisive event in modern history that had changed the global balance of power between the 'oppressors' and the 'oppressed' of the world – the process of revolution itself seemed to unleash an almost mystical power and exert a 'romantic' appeal that could overcome seemingly impossible obstacles. As he put it: 'for those who join in that mighty current of the Revolution, the dynamic spirit of the Revolution becomes a Romanticism arousing a passionate spirit' (Sukarno 1960a: 83).

The slow procedures of parliamentary democracy were anathema to Sukarno, not so much because he was an instinctive autocrat, but because he was an instinctive revolutionary. The concentrated force of revolution never, as Trotsky once admitted, 'coincides with the rhythm of formal representative democracy' – and it could be argued that Sukarno's main objection to Western-style liberal democracy was not that it violated the traditional political norms of Indonesian society, but that it was incompatible with revolutionary politics.

Sukarno's revolutionary instincts were inextricably combined with his internationalism. Far from arguing that the Indonesian Revolution was *sui generis*, he asserted (as noted in chapter 9) that the principles of *pancasila* had universal application, and were in fact a combination and 'pulling up higher' of the universal values expressed in the American Declaration of Independence and the Communist Manifesto (Sukarno 1960a: 116). Since, ultimately, no nation could describe itself as completely free until all nations were free of colonialism and of the international capitalist system that underpinned colonialism (Sukarno 1959: 74), Indonesia was participating, not just in a national endeavour, but in an international revolution that could not end till an entirely new world order had been established (Sukarno 1965: 8).

This combination of internationalism and revolutionary politics reveals Sukarno's anxiety that Indonesia should take a leading part in international events. Indeed, Indonesia under Sukarno could be described as a 'theatre nation' deliberately setting out to play a role on the world stage, and Sukarno's dramatic political language was clearly designed to give Indonesians a sense that they as a people were playing a leading role in a revolutionary drama of global significance (Sukarno 1965: 4). In part, this was a result of Sukarno's instinctive sense that all of Asia, Africa and Latin America was 'glowing with the fire of revolution', and that in such a world Indonesians could not afford to 'creep like snails' or 'crawl like tortoises' (Sukarno 1960a: 85). In part, what might be described as Sukarno's 'politics of revolutionary theatre' was designed to overcome the natural sense of inferiority of a people who had endured centuries of colonial rule, and who could so easily have seen themselves as a 'nation of coolies' (Sukarno 1964: 242). Sukarno, like Oswald Spengler in his seminal book, *The Decline of the West*, believed that peoples and civilizations that were not active 'makers of history' would have no history at all, and would 'vanish in the heart of history ... as though they were nothing' (Sukarno 1965: 6).

Given Sukarno's overwhelming anxiety that Indonesia should be a 'maker of history', it is not surprising that 'non-alignment' played an diminishing role in his thinking during the 1960s. In the first place, the role of by-stander in international affairs was clearly anathema to Sukarno, and even the 'revolutionary' non-alignment he advocated did not truly fit his radical world-view (Sukarno 1965: 32). In the second place, during the 'Guided Democracy' period, Sukarno no longer regarded the Cold War confrontation between the USA and the USSR, or between the capitalist and socialist camps, as the central global confrontation. The major confrontation was, by then, that between the 'oppressor' nations of colonialism, neo-colonialism and its puppets in one camp, and the 'oppressed' nations of Asia, Africa and Latin America in the other camp (Sukarno 1965: 16–20). For Sukarno, the epicentre of the world struggle against capitalism and colonialism was no longer in Moscow, but in what was known at that time as the 'Third World'.

THE IDEOLOGICAL FOUNDATIONS OF THE STRATEGY OF THE COMMUNIST PARTY OF INDONESIA (PKI), 1948–1965

Although Sukarno's ideological trajectory was increasingly convergent with that of the communists, the ideological development of the Partai Komunis Indonesia (PKI) in the years after 1948 followed its own logic. In 1948, a combination of a 'dogmatic' strategy and a lack of coordination and discipline within the PKI itself had nearly led to the complete annihilation of the party as a political force. Indeed, a large section of Indonesia's political establishment – including most of the armed forces' leadership – regarded the PKI thereafter as a traitorous movement that had stabbed the Republic of Indonesia in the back at its moment of greatest peril. In the years after the failed Madiun Revolt of 1948, therefore, the PKI's very survival depended on a policy based on caution, and accommodation with other elements in the nationalist movement. The rehabilitation of the PKI was undoubtedly helped by the fact that it gave wholehearted support to the Republic against a series of separatist, Islamic and military revolts that broke out between 1948 and 1953 (Aidit 1955: 31).

This new policy of cooperation was not only dictated by necessity, but was also in line with the general international communist strategy that began to prevail after Stalin's death in 1953. This topic has already been addressed in chapter 9, and may be summed up as the view that communist parties in the colonial world should give wholehearted support for wars of national liberation and newly independent governments that were generally 'progressive' in their political stance, even if those movements and governments were headed by non-communist 'national bourgeois' elements. In other words, the line taken by the Burmese communists in the 'Goshal Thesis' (see chapter 10) was now considered 'sectarian', since it was liable to divide, and thereby weaken, the general anti-colonial movement which Moscow now saw as a vital means of crippling the West's global position.

In March 1954, D. N. Aidit, the General-Secretary of the PKI Central Committee and therefore effective leader of the Indonesian communists, outlined the overall ideological position and strategic objectives of the Indonesian Communist Party. In this survey, he focused on three main areas: the PKI's national policy, and the role it should play at the level of the centre of power; the building by the PKI of a mass base of support among the population; and the re-building of the party itself.

At the level of national policy, Aidit argued that the party should seek to build a 'national united front' with all 'progressive' political elements that, like the PKI, sought 'complete national independence' for Indonesia (Aidit 1955: 30). Like Sukarno, Aidit contended that the independence gained in 1949–50 only gave Indonesia the outward show of political freedom: in reality, Indonesia remained in a 'semi-colonial' condition (Aidit 1955: 24–25). In Marxist-Leninist terms, this meant that the PKI recognized that Indonesia was at the 'bourgeois-democratic' stage of trying to achieve full economic and political independence, and that the party was seeking common cause with the bourgeois-led nationalist movement to achieve these goals, and therefore should not push their policy or their rhetoric beyond this immediate objective.

Simultaneously, however, Aidit urged the party to build a 'mass base' among the population as a whole. This involved, first and foremost, an all-out effort by the party to win support among the peasantry, who constituted the vast majority of the Indonesian population, and would be the ultimate determinant of success or failure for the PKI. Aidit pointed out that, while the Indonesian Revolution was in the 'bourgeois-democratic' phase of national liberation, the bourgeoisie of Indonesia itself was actually divided between those who had benefited from the colonial economic system, and those who wished to achieve complete economic independence from that system. Seen as a whole, therefore, the bourgeoisie was unreliable, and consequently even a slight tilt in the balance of power within its ranks towards its reactionary elements could have disastrous consequences for the political fortunes of the PKI. Strong and firm support from the peasantry could protect them against this danger (Aidit 1955: 44–48).

The key to winning peasant support, Aidit asserted, was the pursuit of a vigorous campaign against 'feudalism' in the countryside, and the demand that land held by feudal landlords be distributed to the 'landless peasants' (Aidit 1955: 30). Such a policy would not only win support from a large section of the poorer peasantry, but would also be ideologically appropriate, since it would be seeking to extend – not eliminate – 'bourgeois' property rights, and it would help to eradicate the traces of that feudal structure on which colonial rule had relied (Aidit 1955: 32–33).

Overall, therefore, Aidit's strategy was to support the creation of a 'national united front' that would include all patriotic and anti-colonial elements, including as wide a section of the 'national bourgeoisie' as possible, while building a firm base of support among the peasantry. Aidit was acutely aware, however, that this alliance would always be inherently unstable, mainly because of the suspicion with which the PKI was regarded by a large section of the nationalist establishment. Success, and even survival, for the PKI therefore depended on what Aidit described as the 'bolshevization' of the core party membership (Aidit 1955: 43). By this term he did not mean the 'radicalization' of the party, but rather the instilling of firm party discipline and a clear and appropriate ideological outlook that could maintain a balance between a grasp of Marxist-Leninist theory and an understanding of the actual social and political situation in Indonesia at any given time. Since party recruits came largely from what Aidit described as the 'petty-bourgeoisie', they tended either to lack a firm intellectual grasp of Marxist theory, and thereby to develop a purely 'empirical' outlook; or, since they lacked any firm roots in the proletariat or the peasantry, they tended to adopt a 'dogmatic' and overly theoretical approach (Aidit 1955: 51). An ability to balance between 'theory' and 'practice' would enable party members to distinguish between 'antagonistic' and 'non-antagonistic' contradictions between the classes in society, and to understand the evolution of these contradictions. Not surprisingly, Aidit recommended Mao Tse-tung's *On Contradiction* as a key text for cadres (Aidit 1955: 54).

The PKI's strategy of trying to build – and ultimately to guide – an anti-colonial and anti-feudal alliance of classes required above all a systematic class analysis. In 1957, Aidit published just such an analysis for use in party training. The overall objective was to identify those classes that fell firmly in the 'reactionary' camp, and therefore were to be isolated and confronted; those 'middle of the road' elements that would play a progressive role during the anti-colonial, anti-feudal period, but would subsequently become 'antagonistic' as the revolution moved to its socialist phase; and those 'progressive' classes that would form a bedrock of support for the PKI in both the anti-colonial and socialist phases (Aidit 1957: 251–53).

The key to the success of the PKI's strategy of maintaining a progressive 'national united front' against feudalism and colonialism would, Aidit claimed, lie in winning over to that front the bulk of the 'middle of the road' elements of the bourgeoisie and middle peasantry. This would require a balance between a political stance that was sufficiently moderate not to alarm the above 'middle of the road' elements, but sufficiently radical on issues such a land reform to maintain a revolutionary momentum and keep the support of the poorest elements of society (Aidit 1957: 259–63). On this basis, it would be possible to 'develop the progressive forces, unite with the middle of the road forces, and isolate the die-hard forces' (Aidit 1957: 265).

When it was installed in 1959, Sukarno's Guided Democracy regime posed a dilemma for the PKI. The PKI had benefited considerably from the party-parliamentary period, and, through the operation of the democratic process initiated in 1955, had managed to build a widespread base of support in the hinterland of Java. In the Guided Democracy system, the PKI would still be permitted to organize politically; but they would no longer be able to convert expanding support among the population into expanding representation and influence at the centre of power. From now on, the level of PKI political influence exerted at the centre would be dependent on President Sukarno, and their policies would have to harmonize with Guided Democracy objectives as outlined by Sukarno.

The balance between the dangers and opportunities presented by Guided Democracy was discussed by a PKI Politburo member, Sakirman, in a series of articles written in *Bintang Merah* ('Red Star'), the theoretical journal of the PKI, between May and August 1960. Given Sukarno's own political vision and his determination to carry the anti-colonial revolution to a conclusion, there could be no doubt that the ideological tendency of the new regime was 'progressive', and generally in tune with PKI strategy. On the other hand, the actual power that sustained Guided Democracy clearly lay with the armed forces, and there was a real danger that any crisis in the regime could lead straight to a 'military dictatorship' (Sakirman 1960: 125). Sakirman concluded that the very fact that the regime was so precariously balanced between progressive and reactionary tendencies made it vital for the PKI to lend support to the regime, and decisively tip the balance of Guided Democracy in a progressive direction (Sakirman 1960: 126).

In a survey of the world situation presented to the PKI Central Committee in December 1963, the Party leader D.N. Aidit observed that two 'mighty currents of contradiction' – the struggle between the socialist and capitalist systems in the developed world, and the struggle between 'the oppressed nations and imperialism' in the 'Third World' – were confronting each other (Aidit 1963: 266). Aidit argued that, because Asia, Africa and Latin America were manifestly the 'weakest links in the chain of imperialism', international revolutionary leadership now lay in the hands of the communist and anti-colonial movements of the Third World (Aidit 1963: 267–68). This obvious convergence between the world-view of the PKI and that of Sukarno cannot be dismissed merely as a tactic on the part of the former to get close to Sukarno. What may be described as the 'Third Worldist' tendency of the PKI sprang from the inner logic of the Party's increasingly overt adherence to the Chinese Communist international position at that time (see chapter 13).

If anything, in fact, it was Sukarno who was drawing closer towards the PKI line. In the last years of Guided Democracy, the PKI found itself in the anomalous and dangerous position of gaining increased 'ideological hegemony' within the regime, without at the same time achieving any hegemony over the instruments of political power. Indeed, it was this evident tendency of Sukarno to align himself with the PKI ideologically that at least partly explains the destruction of the Guided Democracy regime by the fiercely anti-communist leadership within the armed forces.

REVOLUSI ISLAM, OR THE ISLAMIC REVOLUTION IN INDONESIA

Among the ideological elements opposed to the Sukarno-PKI axis were the leaders of the Islamic sections of the nationalist movement, both revolutionary and moderate. In 1948–49, as has already been noted above, a Negara Islam Indonesia (NII), or 'Islamic State of Indonesia', had been established in the strongly Islamic region of southwest Java. This state denied the legitimacy of the Republic of Indonesia, and its Darul Islam ('House/Abode of Islam') rebellion was designed to create a new entity throughout Indonesia that was founded on exclusively Islamic principles. In 1953, when the religious and political leadership of the province of Aceh in northwest Sumatra declared Aceh's adherence to the Negara Islam Indonesia, Aceh thereby became part of the Darul Islam revolt against the Republic of Indonesia.

Aceh was a strongly Islamic region that had – as the former Sultanate of Aceh – fiercely resisted Dutch colonial take-over in a thirty-year war at the end of the nineteenth century. The Acehnese saw this war – at the time and subsequently – not just as a war for the defence of Acehnese independence, but also as a war for the defence of Islam: a *perang sabil* ('war in God's cause') or *jihad*. When the independence struggle began against the Dutch in 1945, the Acehnese leadership gave their full support, with the chief *ulama* (religious scholars) of Aceh giving a religious *imprimatur* to a struggle that was in most of the rest of Indonesia seen in nationalist terms. A *fatwa*, or religious decision, issued by four eminent *ulama* on 15 October 1945 declared, first, that the *perang kemerdekaan* (war for independence) was also a *perang sabil* or *jihad*. Secondly, the *fatwa* made clear that this holy war was a *sambungan*, or 'continuation' of the Acehnese anti-colonial war against the Dutch which began in 1873 (Hasjmy 1989). While Aceh participated wholeheartedly in the independence struggle, therefore, it did so on a basis that emphasized the Islamic nature of the war, and that preserved Aceh's sense of a special identity.

The shift from Aceh's wholehearted support for the Indonesian Republic in 1945 – albeit on its own terms – to outright rebellion in 1953, is explained in a manifesto produced by the Acehnese rebel leadership in that year. The manifesto makes clear that the refusal of the Republic to recognize Aceh's separate identity in its structure of regional government, added to the Republic's withholding of any genuine autonomous rights to the regions, was one of the two major stimulants for the rebellion. Still more important, however, was the issue of Islam. The manifesto pointed out that Sukarno had consistently stated – particularly in his *pancasila* speech of June 1945 – that the actual ideological shape of an independent Indonesia could only be decided *after* Indonesia had won its independence: that, in Sukarno's words, independence was the 'golden bridge' that had to be crossed before Indonesians could address in a democratic manner the structure and ideological basis of their state (Aceh 1953: 213). However – and here the Acehnese rebels got to the heart of the contradiction in Sukarno's thinking – at the very time that Sukarno was apparently leaving this crucial matter for future consideration, he was in fact pre-emptively entrenching *pancasila* as the core ideology of the Republic of Indonesia.

The Acehnese therefore found themselves, at the end of the independence war, in a position of having to comply with a pre-determined set of principles that made Islam a mere aspect or contributory component of the state ideology. It was this that was unacceptable to the Islamic rebels of Aceh – since, as the manifesto expressed it, 'Belief in One God is for us the very source of social life, and every one of its [Islam's] directives must apply here on Indonesian soil' (Aceh 1953: 212). They pointed out that Islam did not distinguish between the religious and secular realms, but constituted an all-encompassing guidance for every aspect of individual, social and political life. The principles of Islam in their very nature, therefore, could not be applied partially or selectively. No area of public or private life could be regarded as beyond the scope of Islam, and any policy that ignored or violated Islamic principles was in effect inviting society to 'deviate' from 'Belief in One God' (Aceh 1953: 212). The manifesto emphasized that the Acehnese rebels did not oppose the legitimacy of the concept of the Indonesian state as such, or the general principle of nationality – but it insisted that their allegiance to this national entity depended on the nation's absolute, unequivocal and exclusive adherence to Islamic values (Aceh 1953: 212–13).

In 1956, one of the leaders of the Darul Islam movement in Aceh, Hasan Saleh, explained its principles and objectives in a book entitled *Revolusi Islam di Indonesia* ('The Islamic Revolution in Indonesia'). Hasan Saleh argued in this book that Indonesian Muslims would have to climb two mountains before they could achieve their ultimate goal of the Islamic state. They had already climbed the first mountain with the establishment of *negara merdeka*, or an independent state. The next and more arduous task, however, was that of climbing the higher mountain by establishing Islamic principles as the foundation of that independent state (Saleh 1956: 97). The problem for the Muslim community was that this second endeavour had stalled, partly because of sheer exhaustion at the conclusion of the independence struggle, and partly because large sections of the overwhelmingly Muslim population of Indonesia had been misled into thinking that the *pancasila* principles sufficiently satisfied their Islamic aspirations (Saleh 1956: 98, 100–1).

Hasan Saleh regarded what he called the '*pancasila* government' as a deadly enemy of Islam, not only because it deceived faithful Muslims, but because it was at the root a secular state pretending to incorporate Islamic principles (Saleh 1956: 99). More important still, it was the contention of Hasan Saleh that behind the vacuous generalities of *pancasila* lurked the most lethal form of secularism: the atheistic communism of the PKI. Ultimately, he saw Darul Islam's holy war as a revolutionary struggle against its most dangerous enemy – communism (Saleh 1956: 17). In fact, two revolutionary forces – those of Islam and communism – based on diametrically opposed principles, were waging a life-and-death struggle for the soul of the Indonesian nation. If communist revolutions depended on the trinity of Party, People's Armed Forces and the 'masses', the *revolusi Islam* was given religious guidance by the *ulama*, was spearheaded by militant Islamic youth organizations, and depended on a broad base of support among the faithful Muslim population as a whole (Saleh 1956: 106). If the communists' revolutionary zeal was sustained by a sense that they represented a force that was destined to triumph through the inevitable scientific laws of historical development, the spiritual zeal of the *mujahidin* (Islamic warriors) was vindicated by their knowledge that they were instruments of a divine purpose (Saleh 1956: 107).

On-and-off negotiations eventually brought the Darul Islam rebellion in Aceh to an end in the early 1960s. An agreement was reached with the central government in which, at least in theory, Aceh was granted special autonomous rights, and Islam was given a special status within Aceh. As in many other regions of Indonesia, however, tensions between Islam and the PKI escalated in the last years of Guided Democracy. When the armed forces turned against the PKI in late 1965, radical Acehnese Muslims seized the opportunity to wipe out the PKI in their province, and justified this action as a necessary *jihad* in defence of Islam.

PANCASILA, GUIDED DEMOCRACY AND ISLAMIC DEMOCRACY

Although Muslims constituted the vast majority of the population of Indonesia, not all of them saw politics through the prism of their Islamic faith. Furthermore, even among those who saw politics in Islamic terms, there was a difference between those who adopted a radical approach and supported the general objectives of the Darul Islam movement, and those who, while they opposed the ideological tendencies of *pancasila* and of the Guided Democracy regime, on the whole confined themselves to constitutional opposition.

Among these latter, the most prominent political movement was the Masyumi Party, which was formed as an umbrella Islamic organization during the Japanese occupation, and became after 1945 the principle Islamic party in Indonesia. Masyumi was the foremost element of a general trend of Islamic opinion in Indonesia that found itself at odds with Sukarno's political vision, and countered his version of democracy with a specifically Islamic concept of democracy.

In 1957, Mohammad Natsir, the Chairman of Masyumi, described *pancasila* as a 'vague' political philosophy which had 'nothing to say to the soul of the Muslim community' compared to the 'definite, clear and complete' political prescriptions of Islam (Natsir 1957: 219). Nevertheless, there were clearly points of agreement between the political outlook of Islam and the *pancasila* precepts of Sukarno. In the first place, given the fact that nearly all the Islamic world had fallen under European rule during the imperialist era, the Muslim community shared Sukarno's anti-colonial outlook (Natsir 1954: 2). Sukarno's declaration in his *pancasila* speech of 1945 that Indonesian nationalism should not have a racist or xenophobic outlook bore at least some resemblance to the principle underlying the first Islamic community that Muhammad had founded in Medina in 622 AD: namely, that the traditional ties of blood, kin and tribe should be replaced by the transcending brotherhood of a common faith (Natsir 1954: 10). Furthermore, Sukarno's much cherished idea of *musyawarah*, or consultation and consensus, was an Islamic concept, and was enjoined in Islam on Muslims as the proper means of deciding the correct conduct that should be deduced from the basic principles stated in the *Qur'an* (Natsir 1954: 7). The *pancasila* emphasis on social responsibility likewise coincided with the duty of all Muslims, repeatedly stated in the *Qur'an*, to pay alms (*zakat*) regularly, for the benefit of the whole society, and for that society to provide for widows and orphans in particular.

The major point of divergence between Islamic Democracy and Sukarno was not so much over the *pancasila* principles – which were seen in themselves as inadequate rather than positively dangerous – but over the concept of democracy underlying the Guided Democracy regime. Guided Democracy abandoned the normal foundation of a democratic system – the individual vote – and replaced it with an abstract notion of democracy as the general, rather than merely majority, expression of the popular will, embodied in a national leader and a unifying revolutionary cause.

This idea of the sovereign authority of a 'general will' that was understood in abstract terms offended against Islamic democracy in two important ways. Seen 'from above', it violated the precept that all human action, leadership and institutions were subordinated to the unalterable law of God expressed in the *Qur'an* and the *Hadith* (the reported actions and precepts of Muhammad). This was as true of the Caliphs, or 'successors', who in turn took over leadership of the Islamic community after Muhammad's death, as it should be for any form of democracy devised by humanity (Natsir 1954: 7). Islamic democracy, therefore, was always a strictly 'constitutional' democracy, and that constitutional restraint was precisely provided by the *Qur'an* and the *Hadith*. The notion of 'popular sovereignty' or the 'general will' could only be accepted by Muslims if it was subordinate and accountable to God and the law of God.

Seen 'from below', Guided Democracy's collectivist version of democracy destroyed the idea of accountability – political and moral – in another way, by ending the accountability of society to the individual, and the converse accountability of the individual to society. Despite the fact that the *Qur'an* deals extensively with the general moral responsibilities of the Islamic society, it fundamentally concerns itself with the faith and salvation of each individual soul (Wiranata Koesoema 1948: 225). It is a central tenet of the

Qur'an that each individual human being ultimately stands alone before God's judgement, and that no-one can take the burden of individual moral responsibility off another's shoulders. Just as the individual, therefore, was the fundamental 'unit' in the spiritual sphere, so in Islamic democracy the individual had to be the basic unit of civic responsibility in the political sphere.

It was this abandonment of limits and accountability in Sukarno's political vision that the promoters of Islamic democracy could not accept. Ultimately, Mohammad Natsir argued, despite the apparently dynamic revolutionary rhetoric, Sukarno's political vision actually appealed to a people who had never abandoned the dependency mentality of the colonial period, and had a tendency to abdicate personal responsibility for the future of their society. Faced with the manifold problems of building an independent state, large sections of the population had fallen into what Mohammad Natsir called a *ratu adil* mentality. This was an allusion to the traditional tendency of the Javanese – during periods of tyranny, hardship or chaos – to wait for a *ratu adil*, or 'just king', to take power, liberate the people from their oppressors and alleviate their sufferings (Natsir 1956: 91).

The political outlook of Mohammad Hatta, who as Vice-President to Sukarno from the time of the August Revolution until his resignation in 1956, was deeply influenced by the concepts of Islamic democracy. As one of the co-founders of the Republic of Indonesia, however, Hatta accepted the validity of *pancasila* as the ideological basis of the state. His interpretation of *pancasila* was, however, significantly different from that of Sukarno. Whereas Sukarno's speeches during this period indicate that he regarded 'social justice' as the most important of the five principles, Hatta – like all devout Muslims – naturally saw 'Belief in One God', not just as *primus inter pares* among the five principles, but as the necessary moral foundation for the other principles – as an all-encompassing religious validation for what would otherwise be purely secular political tenets (Hatta 1960b: 30–31).

Hatta's concepts of democracy and socialism, however, owed their origins, not only to Islamic values, but also to Western political ideas and traditional Indonesian political and economic codes of behaviour. He agreed with Sukarno that Indonesian nationalism's emphasis on social justice and internationalism was a commendable attempt to complete the unfulfilled promise of Western liberal democracy to provide genuine 'equality' and 'fraternity' as well as liberty (Hatta 1960b: 22). But also, perhaps to an even greater extent than Sukarno, he saw the communitarian traditions of the Indonesian *desa* (village) as an ideal model for modern Indonesian democracy (Hatta 1960b: 24). In the economic sphere, Indonesian peasants had had long experience in farming the village communal lands on a basis of mutual cooperation, or *gotong royong* (Hatta

1960b: 25). In the political sphere, the traditional village system of reaching communal decisions on the basis of open discussion, – in which the *desa* head guided the debate towards a consensus decision – constituted an embryonic form of the democratic principle. Hatta added that, even in the feudal era, villages also had had the acknowledged right to protest against decisions from above that violated *adat*, or traditional customary law (Hatta 1960b: 26).

These indigenous survivals of economic cooperation and village democracy from the pre-colonial and pre-capitalist era could, argued Hatta, form an ideal basis for a specially Indonesian way of operating 'social democracy' (Hatta 1960b: 27). But, he added, such a system of discussion and consensus clearly could not realistically operate at a central government level, where factors of sheer numbers and size required the formal structures of Western-style representative and majority-based democracy (Hatta 1960a: 9). Indigenous social democracy could only work at a much more local level; and it was precisely here that Guided Democracy's centralized concept of politics utterly stifled all economic and political initiative. One of Hatta's main aspirations throughout this period was for the establishment of genuine local and regional economic and political decision-making bodies, through which Indonesian-style democracy could function beneficially and effectively. He therefore consistently urged the creation of a network of local cooperatives that could restore the principles of *gotong royong*, and the replacement of centrally-appointed *bupati*, the chief administrators at the *kebupaten* or 'regency' level of administration, by locally elected officials who would themselves form the basis for a comprehensive system of regional autonomy (Hatta 1960b: 27).

Hatta agreed with Sukarno that the party-parliamentary era had been a disaster, breeding corruption, disillusion and political fragmentation (Hatta 1960a: 12). He fundamentally disagreed with Sukarno, however, over the appropriate solution to Indonesia's political and economic ailments. Above all, he did not accept that the revolutionary mentality that had emerged in 1945, and that had been necessary for driving out the Dutch, should be encouraged or even intensified. On the contrary, he believed that the continuation of the politics and rhetoric of revolution was breeding anarchy, paralyzing the growth of political maturity, and shaking loose the already fragile foundations of Indonesia's economy and society (Hatta 1960a: 15). By 1960 – with the now overwhelming evidence of complete economic and administrative breakdown – Hatta was more than ever convinced that Sukarno's revolution was leading Indonesia to disaster. To the destructive and hysterical rhetoric of revolution without end was now added the evil of inflation, which Hatta regarded not just as an economic malaise, but as a deeply corrosive force that 'demoralized' society and undermined any remaining stable foundations (Hatta 1960b: 14, 19).

Between Hatta's outlook and that of Sukarno – who regarded the 'uprooting' process of revolution as psychologically necessary for the Indonesian people, but who in the sphere of practical economics was reduced in 1964 to urging the people of Indonesia to eat less rice and more 'maize, millet, cassava, edible roots and so on' – there could ultimately be no common ground. Hatta's prescription for Indonesia's political ills – which bore at least some similarity to those of Sjahrir in *Perjuangan Kita* (see chapter 7) – involved first of all the ending of revolutionary politics. The re-establishment of economic and political stability could provide a suitable environment for the installing of local forms of social democracy, which would in turn gradually educate Indonesians in the all-important goal – democratic 'responsibility' (Hatta 1960a: 15). The question was: How could such economic and political stability be achieved?

* * *

Hatta's question was, in the end, answered by the military under the leadership of General – later President – Suharto, who brought the period of ideological struggle to a decisive end in 1965–66. While the ideological trend of the regime during the decade and a half following independence had been revolutionary, the main force sustaining it – the army – had been essentially anti-revolutionary, and certainly viscerally hostile to the PKI. As the revolutionary rhetoric intensified over the years between 1960 and 1965, the economy and social cohesion gradually collapsed. Finally, in September 1965, this state of institutionalized political confrontation came to an end when the Left made a false move, and the armed forces subsequently used their overwhelming power to annihilate the PKI, and put an end to the Guided Democracy regime. They then established a regime in which the military assumed administrative and political authority, and all ideological debate and political competition was effectively stifled.

CHAPTER TWELVE

Political Ideas in Post-Revolutionary Southeast Asia: Malaysia, Singapore and Regional Cooperation

In the decades after the Second World War, it was virtually *de rigueur* for any political initiative or plan in much of Southeast Asia to adopt the epithet of 'revolutionary'. No doubt this was partly due to the fact that anti-colonial politics involved in its very nature opposition and upheaval; it also reflected the fact that the challenges of modernization and development that the region faced necessitated deep-rooted change – social, political or cultural – not mere 'reform'. The inevitable consequence of this rhetorical tendency, however, was that the ideologies supporting regimes that were conservative in tendency, such as that of Ngo Dinh Diem, also described themselves as 'revolutionary'. This was even true of the frankly patriarchal and traditionalist regime of Field-Marshal Sarit Thanarat in Thailand in the period 1957–1963, even though the *dominant* post-war political trends of Thailand – like those in the Malayan region – had always been deliberately insulated from the revolutionary politics of the surrounding regions.

In the mid 1960s, however, the whole tone of politics in the core region of Southeast Asia underwent a fundamental change. Even though programmes and ideas were still occasionally designated 'revolutionary', the climate of revolution no longer dominated politics and political thinking to the extent that it had in earlier decades. The decisive regional change came in Indonesia in 1965. The new Indonesian military regime that installed itself on the ruins of the PKI and the radical left as a whole, not only put an end to revolutionary politics, but comprehensively de-politicized Indonesian society. The suspension of the constitution had the same effect of de-politicizing the Philippines in 1972. At the edge of the Southeast Asian core, the Burmese military regime (see chapter 10) may have been theoretically guided by a revolutionary ideology: but this very ideology led to the insulation of Burmese politics from the rest of the world. In another corner of the region, the undoubted energies of Vietnamese communism were exclusively concentrated on a protracted struggle for survival directed against the United States.

In order to wage a successful anti-colonial struggle, it had been necessary for the respective nationalist elites of Southeast Asia to 'invite' the 'masses' into the political arena. This was especially true of nations such as Vietnam and Indonesia, where the colonial power had resisted moves to independence; but it was also true of nations such as Malaya, where it had proved to be necessary at times to put pressure on the outgoing colonial power. After independence had been achieved, these nationalist elites faced the challenge of the rapid modernization of the economy and society, not just as a means of satisfying demands for social justice among the population, but also as a way of creating strong states that would no longer be vulnerable to threats from outside. The political energies of the 'masses' were therefore transferred from the national revolution for independence to the new social and economic 'revolution' for rapid modernization and development.

Although it was expressed in different ways, there was a general hope that the common will of a liberated, politicized and mobilized population would be the most rapid and effective means of overcoming the problems of backwardness. In general, the ideological crises of the independence regimes reflected the failure of these expectations, and moreover a fear that the energies unleashed by the different forms of populist mobilization were spinning out of the control of the nationalist elites. The post-revolutionary era, therefore, effectively saw the reclaiming of power by these nationalist elites, and what might be called the 'disinviting' of the masses from active participation in the political arena. This was true of Indonesia after 1965; of the Philippines after 1972; and – despite the populist rhetoric – of Burma after 1962. It was also partially true of Malaysia after 1969–70, and of Singapore in the 1970s. Far from being replaced by more genuinely democratic structures – a course which had been advocated by people such as U Nu, Soetan Sjahrir and Mohammad Hatta – revolutionary politics was supplanted by a new politics that was authoritarian in the political arena, and pragmatic in the economic arena. The problems of national development, unity and security remained, of course; the difference lay in the fact that these problems were now addressed in a post-revolutionary, post-socialist way.

RACE AND NATION IN MALAYA/MALAYSIA

As has already been noted in chapter 8, the issue of race overshadowed the politics of Malaya in the lead up to independence in 1957. After an initial period of turbulence and inter-ethnic confrontation following the Second World War, the negotiations over independence were dominated by the traditional Malay political elite and the leadership of the Chinese community, which was mainly composed of people with a business background. In these circumstances, there was no scope for the development of the kind of radical, revolutionary or socialist solutions that prevailed in other parts of Southeast Asia; all the more so, since such solutions were associated with the Malayan Communist Party, which after 1948 waged a prolonged guerrilla war, first against the British, and then against the independent Malayan state. The road to independence in Malaya was paved by what was essentially a deal between the Malay and Chinese elites, and implicitly, between the two communities that these elites represented. In return for Malay dominance of the symbols of the state and its administrative structure, the Chinese were given free scope in the economic sector. Likewise, special provisions that gave the Malay community privileged access to education and special help in the area of development generally were matched by the concession of rights to citizenship for a large number of the domiciled Chinese community.

This 'deal' had, however, only been reached after a fundamental debate over the question of race and identity in Malaya. And this debate centred on the issue of 'ownership': ownership of the national identity and culture, and thereby ownership of the state itself. The vision of Tan Cheng Lock, effectively the leader of the Chinese community after the war, was of a Malaya in which cultural identity would be separated from the political identity of the overall nation. While the separate communities would be guaranteed their cultural rights, the national identity of Malaya would be culturally neutral – a neutrality that would have been reinforced by Tan Cheng Lock's original advocacy of English as the national language. The national identity of Malaya, as envisaged by Tan Cheng Lock, would therefore have been strictly political, in the sense that it would have emerged out of the common political interests and aspirations of all the people of Malaya as they evolved through a common experience of living together, irrespective of cultural difference.

This notion of common ownership of a culturally neutral Malayan identity was anathema to the Malay political leadership. The absolute bedrock of the Malay position was that the Malay peninsula was *tanah melayu*, the land of the Malay people. This status had been recognized throughout the British period of colonial rule, and the Malay leadership demanded that it should not be altered by the fact that a large immigrant population had settled in Malaya. The Malays insisted, therefore, that ownership of the core identity of the independent Malayan nation should belong to the Malays: that there should be a Malay monarch as head of state, the guarantee of a special status for Islam, the acceptance of Malay as the national language, the granting of certain special rights for the Malay people, and – in more practical terms – a safeguard for Malay predominance in the institutions of the state.

In effect, the Malayan independence agreement created a 'reserved' Malay sector in the symbols of state, in the state institutions, and in the general acceptance of the special position of the Malays in the society as a whole. In return, the Chinese had unrestricted access to the private sector of the economy. This in itself explains why independent Malaya was inhibited from following the socialist, state-controlled road to development that was taken by most other Southeast Asian countries. In addition, the domiciled Chinese who had acquired the right to citizenship had free access to what might be called the 'contested', as opposed to the 'reserved', sector of politics. Since it was inevitable that politics in Malaya would take the form of racial politics, an arrangement emerged that was designed to avert the danger of racial confrontation in the contested area of politics: namely, the creation of an umbrella alliance that would enable the main parties representing the different races to moderate their differences peacefully and at the same time pursue a general national strategy.

MAHATHIR MOHAMAD: MALAY RIGHTS AND THE 'MALAY DILEMMA'

In 1963, however, after prolonged negotiations, the political landscape of Malaya was radically changed when the former British colonies of Singapore, Sabah and Sarawak joined the Federation of Malaya to form a new entity, the Federation of Malaysia. In retrospect, it is clear that the addition of Singapore – where ethnic Chinese constituted the vast majority of the population – seriously disturbed the ethnic balance, and increased the fears of the Malay community that they would lose political as well as economic control of the new enlarged federal state. The years 1963–1965 were marked by escalating racial tension between the Chinese and Malay communities.

By 1965, the friction between Singapore and the Malay political leadership of the Federation – which was as much a matter of personalities as it was a dispute over the nature of the Malaysian state – had reached breaking point, and Singapore was effectively expelled from Malaysia. This event did not, however, end the racial conflict in Malaysia. From the Chinese side, there was increasing resentment at what was seen as the permanent second-class status of non-Malays in their own country. The Malay community, on the other hand, felt that the Chinese were using their control over the economy, and indeed their growing strength in the 'contested' sector of the political system, to challenge Malay 'ownership' of the state and its symbols. In 1969, these tensions burst out into the open, and extensive racial riots threatened the stability of the whole political system.

From one perspective, it could be said that the political leadership of Malaysia– and indeed the country as a whole – subsequently recoiled from the abyss, and hurriedly reinstated the inter-ethnic political system that had been set up in 1957; a system that had its imperfections, but at least was a barrier against inter-racial civil war. From another perspective, what happened after the riots of 1969 was that the Malay leadership used its control over the 'reserved' sector of the state – particularly the administration and the security forces – to impose order and reinstate the concept of Malaysia as *tanah melayu*, but at the same time to withdraw the whole question of race from political debate. By setting out in the *rukunegara*, or 'pillars of the nation', the basic principles that should govern Malaysian politics and society, and putting both these and the symbols of the nation beyond public discussion or questioning, the Malay leadership was emphatically asserting ideological as well as political hegemony (Malaysia nd.).

It was in this highly sensitive climate that Dr. Mahathir Mohamad published his analysis of the racial situation in Malaysia entitled *The Malay Dilemma* (1970). This book is both a defence of Malay rights and a critique of Malay culture. Taken as a whole, however, it presents a forthright and at the same time a sophisticated thesis on the relationship between race and national identity; a thesis that is particularly relevant in a modern world where mass movements across national borders have become a widespread phenomenon.

This thesis begins with an attempt to explain why, despite the fact that in Malaya – and subsequently in Malaysia – the Malays had managed to secure the concept of *tanah melayu*, they still had the sense that they had been 'dispossessed in their own land' (Mahathir 1970: 3). Mahathir traces the reason for this sense of 'dispossession' back to the impact of British colonialism in the Malay region. The particular character of colonial rule, he argued, had had the fatal effect of disconnecting economic development from national development. Mahathir pointed out that there *had* been Chinese immigration into the Malay region well before the imposition of British power: but – precisely because the Malays then had control over their political destiny – the *levels* of immigration could be controlled, and, on the basis of this absorbable level of immigration, a steady pattern of intermarriage and integration into Malay culture had begun to take root (Mahathir 1970: 134).

This process, if it had been allowed to continue, could have enabled the Malay region to evolve into a modern united nation with a coherent identity, while at the same time enabling the development of a modern economy. Instead, the various protectorate treaties that the Malay sultans of the peninsula signed with the British had given the latter overall control over policy – including immigration policy – and had left the former with only the 'shadow' of power (Mahathir 1970: 158). In consequence, while the Malays – under the leadership of their various sultans – remained cocooned in their traditional rural world, mass Chinese immigration had been encouraged in order to work the modern urban economy. Since these Chinese immigrants had been encouraged, until very late in the period of colonial rule, to regard themselves as mere 'sojourners' who would return to China, the issue of integration had never seriously been addressed (Mahathir 1970: 148–49).

At the end of the Second World War, therefore, the Malays had entered the independence era in a situation in which they shared their land with immigrant communities that lived in entirely separate cultural worlds, and that had entirely different political loyalties. Furthermore, the better organized and more economically competitive Chinese had effectively absorbed control of all those areas of the economy that were not dominated by British business interests (Mahathir 1970: 24–26). In the long ensuing process of defining Malayan nationality and creating the structures of the independent Malayan state, the Malays had discovered that they could not merely assert their core and central status as of right, but had had to bargain – for example, over the issue of defining citizenship – with the other ethnic groups (Mahathir 1970: 133–34). It was true that the Malay leadership had been able, after the mass mobilization of the Malay community, to secure Malay rights in the area of government and control of the symbols of the state. But the Chinese had continued to control the economy, and indeed had moved in after independence to absorb those vital sectors of the economy that had been vacated by the British (Mahathir 1970: 48–52). Mahathir argued that once again – as in the colonial period – the Malay political leadership had allowed itself to be fobbed off with the illusion of power, while the substance was being steadily accumulated in other hands (Mahathir 1970: 31).

Mahathir agreed with the Malay political establishment of that time that it was vital for the Malays to maintain control of the state. What he rejected was the complacent notion of some of the leadership that this political control was sufficient of itself to guarantee the Malays' predominant status in Malaysia. It was central to Mahathir's thesis that Malay rights could not be sustained unless they gained a full stake in the economy; but that, in the area of the economy, a situation of free competition existed only in theory, not in fact. In practice, he argued, the Chinese community was able to use its closed networks of affiliation to advance its interests and protect itself from outside competition, and had thereby used racial solidarity to gain an unfair advantage over the Malays (Mahathir 1970: 52). As a counter-weight to Chinese economic organization, therefore, it was absolutely essential for the Malays to use their political power to force the opening up of economic opportunity for Malays, and to ensure their 'constructive protection' in a highly competitive and hostile environment (Mahathir 1970: 31, 77–78).

However, in Mahathir's view, state *intervention* in the economy did not imply state *control* or running of the economy. He was clear that free enterprise provided the best framework for 'self-sustaining and self-correcting' economic development (Mahathir 1970: 52). The role of the state, therefore, should not be to obliterate the rights of free enterprise generally, and create a new economy run by government functionaries, but to ensure that the inherent right of the Malays to participate equally in the economy could be freely exercised. This objective would require a 'period of adjustment', during which the Malay community would be 'modernized' and urbanized, to prepare it to play a full part in a developed economy. Accordingly, the state would need to accelerate 'positive steps' to bring Malays into the higher levels of education, give access to technical training, provide special help for business ventures, grant priority in government contracts, and eventually develop a self-sustaining Malay economic network (Mahathir 1970: 67–74).

This system of promoting Malay rights in the economic sphere through what was later to be described as 'positive discrimination' was part of the independence 'deal', and in a sense Mahathir's arguments were defending a system that already existed. What was different, however, was Mahathir's sense of urgency, and his belief that an inert leadership had merely contented itself with defending Malay rights rather than actively seeking to advance them.

At one level, *The Malay Dilemma* can be read as part of an internal debate within the Malay community. However, Mahathir was equally concerned to defend the concept of Malay rights against those outside the community who questioned whether the assertion of such rights could genuinely be justified. This latter dispute ultimately centred on the relationship between 'indigenousness' and national identity. From one perspective, those who questioned the legitimacy of a prior Malay 'right' in Malaya/Malaysia over the immigrant community argued that rights based on 'indigenousness' were matched by rights that had been earned by the immigrant communities through their contribution to the development of the economy, their common sharing over the generations of the good and bad times, and their common commitment to the nation's well-being. From another perspective, the very assertion of the Malays' primary indigenous status was questioned: if indigenousness was to be the yardstick for determining national status, it was argued, did not the minorities living in the interior of Malaya – the *orang asli*, or 'original people' – have a prior claim that had been usurped by the Malays? (Mahathir 1970: 122–23).

Mahathir's response to these challenges makes particularly interesting reading in a later age during which, in the West at least, the orthodoxies of 'multiculturalism' prevail. In the first place, he argued that political legitimacy – the right, that is, to define the national identity in a particular nation – did not necessarily lie with the original people, but rather with the racial group that first created a coherent state system that was recognized and treated as such by outside powers. Mahathir described the peoples who set up these original recognized state systems as 'the definitive people', and on this basis asserted that the White Australians were the 'definitive people' in Australia, *not* the native Australians; the Anglo-Americans were likewise the 'definitive people' in the United States; and, by the same token, the Malays were the 'definitive people' in the Malayan peninsula (Mahathir 1970: 122–26). However, he reinforced the Malays' claim to a special indigenous status with the observation that, whereas the recent immigrant communities had homelands other than Malaysia, the Malays had no other homeland, no other place to which they could claim 'ownership' (Mahathir 1970: 133).

For Mahathir, therefore, Malay rights were based on their position as the 'original definitive race' and on the fact that Malaya was their sole homeland. Their status as the 'definitive race' gave them the right to be the 'national definers of identity' in the areas of culture, language and the political system. This status did not mean, however, that there could be no accommodation between Malay identity and immigrant identity, or that immigrant communities would forever be condemned to second class status in the Malay state. But it did mean that any process of integration had to be on Malay terms, and had to 'ensure the perpetuation of the characteristics of the definitive race' (Mahathir 1970: 133–35).

In this context, Mahathir observed that acceptance by the other communities of Malay 'ownership' of identity based on a prior right would have the paradoxical effect of making it easier for the Malays to accommodate to other identities (Mahathir 1970: 153). Much of the racial tension of post-war Malaya centred on Malay anxiety that their weaknesses as a community would ultimately lead to their being deprived of the thing that mattered to them most: their racial birthright in their own land. Once they had been relieved of anxiety on this point, it would become far easier for them to 'adjust' to the other races on a relaxed basis of 'understanding' and 'good will' (Mahathir 1970: 97).

MALAY RIGHTS AND MALAY CULTURE

In general, what Mahathir had in mind in *The Malay Dilemma* was a Malaysia in which the national identity would be Malay in its essential characteristics, but in which there would be a gradual process of cultural adjustment and integration over time. Clearly, therefore, Mahathir's vision was different from that, say, of Tan Cheng Lock, who had drawn a distinction between a unified *political* identity and diverse *cultural* identities. What Mahathir ideally envisaged was a return to the kind of integrative process he believed to have been under way in the Malay region before the colonial era. 'The people', wrote Mahathir,

> 'must truly integrate. Every barrier which tends to distinguish between racial, ethnic and other origins must be broken. Discrimination in all walks of life must be eliminated. And finally, inter-racial marriages should be encouraged. These are the basis of national unity, the understanding of which is the *sine qua non* of a multiracial society desirous of building a stable and viable nation' (Mahathir 1970: 102).

This was itself a radical proposal. More radical still, however, was Mahathir's insistence that this process of cultural adjustment and integration absolutely necessitated fundamental change in the value system that underpinned Malay culture. In other words, the protection of Malay rights in the modern world required the abandonment of many aspects of traditional Malay culture. Mahathir by no means advocated the complete abandonment of traditional values. But he did advocate the elimination of practices, grounded in traditional values, that hindered Malay adjustment to the modern world. Whether one liked it or not, he wrote, 'those who have adjusted to Western values have survived and done well'; conversely, clinging to the traditional 'value system' impeded 'the progressive and competitive abilities of the Malays in a multiracial society' (Mahathir 1970: 172–73).

A central task of *The Malay Dilemma*, therefore, was a critical examination of Malay 'character, culture and abilities'. Mahathir singled out the three main pillars of Malay culture as Islam, loyalty to the sultanate, and *adat*, or the customary rules governing everyday behaviour. Mahathir was clear that Islam itself was an immutable core to Malay existence (Mahathir 1970: 104–5). However, he drew a distinction between the faith and doctrine of Islam on one side, and the tendency over time of Malays to give an Islamic gloss to traditional practices – and he focused his criticism on the latter (Mahathir 1970: 155). On the whole, Mahathir avoided the issue of Islam in his discussion, not only because he did not wish his critique of the Malay mentality to become a critique of Islam, but also because the issue of Islam – and indeed religion in general – seriously complicated discussion of inter-racial harmony, cultural integration, and inter-marriage (Mahathir 1970: 152). In a sleight-of-hand that could perhaps be justified by the fact that political debate was more secular in the Malaysia of 1970 than was to be the case in later years, the issue of Islamic values was kept by Mahathir largely outside the scope of his analysis in *The Malay Dilemma*.

The second pillar of Malay behaviour to which Mahathir alluded was the culture of deference in the political sphere, embodied in the importance attached to loyalty (*setia*) to the sultan or raja of the traditional state, and by extension to the monarchy of independent Malaysia. Perhaps surprisingly, given the general trend of his thinking, Mahathir believed that this deference culture could play a beneficial role, even in the modern age. In part this was because such a culture could form the ideal basis for a society that was law-abiding and stable (Mahathir 1970: 170). More important, perhaps, was his perception that no thoroughgoing change in Malay habits and attitudes could take place except from above. Everything, therefore, depended on the quality of Malay leadership. If the leadership was complacent and inert, the cultural stagnation of Malay society would be correspondingly complete. If, however, there was 'dynamism at the top',

Malay society could be led without resistance along the path of rapid and radical change (Mahathir 1970: 170–71).

Mahathir directed the whole force of his criticism, therefore, at Malay *adat* or traditional codes governing everyday behaviour: what might be called the 'Malay mentality' in general. Although Mahathir rejected Darwin's non-Islamic explanation of the origins of humanity, he accepted the 'logic' of his general thesis of the essentially competitive foundation of human and natural development (Mahathir 1970: 19). From this perspective, he warned the Malay community that failure to adapt to the modern world would condemn it to permanent backwardness (Mahathir 1970: 2).

Looking first at the area of marriage and the family, he suggested that the Malay tradition of 'first cousin marriages' had contributed to a pattern of in-breeding – a common feature of many rural communities – that had led to the reproduction and intensification through the generations of 'weak' characteristics. This contrasted sharply with the Chinese community, within which 'out of clan' marriages helped to maintain hybrid vigour (Mahathir 1970: 18, 24, 29). Further, unhelpful hereditary traits were exacerbated by the Malay environment in which these marriages took place. The traditional Malay abhorrence of celibacy led to early marriages, and the production of children by parents who were too young to take on the responsibilities of parenthood. The consequence was that children tended to be brought up by indulgent grandparents who reinforced traditional modes of behaviour (Mahathir 1970: 27–29). This whole pattern of upbringing revealed a key weakness in the traditional Malay mentality: a failure to plan ahead in a rational manner.

Moving beyond the realm of family life to that of education, Mahathir noted the traditional Malay tendency to value form over substance. Wisdom was associated with old age, and learning was associated with the ability to recite by rote. Such a mentality naturally excluded scepticism, *a priori* reasoning, or a general spirit of innovation and enquiry (Mahathir 1970: 156–59). In these circumstances, the Malay attitude to education, far from liberating a younger generation, served to chain them firmly to the traditional world.

In the everyday world of work, Mahathir observed that the Malays tended to treat such economic activities as rice-production as part of a customary 'way of life' rather than as a 'business proposition'. Economic activity, therefore, was not susceptible to innovation, improvement or rational calculations of profit and loss (Mahathir 1970: 168). In the same way, the Malay mentality put no clear value on time: meetings and discussions among Malays had no defined beginnings or ends, and consequently no organized pattern of discussion, decision and implementation within a set time frame (Mahathir 1970: 163). Mahathir's attitude to the *gotong-royong* tradition of the Malayo-Indonesian world could not, therefore, have been more different from that of Indonesian nationalists such as Hatta and Sukarno. Far from seeing this *gotong-royong* mentality as a traditional value on which an economic and political system could be built, Mahathir regarded it as an impediment to modernization and engagement with a competitive world (Mahathir 1970: 168).

Above all, Mahathir noted that the Malays had a fearful attitude to life: a compound of religious piety and an anxiety about death that became more pronounced in middle-age, and that led to a conflict-avoiding and fatalistic psychological outlook. It was an attitude that was more attuned to coping with failure than striving for success (Mahathir 1970: 162).

In short, Mahathir argued that the Malay mentality prevented genuine and productive self-examination, stifled the development of a mode of thinking that 'related cause to effect', and inhibited the desire to improve one's condition (Mahathir 1970: 159, 164–65). The paradox in Mahathir's analysis and prescription for change lay in the fact that he advocated exploiting the Malay culture of deference – which was itself a manifestation of the Malay mentality he criticized – to drag the Malay community 'from above' into the competitive and rationally organized modern world. What he did not make clear was how, or whether, that deference culture itself could survive such a radical upheaval.

Mahathir's analysis of the racial problem in Malaya clearly had an anti-colonial basis. But the solutions outlined in *The Malay Dilemma* did not conform to the general pattern of anti-colonial solutions to race and minority problems that were emerging elsewhere in the decolonizing world at that time. In Burma, Vietnam and Indonesia, for instance, the prevailing notion was that, since colonialism had deliberately used a policy of 'divide and rule' – between ethnic groups, and between majorities and minorities generally – the removal of colonial rule of itself would create a healing environment in which inter-racial concord could begin to be restored. Following the precepts of both Western and communist models of nation-building, most nationalists believed that accelerated plans for education and development in backward and minority areas would help complete a process of national integration, through which cultural diversity could be harmonized with undisputed national unity. While Mahathir certainly agreed that colonialism had exacerbated racial problems, the sheer immensity of the racial problem in Malaysia made the other parts of the anti-colonial approach utterly inadequate. Mahathir's book was most radical in the fact that it moved beyond the anti-colonial way of thinking about political issues.

BEYOND ANTI-COLONIALISM: LEE KUAN YEW AND THE DEMOCRATIC SOCIALIST PERSPECTIVE

In isolated instances in the 1950s, but with much greater confidence in the 1960s, there began to emerge in Southeast Asia what might be called 'post anti-colonial' thinking. Such an approach appeared in the writings and speeches of such figures as Soetan Sjahrir, Mohammad Hatta and U Nu, all of whom were in one way or another adherents to the democratic socialist tradition. But the most clear-cut case of a political leader of that time who thought in 'post anti-colonial' terms was Lee Kuan Yew, the Prime Minister of Singapore from 1959 to 1990, who also came from a democratic socialist intellectual background. It would be a mistake, however, to suggest that the democratic socialist approach was uniform. Lee Kuan Yew shared Mahathir Mohamad's impatience with the tendency of some nationalists – of whom Mohammad Hatta was a classic case – to idyllicize pre-colonial political systems and hark back to a 'natural socialism' that could be reconstituted in the independent states of modern Southeast Asia (Lee Kuan Yew 1966a: 28).

What the other democratic socialists had in common with Lee Kuan Yew, however, was their criticism of the tendency of Asian nationalism to see anti-colonialism as an end in itself, or to use imperialism as a standing alibi for post-independence political and economic failure (Lee Kuan Yew 1966a: 34). In 1968, Mohammad Hatta suggested that the obstinate refusal of some colonial powers to concede independence had exacerbated these tendencies. The very intensity of the independence struggle in Indonesia, for example, had had the effect of focusing attention exclusively on politics and 'revolution' as the solution to post-independence problems (Hatta 1968: 584). This, argued Lee Kuan Yew in a different context, had led to a mentality that assumed that the mere fact of independence would of itself ensure a 'more equal and more just society' (Lee Kuan Yew 1966b: 12). Such a way of thinking encouraged the notion – promoted by such leaders as Sukarno in Indonesia (see chapter 11) – that residual problems in an independent state could be resolved simply by a continuing political struggle against all national, regional and global traces of colonialism, until some kind of absolute independence could be achieved. A utopian outlook of this sort completely ignored the mundane problems of creating 'a sound administration' and 'an economy that ticks' (Lee Kuan Yew 1963b: 15).

What the democratic socialists could detect in the anti-colonial political outlook was a sense that in some way colonial oppression gave a moral status to its victims, and that resistance to that oppression conferred intrinsic moral superiority. As early as 1953, Soetan Sjahrir had lamented the self-glorifying and egocentric tone of anti-colonial nationalism, particularly in the immediate aftermath of independence (Sjahrir 1953: 234). Lee Kuan Yew noticed the same outlook in the rhetoric surrounding the whole non-aligned movement, and that of the Bandung Conference in particular. As he pointed out in 1965, there was at the heart of post-independence Asian thinking a presumption that the newly decolonized regions – once they were fully liberated from colonialism and had disentangled themselves from the ideological conflicts of Europe – would create a new moral world order in which differences between nations would be resolved peacefully, and in which 'power politics' would somehow become redundant (Lee Kuan Yew 1965b: 8). It had taken a full-scale war between two main protagonists of the 'Bandung spirit' – India and China in 1962 – and the conflict between Indonesia and Malaysia in Borneo in the period 1963–65, to show that Asians too were 'human beings, just like the others, as much prisoners of their past as apostles of the future' (Lee Kuan Yew 1965c: 40).

Lee Kuan Yew argued that the danger with the anti-colonial mentality and its offshoot, the non-aligned world view, lay in the fact that it had prevented Southeast Asia from addressing its very real post-independence internal and international problems in a pragmatic way, shorn of alibis and ideological illusions. He considered one of the immediate local dangers to be the possibility of political instability triggering ethnic conflict, leading ultimately to the 'Balkanization' of the region (Lee Kuan Yew 1963a: 10). The anti-colonial axis of confrontation was simply irrelevant to this kind of post-independence challenge. The anti-colonial outlook, moreover, masked the fact that the primary danger to the stability and welfare of the region came, not from the West, but from Asian communism. Chinese communism, asserted Lee Kuan Yew, had a direct interest in using local communist movements such as the Indonesian Communist Party (PKI) to subvert and destabilize the region, and thereby prevent the emergence of 'self-sustaining' and 'self-generating' non-communist states in Southeast Asia that would serve to discredit the communist model for development (Lee Kuan Yew 1965b: 14–17).

In the face of these very real and immediate dangers, whatever their other differences of outlook, Lee Kuan Yew, Mahathir Mohamad and Mohammad Hatta were agreed in the 1960s that the region required a new form of international cooperation that looked beyond the vapid global formulations of anti-colonialism and non-alignment, and was based on the actual mutual needs and interests of the countries of the region (Mahathir 1970: 185–88; Hatta 1968: 591). In Lee Kuan Yew's eyes, this was not only a matter of ensuring regional stability, but also a vital precondition for a level of economic cooperation and development that would enable Southeast Asia to compete effectively in a world increasingly divided into regional economic blocs (Lee Kuan Yew 1966b: 10). The formation of the Association of South-East Asian Nations (ASEAN) in 1967 was a consequence of this new outlook.

Lee Kuan Yew argued that regional cooperation and stability was a necessary precondition for finding what he called a 'meeting ground with Western interests' on a basis that would not be subordinate, but genuinely equal (Lee Kuan Yew 1965b: 20). Links with the West were, in Lee Kuan Yew's eyes, an absolutely vital means of achieving development within a democratic-socialist framework. 'Natural resources', 'human resources', and 'technological skills and capital equipment' were the three essential preconditions for development, but democratic socialism of the Asian variety did not have communism's capacity ruthlessly to mobilize the population for development goals, or to allocate resources for long-term economic ends without reference to the immediate consumer needs and desires of the people it governed. On the other hand, democratic-socialist states could not rely on the massive levels of aid provided to the Asian states that had formed a Cold War alliance with the United States (Lee Kuan Yew 1966b: 2–3, 12, 14). The only way, therefore, for democratic-socialist states to develop at a rate that would enable them to keep up with communist or pro-American states was through 'trade and the borrowing of technological and capital resources' in the open world economy (Lee Kuan Yew 1966b: 14–16).

This required an abandonment of the idea, instilled by decades of anti-colonial thinking, that Western trade and investment constituted a 'neo-colonial' trap that would destroy self-reliance (Lee Kuan Yew 1966b: 6; 1963b: 16–17). What democratic socialism in Asia desperately needed, argued Lee, was the instillation of a new ethos that emphasized, not so much self-reliance, but self-discipline within a society. Democratic socialism constituted an attempt to ensure social justice within a society by the distribution of wealth, without at the same time destroying 'individual human values' (Lee Kuan Yew 1965d: 10). However, as Lee Kuan Yew pointed out, wealth could not be distributed until it had been accumulated; and this required in the Asian context an intensive and disciplined process of development. What was needed, therefore, was a policy that emphasized the 'duties' involved in economic growth over the 'rights' associated with distributing the fruits of that growth; a policy, in other words, that put development before welfare. This in its turn required the instilling of what might be called a 'delayed gratification' mentality among the population of a democratic-socialist state; a recognition that, before the socialist ideal of 'from each his best, to each his need' could be achieved, there would have to be an intermediate stage based on the principle 'from each his economic best, to each his economic worth' (Lee Kuan Yew 1965d: 8, 25).

However, an examination of Lee Kuan Yew's speeches and statements in the mid-1960s period reveals the gap that was steadily emerging between his democratic socialist ideals and the actual pragmatic policies he had to pursue in order to ensure Singapore's economic survival. As he put it in 1965, while democratic socialism necessarily gave priority to the creation of 'democratic, parliamentary practice', and the formation of a 'welfare state', the leadership of a weak, unstable and vulnerable country newly emerging into independence had to address the more imperative issues of 'the mechanics of power' and the 'problems of development' (Lee Kuan Yew 1965d: 25). Experience of running the Singapore economy showed all too clearly that the nationalized sectors of that economy, in which salaries and wages were fixed, ran less efficiently than those sectors in which there were incentives for performance; and, ultimately, that the model of public ownership could not work in an entrepot economy (Lee Kuan Yew 1965d: 25, 35).

Moreover, Lee Kuan Yew contended that engagement with the West in economic terms did not mean that Asia had to 'slavishly follow Western parliamentary forms' (Lee Kuan Yew 1965c: 60). Neither could Asian states afford the luxury of viewing 'Asian problems of poverty and under-development through the rosy spectacles of the Western European socialists' (Lee Kuan Yew 1965d: 10). In the context of existing Asian realities, socialism in the sense of the creation of a welfare state could only be a distant goal far beyond the horizon. The preliminary task of socialism was the creation through a universal education system of a society of equal opportunity in which the pool of talent could be widened to encompass the whole society. In the end, Lee Kuan Yew's socialism was not so much a socialism based on the satisfaction of individual rights and needs, but rather a way of 'mobilizing human resources' without going along the communist road of dragooning the society into a system in which all the resources of society – including human – were under the control, and at the disposal, of the state (Lee Kuan Yew 1966b: 8).

CHAPTER THIRTEEN

The Triumphs and Tribulations of Marxism-Leninism in Southeast Asia

When the French withdrew from Vietnam in 1954, they left behind two Vietnamese states: the communist-dominated Democratic Republic of Vietnam in the north, and the anti-communist State of Vietnam in the south, later to become the Republic of Vietnam (see Chapter 10). The unification elections projected for the summer of 1956 did not take place, and by 1958–59 the southern regime of Ngo Dinh Diem faced a full-scale rebellion, which was supported by the Democratic Republic of Vietnam. The United States saw this insurrection as the beginning of a concerted effort, not only by communist Vietnam, but also by communist China, to bring South Vietnam – and, indeed, neighbouring Laos and Cambodia – within the communist camp, and ultimately to use Indochina as a *point d'appui* for the subversion of the remainder of South, Southeast, and East Asia.

From 1958 onwards, the United States tried to shore up the South Vietnamese regime, and from 1965 onwards effectively took over the conduct of the war against the National Liberation Front for South Vietnam (NLFSVN) and North Vietnam itself. By 1967–68, it was becoming apparent to the United States Government that the price that would have to be paid to prevent a communist take-over in South Vietnam was too great in terms of resources, military commitment, economic and social stability, and the maintenance of the United States' international standing and interests. The great American fear, however, was that the process of unravelling their commitment to Vietnam would lead to an unravelling of their global position. They therefore sought, through a combination of enlarged military activity in Indochina and bold diplomatic initiatives directed at the communist camp, to prepare the ground for a 'post-Vietnam' international environment favourable to the United States; or, at least, one in which the damage inflicted on the United States by defeat in Vietnam could be minimized. By 1973, the United States had disengaged militarily from Vietnam: in 1975, deprived as it was of the American air support on which its survival ultimately depended, the South Vietnamese regime collapsed, and Vietnam was rapidly unified as a communist state, now called the Socialist Republic of Vietnam (SRV).

THE INTERNATIONAL SIGNIFICANCE OF COMMUNIST VICTORY IN INDOCHINA IN 1975

Vietnam had not been the only state affected by the war, nor was it the only state whose fate was determined by its outcome. Laos and Cambodia, because of their vital strategic position in the Vietnam War, were inevitably drawn into the conflict. In Laos, ineffectual efforts had been made between 1953 and 1964 to patch together a coalition government that would include rightists, leftists and neutralists. Between 1964 and 1975, however, Laos was effectively partitioned between a rightist Royal Lao Government (RLG) supported by the United States, and a communist Pathet Lao ('Lao Nation') movement supported by the North Vietnamese. In 1975, as a consequence of the communist victory in Vietnam, the Pathet Lao leaders established the People's Democratic Republic of Laos.

In Cambodia, Prince Sihanouk was, after 1954, able – by pursuing a non-aligned policy that nevertheless turned a blind eye to Vietnamese communist activity on the Cambodian-Vietnamese border – to maintain a delicate balance, in which it was neither in the interests of the Vietnamese communists to subvert the Cambodian regime, nor of the United States to incur international odium by violating Cambodian neutrality. The situation changed dramatically in 1970, however, when the anti-communist section of Sihanouk's government staged a coup against him and established the Khmer Republic. This new regime sought the military protection of the United States against Vietnamese communist violations of Cambodian sovereignty; for their part, the administration of Richard Nixon in the United States saw this development as a golden opportunity to destroy communist 'sanctuaries' in Cambodia, and thereby weaken the whole communist war effort in South Vietnam. Just as the United States lent full support to the anti-communist Khmer Republic, so China and North Vietnam no longer had any inhibitions about supporting the Khmer communist movement, or Khmer Rouge, which – nominally at least – formed part of a patriotic front headed by the deposed Sihanouk. In practice, the Khmer Rouge took control of the increasingly bitter war against the Khmer Republic. At the same time, they demonstrated their independence from their neighbours by refusing to follow the diplomatic 'line' pursued between 1970 and 1975 by the Vietnamese and Lao communists. In April 1975, the Khmer Republic collapsed, and in 1976 the Khmer Rouge established the State of Democratic Kampuchea.

At the time, these spectacular victories for communist movements, and defeats for the most powerful Western state, were seen to have an international significance. Matched as they were by the economic crisis of the West that had been brought about in 1973 by the dramatic rise in the price of oil engineered by the Arab-dominated Oil-Producing and Exporting Countries (OPEC), it was tempting even for anti-communist international pundits to see the beginning of the decisive period of that much-predicted event: 'the decline of the West'. Westerners with a classical education saw a reconfirmation of that historical law that had determined Sparta's victory over Athens: that 'Spartan' militarized states would in the end overcome more vulnerable 'open society' democracies. Historians of empire noted that – as in the recent cases of Britain and France – the first stages of retreat from empire could rapidly and inexorably lead to the unravelling of entire imperial structures.

For the Marxist Left as a whole, whether orthodox Marxist-Leninist or unorthodox, the communist victories in Indochina seemed to indicate the opening of a new global era. One of the most respected of Marxist thinkers, the Hungarian Georg Lukacs, suggested in 1971, shortly before his death, that the imminent defeat of the United States in Vietnam signalled the beginning of a seismic shift in world history (*New Left Review* 1975: 1). *The New Left Review*, possibly the most eminent and authoritative Marxist-influenced theoretical journal of that time – at least in the English-speaking world – asserted that 'the ultimate victory of the Indochinese revolution has profound significance for the global order that emerged from the Second World War' (*New Left Review* 1975: 3–4). Significantly, the journal's contributors did not see the Indochina events as a victory for orthodox world communism embodied in the competing versions promoted by the Soviet Union or China, but rather as a triumph for a combined global grass-roots struggle of 'national-liberation' and 'social revolution'. For many Western Marxists, there was an umbilical link between the Vietnamese struggle for national liberation and events such as the May 1968 student demonstrations in Paris. Both weakened and discredited a common enemy: international capitalism, dominated by the United States.

After the initial euphoria, the disillusionment of the Western Left came rapidly. Anti-communists had warned of the horrors that would follow in Indochina 'when the communists came', but even the most fertile inventions of anti-communist propaganda could not have envisaged the Khmer Rouge regime that terrorized Cambodian society between 1975 and 1978. In respect to Vietnam, the Western Left had for years asserted that the National Liberation Front for South Vietnam was allied but not subordinate to communist North Vietnam, and that the new post-liberation regime in the South would be more open, more inclusive and less dogmatic than that of the North. In fact, the real status of the NLF was revealed by the almost immediate imposition of direct northern orthodox communist control over the South. The subsequent mass outflow of refugees from Vietnam and Laos further discredited these two regimes in the eyes of the Western Left.

Beneath the outward show of international socialist solidarity, moreover, it quickly became apparent after 1975 that relations between the Asian communist regimes were anything but friendly. This hostility burst out into the open at the very end of 1977, when the Khmer Rouge regime of Democratic Kampuchea accused Vietnam of seeking to take over Cambodia by force and incorporate it within an 'Indochinese Federation' (*Survey of World Broadcasts* 3 January 1978: 2–3, 8). For strategic as well as ideological reasons, China supported the position of Democratic Kampuchea, while Vietnam gravitated towards full commitment to the opposing Soviet camp. Years of 'armed struggle' had inclined these Asian communist regimes to resort to force as a means of meeting perceived external threats; and, with alarming rapidity, war erupted between Vietnam and Democratic Kampuchea, and then between China and Vietnam, at the end of 1978 and the beginning of 1979. Vietnam swiftly occupied Cambodia, and the border war between China and Vietnam ended in a bloody stalemate.

International developments in the ensuing decade of the 1980s – when revolutionary regimes in the 'Third World' found themselves successfully undermined by the United States and its allies, and the Soviet Union itself began to disintegrate – suggested that if 'the reverberations of the liberation of Indochina' were, as the *New Left Review* put it in 1975, 'silently making history' (*New Left Review* 1975: 4), the direction of that historical destiny was exactly opposite to that anticipated by the Western Left. If the communist victories in Indochina in 1975 gave a new lease of life to the ideological prestige of Marxism-Leninism, the blow delivered to that prestige by subsequent events was correspondingly severe. It could be said, in fact, that the international credibility of Marxism-Leninism collapsed before the Soviet Union itself, and that the events of post-1975 Indochina made a decisive contribution to that collapse.

Following this ideological debacle, it is not surprising that the Left in general sought to dissociate both itself, and Marxism proper, from the post-1975 Indochina events. The Marxist-Leninist foundations of the Asian communist regimes, and of the conflicts that emerged between these regimes, tended to be heavily downplayed by leftist analysts in the course of the 1980s. The nature of, and relations between, the communist states of East and Southeast Asia tended more and more to be explained in pragmatic terms. The unfortunate consequence has been that important ideological factors affecting the policies and relations of these states have been ignored, creating a dangerous gap in our capacity to understand the motivations and behaviour of these states.

THE IDEOLOGICAL FOUNDATIONS OF THE CHINESE COMMUNIST WORLD-VIEW

In order to understand the ideological differences between the communist regimes of China, Vietnam and Democratic Kampuchea, it is first necessary to clarify the shared ideological characteristics of their respective communist parties. The most important of these shared characteristics was the fact that they were *Leninist* in inspiration: they all generally subscribed to the Leninist solutions to the problems posed to orthodox Marxism by the phenomenon of imperialism and the associated phenomenon of the 'uneven development of history'.

In Lenin's view, if history had merely involved the separate evolution of societies along with their respective class structures, then it would have been possible to envisage a relatively even world-historical development, with societies – as it were – queuing up to take their place in the steady progression from backwardness, to industrial development under capitalism, and thence to socialist society. In these circumstances, the role of a communist party would simply have been to lend support to the evolutionary process, but not to try to pre-empt it. Communist parties could, in fact, have been compared to legal trustees who protect the estate and the interests of a minor, and in due course hand over responsibility for the estate when the minor comes of age. Such a notion of the even development of history was nullified, however, by the fact that capitalism did not operate independently in different societies, but – through the operation of imperialism – created a global phenomenon linking the most developed to the most 'primitive' societies in a world-wide network. In consequence, as in the cases, for instance, of Singapore or Shanghai, the most sophisticated examples of modern industrial society could exist side-by-side with societies that were still – in Marxist terminology – 'feudal' in character.

The uneven development of economies and societies brought about by imperialism inevitably also brought about the uneven development of the class struggle. In these circumstances, the role of the communist party was no longer to act as the long-term 'trustee' of the guaranteed inheritance of a working class patiently waiting for social and economic evolution to run its due course. As Lenin outlined in his polemic entitled *What is to be Done?* (1902), described by Georg Lukacs as 'a preliminary thesis of his whole world outlook' (Lukacs 1972: 9), the true task of a Marxist party was not simply to represent the interests of the proletariat at various stages of economic evolution, but to understand the complex interrelationship between political, economic and social developments on a global scale, and to take advantage, on behalf of the proletariat, of favourable revolutionary situations as and when they occur.

It was, of course, on this basis that Lenin masterminded the Bolshevik/Communist take-over of power in the Russian Revolution of 1917. Just as capitalism had created a world-wide imperial network encompassing all stages of economic development, so now the Soviet Union under the leadership of Lenin set up a competing world-wide revolutionary network. The essential tasks of this alternative revolutionary and socialist world order were, first, to seek all means to weaken and ultimately destroy the global capitalist system; and, second, to provide a model and support for the socialist alternative to capitalist development, through which socialist 'planning' would enable a society to modernize and industrialize in a rational and rapid way, without the attendant suffering and injustice of the capitalist mode of industrialization.

It was therefore a common position of all Leninist parties that, after 1917, two competing world orders confronted each other; that, ultimately, the 'progressive' socialist world order was destined by the laws of history to prevail; but that the road to victory would be uneven, and would depend on the firm maintenance of a revolutionary world-view on the part of communist parties. Following the precepts and the example of Lenin, communist parties were also agreed that the uneven and sometimes unpredictable evolution of international events would occasionally require compromise and negotiation with the opposing capitalist camp. Short-term concessions and negotiations, however, could only be justified to the extent that they contributed to the ultimate goal of the complete defeat of world capitalism. It was the duty of a communist party to use its historical perspective to maintain a balance between short-term flexibility and long-term intransigence.

In considering the overall Chinese world-view, as it evolved between 1958 and 1975, the first point to note is that the significance of 1917 and the subsequent creation of two opposing international systems was not only accepted by the Chinese leaders, but was absolutely central to their outlook. The Chinese leadership also gave full credit to the Soviet Union for challenging and overcoming fascism, the most deadly threat, in the period 1941–45, to the socialist camp. Significantly, they also pointed out that this anti-fascist struggle had illustrated the ultimate superiority of the Soviet 'people's war' over the more advanced technology of fascism, and had thereby confirmed the historical inevitability of the eventual victory of the socialist camp (*Peking Review* 14 May 1965: 15–16).

It was a central part of what might be called the Chinese 'thesis', however, that, after the death of Stalin, the leadership of the Communist Party of the Soviet Union had abandoned its role as the 'vanguard' of the working class in the Soviet Union, and of the global socialist camp, and had in effect metamorphosed into a 'new class' with its own interests separate from those of the working class (*Peking Review* 12 November 1965: 20). While this 'new class' had its own class interests, it now claimed to be a 'party of the entire people' guiding, not a workers' state, but what the Soviet regime itself called a 'state of the whole people' (*Peking Review* 14 May

1965: 17). Thus, the Chinese leaders regarded the USSR no longer as a leader in the global revolutionary struggle, but as a super-power protecting and advancing its own interests. A symptom of this, argued the Chinese, was the fact that the Soviet Union, in retrospect, now viewed the victorious war against fascism not in revolutionary, but primarily in patriotic, terms (*Peking Review* 14 May 1965: 20).

The first clear sign of this transformation, the Chinese thesis continued, had come with the Soviet espousal of the doctrine of 'Peaceful Coexistence' with the West. What others, including China, saw at first as a temporary tactical measure – in the Leninist spirit – designed to weaken the reactionary camp and advance the interests of the socialist camp, had proved in fact to be something quite different: a permanent and complete transformation of the relationship between the Soviet Union and the West. Within a few years, the Soviet leadership had, in effect, abandoned the struggle *à outrance* against the United States and the West, and had tried to convert the global class struggle into a normal competitive relationship between big powers (*Peking Review* 14 May 1965: 18).

The Chinese thesis, as it had evolved by 1965, did not see this 'appeasement' as a temporary and remediable lapse by a fundamentally socialist state, but rather as the inevitable consequence of the fact that the Soviet leadership had completely – but covertly – abandoned its Leninist class and revolutionary role, and effectively moved across into the capitalist camp. It therefore followed that the 'contradiction' between the Soviet Union and the socialist camp was now 'antagonistic' (*Peking Review* 12 November 1965: 12–13). The Soviet leadership had, in fact, become a lethal danger to the socialist camp, precisely because it continued to exploit the rhetoric of Marxism-Leninism as a means of maintaining support from global revolutionary forces, and then used this revolutionary support as a highly effective bargaining counter in its big-power competitive relationship with the United States (*Peking Review* 12 November 1965: 15).

In these circumstances, the Chinese thesis continued, it was imperative that China should take over the role of global revolutionary leadership that had been betrayed by the Soviet leadership. This was all the more important since, while the immediate threat confronting the socialist camp was greater than ever before, the long-term international situation was conversely extremely favourable. Since the defeat of fascism in 1945, it was now the United States that had taken over leadership of the world reactionary camp, and was now 'the main force of aggression and war' (*Peking Review* 14 May 1965: 18). Following the Leninist line of identifying and confronting the main enemy of the socialist camp at any given historical moment, it was therefore the duty of China and the socialist camp to construct a global alliance against the United States (*Peking Review* 12 November 1965: 14).

The locus of this struggle between the two camps was no longer Europe – as it had been up to and beyond 1945 – but the decolonizing world of Asia,

Africa and Latin America. Here, while the United States might have a temporary advantage because of its technological superiority, in the long run sheer numbers and revolutionary will-power would inevitably triumph (*Peking Review* 12 November 1965: 21). The victory of the Soviet Union in 1945 had shown that space and numbers, coupled with the infusion of a revolutionary spirit and mass mobilization, would eventually encircle and grind down a system that ultimately depended on technology alone to maintain its domination (Lin Piao 1965: 399–400).

If the focus of this new arena of revolutionary struggle and 'people's war' was Asia, Africa and Latin America, then, the Chinese thesis asserted, the war between the Vietnamese people and the United States was the epicentre of that struggle. As the *Peking Review* put it in 1965: 'The Viet Nam question is the focal point in the present world wide struggle between the revolutionary forces of the people and the forces of counter-revolution, between the forces of peace and the forces of war' (*Peking Review* 14 May 1965: 21). Although the Soviet Union continued to support the Vietnamese war effort, this was not for genuinely revolutionary reasons, the Chinese thesis insisted, but as a means of maintaining credibility in the socialist camp, and thereby as a way of using Vietnam as an effective bargaining counter in its relationship with the United States (*Peking Review* 12 November 1965: 15, 17). For China, on the other hand, the Vietnam War was not a side-show in big-power manoeuvring; nor indeed was it simply the struggle of one people to achieve national liberation. Rather, it was a vital front in an international struggle against the United States and all that the United States embodied. Seen from this perspective, the Vietnamese were fighting for all oppressed mankind, and, given the fact that 'it is people and not weapons, of whatever kind, that decide the outcome of war', Vietnamese victory was certain (*Peking Review* 14 May 1965: 18).

THE IDEOLOGICAL FOUNDATIONS OF THE VIETNAMESE-CHINESE CONFLICT

Even in their militant anti-Soviet rhetoric, the Chinese had to concede that the Soviet Union was lending vital aid to the Vietnamese communists in their war against the United States. Their argument was that this aid was no longer a genuine expression of 'revolutionary solidarity'; in this context, the very fact that the Soviet Union was providing a level of military technological aid that China could not hope to match could itself be used to imply that the Soviet Union was trying to convert a 'people's war' into a conventional war, and thereby to dilute the revolutionary essence of the Vietnamese struggle (Lin Piao 1965: 396–98).

If China and the USSR were in effect competing to lend aid – both ideological and technological – to the North Vietnamese war effort in an attempt to retain their respective claims to lead world socialism, it manifestly made sense in pragmatic terms for the Vietnamese communist leadership to maintain good relations with both sides, and therefore not to become embroiled in their ideological dispute. It is clear, however, that Ho Chi Minh's view on the ideological 'discord', as he put it, was driven by more than merely pragmatic considerations. As one of the most senior world communist leaders, he deplored the devastating blow that the dispute had given to international communist unity. As an essentially pragmatic political thinker, he genuinely believed that the differences in international perspective between China and the Soviet Union could still be resolved in a 'non-antagonistic' way (Ho Chi Minh 1965: 37–38).

There were nevertheless signs, particularly from 1965 onward, that Vietnam inclined towards the Soviet 'line', although this preference was not – for obvious reasons – expressed openly. This inclination toward the Soviet Union can be explained in simple terms of military expedience: the Soviet Union offered modern arms that could match American technology, while China – undergoing as it was the turmoil of the Cultural Revolution (see below) – was less and less favourably placed to aid the Vietnamese war effort. The very fact that North Vietnam was relying increasingly on high technology to resist the United States had ideological implications. It signalled that the Vietnamese communists were not prepared to fight the kind of long-haul, low technology 'people's war' that China believed was the only way to maintain genuine revolutionary zeal and at the same time ensure that the United States became increasingly bogged down in a war they could not win. There was a limit, in other words, to the extent that the Vietnamese leadership was willing to sacrifice its own people, and play the role of 'revolutionary vanguard' in a potentially endless Chinese-led global struggle against the United States.

Even after the communist victory in Vietnam in 1975, the differences of ideological perspective between China and Vietnam did not come out into the open immediately. However, the Chinese interpretation of the international significance of the Vietnamese victory was so much at variance with the Vietnamese world-view that an open ideological break was only a matter of time. For their part, the Chinese argued that the American defeat in Vietnam, coupled with other signs of the international retreat and weakness of the United States and the West, meant that the United States – even if it still constituted a formidable danger – could no more be considered by the socialist camp as the main or most aggressive global adversary. What the Chinese described as 'the uneven political and economic development of imperialism' had transformed the Soviet Union into what they called a 'social-imperialist' state; a state, that is, that retained the outward form of socialism, but had, under the cover of this term, entered into the reactionary camp and was now pursuing an active imperialist agenda in Asia, Africa and Latin America. As such, it was the

Soviet Union, not the United States, that was the 'most dangerous source of a world war today' (*Survey of World Broadcasts* 29 January 1976: 1–2)

On the basis of this perspective, China summoned the 'Third World', which had now emerged as a 'great motive force propelling the wheel of history', to resist the 'hegemonic' attempts of both the USSR and the USA to 'dictate the destiny of the world' (*Survey of World Broadcasts* 29 January 1976: 3). While the Chinese congratulated the Vietnamese on their victory, they warned them against assuming that, because of their victory over the Americans, the threat of imperialism had ended. The Vietnamese may have driven the American 'wolf' from the front door; they now had to guard the 'back door' against the far more malignant Soviet 'tiger' (*Survey of World Broadcasts* 30 July 1975: i).

Outwardly, the keynote speech after victory, made by Le Duan, General-Secretary of the Vietnamese Communist Party, still maintained a careful equidistance between the Soviet Union and China. Both countries were thanked equally in the speech for the aid they had lent the Vietnamese communists in their war against the United States (Le Duan 1977a: 532). However, the speech went on to hail a victory which had been achieved by a party that had adhered throughout the struggle to Marxism-Leninism, 'the culmination of the intelligence of mankind'; which had not only liberated Vietnam, but had made a 'positive contribution to strengthening the forces of world socialism'; and which had been crucially supported by the three 'revolutionary torrents of our time' – namely, the whole socialist bloc including the Soviet Union, 'progressive elements' in the West, and anti-colonial forces in Asia, Africa and Latin America (Le Duan 1977a: 531, 534–35). Although Le Duan ascribed an international significance to the Vietnam victory, his speech studiously ignored the Chinese world-view, and in fact specifically endorsed the umbilical link between the Soviet Union and revolution in the 'Third World'.

It was, however, two speeches by Le Duan and Truong Chinh, made in October 1977 to commemorate the sixtieth anniversary of the October Revolution, that most clearly indicated the Vietnamese alignment with the Soviet, not the Chinese, world-view. Both speeches bristled with socialist militancy and international commitment. Vietnam, they announced, would push forward, via a 'planned national economy', to establish 'socialist relations of production', and thereby by-pass the capitalist phase of development (Truong Chinh 1977: 24–25). This in itself would not have caused any problem with the Chinese line. But what set these statements completely at odds with the Chinese world-view was the fact that they depicted this rush to socialism as part of an *unbroken* historical sweep from the international objectives of the October Revolution to their imminent realization in a future whose direction was indicated by the Vietnamese victory. The Soviet Union – a renegade formerly socialist state in the eyes of the Chinese leadership – was described by the Vietnamese communist leaders as the historical force that was leading mankind 'from an era of necessity to one of liberty' (Le Duan 1977b: 2). For the Vietnamese communists, the fault-line created by the October Revolution between the progressive and reactionary world camps remained intact.

Up to the end of 1977, the expression of ideological differences was largely confined to the public assertion of differing world-views without direct criticism of each other's position. This changed, however, after the public attack on Vietnam by the Khmer Rouge regime of Democratic Kampuchea at the very end of 1977. Thereafter the Vietnamese openly attacked the Chinese leadership and its ideological stance. The basic position of the Vietnamese was that the Chinese communists had allowed their historically driven national instinct to dominate the East Asian region to overcome their internationalist viewpoint as communists. Worse than this, they had used the 'revolutionary rhetoric' of Marxism-Leninism to cloak their 'great-power chauvinism'. Indeed, their radical attempts to push forward at break-neck speed towards the creation of a socialist society – manifested in the 'Great Leap Forward' of 1959 and the 'Cultural Revolution' of 1965 – had had little to do with advancing world socialism, as claimed by the Chinese leaders, and everything to do with attempting rapidly to increase the national power of China (SRV 1979: 10–13). It was this instinct of 'great-power chauvinism' that had led China to challenge the ideological authority of the Soviet Union, and it was this challenge – nationalist at heart, but ideological in language – that had eventually trapped China in the anomalous position of effectively supporting the USA rather than the Soviet Union in its international diplomacy.

In the eyes of the Vietnamese leadership, perhaps the most damaging of all the actions of China had been its breaking of the unity of the revolutionary camp facing imperialism, thereby creating a confrontation between the revolutionary movement of the 'Third World' on one side, and the socialist states and progressive movements of the USSR, Europe and the West in general on the other (*Vietnam Courier* August 1979: 1–2). Vietnam's open alignment with the Soviet Union in 1978 may indeed have been driven by pragmatic considerations – but it was also undoubtedly motivated by a desire to reassert the unity of the socialist idea, and prevent it from being tainted by what was known at the time as 'Third-Worldism'.

REVOLUTION AND CULTURE IN CHINESE AND SOUTHEAST ASIAN COMMUNISM

In order to understand the ideological dynamics of the socialist regimes and revolutionary movements of Southeast Asia, it is important to understand the role of culture in Marxist-Leninist thinking, and especially the relationship between culture, class and power. Since the Chinese ideological line on culture in the period from the 1940s to the 1970s had a great influence, not only on Southeast Asian Marxism, but Marxist thinking world-wide, the general theoretical background to events such as the 'Cultural Revolution' must also be understood – particularly as a key to understanding the ideology of the Khmer Rouge.

It could be argued that it is a basic tenet of orthodox Marxism that every class society – that is, a society in which a particular class dominates the economy at a given historical stage – will have its own culture, just as it will have its own particular political system, and that the values that inform that culture will reflect the general interests of the dominating class. It would therefore follow that a feudal society will be dominated by a feudal culture that reflects in its basic world-view the interests of feudal land-holders; and that the same would be true of capitalist society, in which the overall values, (religious or secular), ways of thinking about the world, forms of artistic expression, and the customs regulating everyday life, would collectively reflect the bourgeois world-view, and therefore the general culture.

This very general view of the relationship between class, culture and power naturally raises important questions. In the first place, to what extent does this analysis have to take into account the continuity through history of a particular culture – national, racial, religious or ethnic – in a particular region? Out of this issue emerges, of course, the whole debate on the relationship between class and ethnic or national identity, and the different question of the extent to which international economic systems – for example 'global capitalism' – inevitably create a matching global cultural outlook that may leave traces of local cultural differences, but in general overrides them.

There is also the question of the actual relationship between culture and class. To what extent, for example, can it be argued that culture at any given stage completely 'belongs' to the dominant class? Would it not be more true to Marx's original moral perspective to suggest that cultures, like economies, represent the cumulative achievements of a given society, and that dominant classes merely seize temporary control of these economies and cultures, and in a sense distort them to suit their particular ends? This question looms large in considering the concept of 'proletarian culture' or 'socialist culture'. One approach to the relationship between class and culture – the line generally taken by Chinese communism in the 'Maoist' period, and by the Khmer Rouge – asserts that a 'socialist culture' driven by a 'proletarian mentality' must entirely replace 'bourgeois culture' and the 'bourgeois mentality' before a society can be described as completely transformed. The other approach asserts that if it is accepted that culture, like the economy, is the common achievement and inheritance of a society temporarily controlled by a particular class within a society, then it would be nonsense to talk about a separate 'proletarian culture'. Rather, since the very fact of class oppression involved the denial of access to that common cultural and economic inheritance, a socialist revolution would entail the acquisition by the whole society of that inheritance.

Thus far, this debate about culture could be considered a Marxist rather than a specifically Leninist preoccupation. For Asian communism, however, the question of culture was tied in with the essentially Leninist issues of the uneven development of history and the overcoming of backwardness. This is best illustrated by the ideological history of the Chinese Communist Party after 1940. As noted in chapter 7, the Chinese communists sought, through the establishment of a 'New Democracy', to ensure communist supervision of the normally bourgeois-dominated stage of industrialization. Although this was seen as an absolutely necessary means of moving society to socialism without any political challenge from bourgeois political forces, it was Mao Tse-tung's contention that this did nevertheless create an uneven relationship between the economic 'substructure' that was progressing rapidly towards socialism, and the cultural 'superstructure', in which habits of thought and cultural attitudes – particularly among the educated elite of society – often remained rooted in the bourgeois era (Mao Tse-tung 1967: 368). As a consequence of this cultural 'lag', the whole revolutionary process remained in constant peril of being infiltrated and eventually subverted by bourgeois cultural traits that had not been eradicated (Mao Tse-tung 1964: 367). As the *Peking Review* put it in 1975, since 'the historical period of socialism is a long process of struggle between nascent communism and dying capitalism', what it called the 'birth-marks' of the old society remained embedded in the socialist society that was gradually being formed (*Peking Review* 18 April 1975: 4–5).

It was therefore necessary – in order to save the revolutionary process from stagnation, backsliding, and even eventual counter-revolution – to encourage the proletariat and peasantry to develop their own 'ideas, cultures, customs and habits', and thereby bring 'education, literature and art and other parts of the superstructure' into line with 'the socialist economic base' (CCP 1966: 405–6). However, it was clear that this need to develop a 'socialist consciousness and culture' was not just a matter of aligning a lagging cultural superstructure with an advanced substructure (CCP 1966: 413). It was also regarded as an ideologically appropriate way of overcoming China's backwardness. Just as history had shown that revolutionary zeal combined with mass mobilization could defeat superior technology in the military sphere, so it was believed that the same combination would enable China to transcend the technological obstacles in the way of modernization (Mao Tse-tung 1958: 351; CCP 1966: 414–15).

What, however, was the content of this peasant and proletarian culture on which Mao Tse-tung hoped to build a revolutionary China? Mao Tse-tung famously asserted that, precisely because the Chinese masses were exclusively preoccupied with a day-to-day struggle for survival, their culture was, as he put it, as 'blank' as 'a clean sheet of paper' (Mao Tse-tung 1958: 352). Mao, however, regarded this as a positive advantage, since it meant that, for the vast majority of the Chinese people, no detritus of bourgeois culture had to be cleared away. It would, therefore, be all the more easy for the Party to instil in the people an entirely new socialist outlook based on socialist values. This would be achieved through a thoroughgoing inculcation of 'Maoist'-Marxist-Leninist ideas, and an attempt to relate this all-embracing Maoist world-view to the everyday life of the peasant and worker. Ideally, every single aspect of the world of work – right down to such issues as the storage of onions, the increase of peanut yields, or prediction of the weather – should be faced by the peasant, not in the first instance as a technological, but as an ideological challenge, in response to which the adoption of the 'correct' political line, based on the revolutionary ideas of Maoism, would of itself create the essential psychological precondition that would ensure the overcoming of technological obstacles (CCP 1972).

The Vietnamese communists did not carry their notion of cultural revolution to these radical lengths. Indeed, Ho Chi Minh and his successors were careful to stress that a correct political-ideological mentality driven by revolutionary will-power had to be balanced by a respect for technological expertise (Ho Chi Minh 1965: 37–38). Nevertheless, the Vietnamese leadership emphasized in 1977 the pressing need to remove what Truong Chinh called the 'backward and reactionary culture' of the 'exploiting classes', and to encourage the creation of a 'new culture' that would transform 'cultural and moral values' (Truong Chinh 1977: 24). In the eyes of the Vietnamese communists, however, the main threat to the inculcation of a socialist culture came, not – as in the case of China – from traditional indigenous value systems like Confucianism, but from the pervasive influence of the 'neo-colonialist' culture that had taken root in South Vietnamese society during the period of the war against the United States (*Vietnam Courier* 70, March 1978: 21).

THE IDEOLOGICAL CHARACTERISTICS OF THE KHMER ROUGE REVOLUTION

In April 1975, the Khmer Rouge – the general description of the movement that had been formed by the Communist Party of Kampuchea (CPK), officially founded in 1960 – took control of Phnom Penh and the whole of former Cambodia, renaming the state Democratic Kampuchea. There then followed a reign of terror that lasted until Vietnam occupied Cambodia at the end of 1978, and forced the Khmer Rouge to the mountain fringes of the Thai-Cambodian border.

The crude ideological explanation for this horrific episode in Cambodian history was that the communist regime in Cambodia had carried 'class struggle' to its logical conclusion, with the physical elimination of all whom it deemed to be class enemies. In a classic example of the uneven development of the class struggle, the Communist Party of Kampuchea had seized power in an undeveloped society. Indeed, in the eyes of the Khmer communists, the extreme backwardness and national vulnerability of Cambodia had meant that three massive tasks – the creation of a modern economy; advance towards a socialist society; and defence of national sovereignty from outside threats and internal subversion – had to be carried out simultaneously and at break-neck speed. The Khmer Rouge leadership, therefore, considered itself to be fighting a desperate class war and national struggle in which the outcome was uncertain. This sense of imminent threat, coupled with the fact that the Khmer Rouge exercised absolute authority over Cambodian society, meant that this envisaged 'class struggle' actually took the form of a endless massacre.

Because of this appalling outcome, the Western Left was anxious to dissociate the Khmer Rouge from Marxism and Leninism. It was argued by the former that the Khmer Rouge leaders were using an imperfectly understood Marxism-Leninism as a cover for what in fact were purely xenophobic policies; or it was suggested that the level of American bombing of the Khmer Rouge areas had in a sense 'unhinged' the leaders and followers of that movement, and driven them into an uncontrollable paranoid and vengeful reaction. Since the ideological foundations of the Chinese Cultural Revolution still had considerable intellectual respectability among certain sections of the Left in the West in the mid to late 1970s, an attempt was also made to downplay the ideological links between 'Maoism' and the Khmer Rouge. In other words, it was very much in the interests of Marxist-Leninists – world-wide as well as in the West – to treat the Khmer Rouge regime as *sui generis*; as a monstrous and alien child spawned by American imperialist depredation in Indochina.

It is all the more necessary, therefore, to understand the ideological foundations of the Khmer Rouge regime. In the first place, it is important to note that the intellectual influences over the section of the Khmer Communist Party that eventually dominated the party were not Vietnamese, but primarily Chinese and French. The Khmer communist leadership was classically Leninist in its analysis of the uneven impact of imperialism, and its view of the role of the Leninist party as a force for the rapid realization of 'inevitable' historical developments, rather than a mere passive defender of working-class interests in that process of evolution. At the same time, the leadership was Maoist in its preoccupation with the issue of culture, and its belief that only through the implantation of an entirely new revolutionary consciousness and will could society eradicate all traces of reactionary culture, overcome the problems of backwardness and build socialism. The Khmer Rouge, however, carried these orthodox traits to extremes.

Although it cannot be described as an expression of Khmer Rouge ideology, an academic thesis written by Khieu Samphan – who became the main intellectual, and public 'voice' of the Khmer Rouge – written in France, and submitted in 1959, does provide an insight into the general Khmer communist analysis of the impact of imperialism and 'neo-colonialism' on Khmer society (Khieu Samphan 1979). This analysis was, in fact, very close to one of the main academic orthodoxies that prevailed in the social sciences at that time: namely, that the era of European colonial rule had 'distorted' the economies and societies of the colonized world, and that this distortion had been perpetuated by the 'neo-colonial' economic strategies of the West, the United States in particular (Khieu Samphan 1979: 64, 48).

In his dissertation, Khieu Samphan argued that the confrontation brought about by French colonial rule, between the traditional Khmer economy and a modern industrialized economy, had had the effect of rapidly modernizing only one sector of the economy: the essentially 'alien' commercial, import-export sector. The modern economic infrastructure created by France had been designed to facilitate the efficient export of certain raw materials of Cambodia, which had accordingly been locked into the international market (Khieu Samphan 1979: 34, 44). On the other hand, France had left the traditional rural world of the subsistence economy relatively undisturbed; and France's cheaper imported manufactured goods had stifled the development of the small and traditional manufacturing sector of Cambodia's economy (Khieu Samphan 1979: 41). The inevitable consequence had been the creation of a 'distorted' economy, in which the commercial sector burgeoned, the agricultural sector stagnated, and the embryonic manufacturing sector had been more or less destroyed. Normal patterns of growth, and the indigenous economic relationship between the productive, commercial and agricultural sectors had been disrupted. Khieu Samphan's conclusion was that 'international integration', the main economic consequence of colonial rule, far from truly modernizing Cambodia, had been 'the root cause of [the] under development of the Khmer economy' (Khieu Samphan 1979: 44).

This economic distortion, continued Khieu Samphan, had had disastrous social consequences for Cambodia. At the top level, Cambodia's link to the international economy had created a parasitic stratum of non-productive traders and middle-men, whose activities actually helped seal the fate of the indigenous productive economy. At the lower levels, the rural population poured into the towns to find work as peddlers and stall-holders, or to scratch a living by providing demeaning services for the wealthy (Khieu Samphan 1979: 53). In the semi-feudal agricultural sector, landlords used the profits from rent and money-lending, not for investment in agricultural improvement, but for the conspicuous consumption of imported luxury goods (Khieu Samphan 1979: 63).

Khieu Samphan's thesis was an academic work, and his solution for the backwardness of Cambodia was stated in economic rather than political terms. Nevertheless, this solution did point the way to Khmer Rouge thinking in the ensuing decades. Fundamentally, it involved the use of the state to protect the 'productive' agricultural and manufacturing sectors of the economy, and the drastic curtailing of the 'unproductive' commercial sector. This required the encouragement of 'autonomous development' and a conscious effort to disentangle the Cambodian economy from 'international integration' (Khieu Samphan 1979: 67). In his 1959 thesis, Khieu Samphan did not advocate a policy of outright 'autarky', but, rather, strict state regulation of Cambodia's foreign trade, and a guarantee that such foreign trade would be subordinated to the needs of the indigenous 'productive' sectors of the economy (Khieu Samphan 1979: 72–75).

Although Khieu Samphan's 1959 analysis was primarily economic, it introduced a broader political theme that, again, was to point to later Khmer Rouge thinking. He emphasized that, if a national plan for 'launching the economy out of its backwardness' was to succeed, it would require more than mere economic planning (Khieu Samphan 1979: 80). There was, in fact, a distinct moral tone in Khieu Samphan's economic thesis: a sense that the ending of a parasitic economy also required the elimination of a parasitic mentality within society (Khieu Samphan 1979: 98–103). This idea that the damage inflicted by colonialism was as much a matter of moral degradation as economic obstruction was later reflected, for example, in a 'History of the Kampuchean Revolutionary Movement' produced by the Khmer Rouge in 1977. While this history admitted that the people of Cambodia may have had what it called a 'sufficiency' in economic terms before the period of the revolutionary regime, it asserted that the moral price that had had to be paid was a condition and mentality of degrading dependency. 'Independence mastery', therefore, was a moral as well as a purely economic goal (CPK 1977/VII: 225).

It is evident that in the formative period of the Communist Party of Kampuchea, the leadership hesitated between following a policy of working within the Sihanouk regime and attempting to push it in a radical direction, or taking the more militant line of confronting the regime and seeking to overthrow it. By the mid-1960s, however, it was apparent that there could be no accommodation between Sihanouk and the CPK. Thereafter, the party leaders – including Khieu Samphan – conducted an armed struggle against first the Sihanouk regime, and then its successor, the Khmer Republic of 1970–75. Although the Khmer Rouge were prepared, in classic Leninist fashion, to make tactical alliances with other political forces as and when circumstances demanded, they also took the equally Leninist line of ensuring their complete control over the revolutionary forces and the revolutionary momentum in Cambodia, while at the same time maintaining a secret party structure (CPK 1977/VII: 221). This strategy had the double advantage of preventing the penetration of the party structure by unsuitable and possibly treacherous elements, and ensuring that tactically useful policies could be pursued without endangering or becoming confused with secret long-term party objectives.

The two prevailing characteristics of the Khmer Rouge in the 1970s, conspiracy and militancy, were consequences of a strange combination of extreme apprehension and extreme confidence. Like Sihanouk (see chapter 9), the Khmer Rouge leadership was haunted by a conviction that Cambodia's neighbours – Thailand and Vietnam – had expansionist ambitions against Cambodia, and that, in the case of Vietnam, this expansionism had been given a new lease of life by communism, in the sense that it now felt it had an ideological mission. Cambodia's innate weakness and the backwardness of its economy made it all the more vulnerable to these predatory neighbours, and it was therefore urgently necessary to create a modernized economy, not just as a socialist goal, but as a matter of national security (CPK 1976/II: 24). Khmer Rouge confidence, on the other hand, was boosted by the sense that the movement had not only conducted a successful armed struggle against the most powerful nation in the world, the United States, but that it had achieved this – particularly in the period between 1973 and 1975, when communist Vietnam had concluded a cease-fire agreement with the United States – on the basis of uncompromising self-reliance (CPK 1976/II: 24–26).

The Khmer Rouge therefore confronted the dangers and the tasks that faced them after they seized power in the same spirit that they had conducted the armed struggle: a combination of uncompromising militancy and extreme vigilance. In a clear deviation from the policy that Mao Tse-tung and the Chinese communists had pursued in China, they dispensed with the notion of installing a 'People's Democratic Dictatorship', through which a communist-dominated but initially multi-class state would supervise the transition of the economy and the changing class relations of society through the stages of industrialization to eventual socialism. Instead, the sense of urgency driving the Khmer Rouge compelled them to create socialist forms immediately, and use this collectivized socialist system to modernize the society rapidly in the areas of agriculture, light industry and, eventually, heavy industry (CPK 1976/III: 46–47).

The Khmer Rouge outlook, however, *was* 'Maoist' – one might say 'ultra-Maoist' – in the sense that it relied on revolutionary consciousness and revolutionary will to achieve this immediate and giant transformation in Cambodian society. Again, it is possible to detect the interplay of an aggressive and defensive approach. On the one hand, it was argued by the Khmer Rouge that the rapid development of socialist forms had created a lag in the cultural 'superstructure', where remaining traces of reactionary and traditional 'consciousness' could contaminate the goals of the revolution if they were not rooted out (CPK 1976/II: 22). On the other hand, the Khmer Rouge clearly saw the development of the right 'consciousness' as the necessary prelude to, not the consequence of, the creation of a fully socialist society. A 'socialist consciousness', in which all vestiges of former cultural outlooks had been removed, would serve as a battering-ram – the ideological equivalent of armed struggle – that would bring socialism to complete fulfilment, not just in its outer form but in its inner content (CPK 1976/II: 19; CPK 1977/VII: 223).

A key ingredient in the development of an all-embracing revolutionary, socialist mentality was self-reliance or 'independence-mastery', as it was called by the CPK (CPK 1977/VII: 225). In part, 'independence-mastery' was seen as a means of preventing outside subversion. Principally, however, it served as a means of linking complete self-reliance in the economic sense with a self-reliant mentality, in a 'revolutionary cohesion' (CPK 1976/III: 47). 'Independence-mastery' would be both a revolutionary means and a revolutionary goal; and 'independence' meant independence, not just from outside influences, but from pre-socialist ways of thinking. The problems of technology and production would henceforth not be solved *for* the masses by experts, but *by* the masses for themselves, through an interaction of socialist theory and everyday practice (CPK 1976/IV: 159–60). In this way, a socialist mentality would form the basis, in the heart of everyday life, for a genuine socialist society.

The other ingredient for developing socialism was 'collective mastery'. The key to solving the contradiction between socialist and pre-socialist mentalities was the confrontation between a 'collective' and an 'individual' way of thinking. The primary task of party cadres, therefore, was to live and think collectively and to, as it was put, 'seep' this collective mentality through to the people as a whole (Carney 1988: 28; CPK 1976/IV: 161). The development of 'collective mastery' was seen almost in physical terms as the creation of a new, live organism, that was, however, in constant danger of being penetrated by the cancer of individualism, which could then multiply from small beginnings and eventually destroy the socialist organism that had been created. This sense of threat from small things is perfectly illustrated by the Khmer Rouge attitude to 'collective eating' (CPK 1976/III: 112). In a departure from their normal insistence on the priority of the correct revolutionary attitude over expertise, the Khmer Rouge insisted that cooking in the collectives should be entrusted to experts (CPK 1976/IV: 156–57). Poor cooking – the possible result of an excess of revolutionary zeal over expertise – might undermine arrangements for collective eating, which, in turn, would encourage 'individual' arrangements: and gradually, a mentality would spread that would be 'antagonistic to the revolution' (CPK 1976/VI: 185).

Despite its rhetoric of 'collective mastery' and 'independence-mastery', the Khmer Rouge regime disintegrated with astonishing rapidity when the Vietnamese communists invaded Cambodia in December 1978. But it will take generations for Cambodia to repair the damage that the regime left behind.

CHAPTER FOURTEEN

The Persistence and Paradoxes of Anti-Colonial Thinking: The Example of East Timor

EAST TIMOR 1974–1975: THE CULTURAL FOUNDATIONS OF THE FRETILIN REVOLUTION

Long after other European powers had decolonized, Portugal still clung to its lonely Southeast Asian outpost of empire, East Timor. After the Second World War, the ultra-conservative Portuguese government of Dr. Salazar sought to push forward the cultural and political assimilation of the overseas territories of Portugal – which principally included the African territories of Angola, Mozambique and Guinea, as well as East Timor – to the Portuguese motherland. This project was interrupted, however, by the outbreak of anti-colonial rebellions in Portuguese African territories in the early 1960s. In the long and bitter ensuing wars of national liberation, Portugal's policy of assimilation through increased educational opportunity simply encouraged the expansion of a radical and well-educated nationalist leadership in Portuguese Africa, and facilitated the penetration of revolutionary ideas among the Portuguese armed forces.

In 1974, the Portuguese dictatorship was overthrown, and the Portuguese empire rapidly disintegrated. The effect of this development was to pitchfork East Timor into a political crisis for which the society was unprepared. Admittedly, the Portuguese authorities had, from the 1960s onwards, opened up greater administrative opportunities for East Timorese, as part of their general attempt to create an 'assimilated' elite stratum of the population that could form the basis for their vision of an 'Overseas Portugal' (Taylor 1995: 32–33). But this elite was tiny, and was mainly concentrated in Dili, the largest town in the territory (Carey 1995: 5). In the rural hinterland of East Timor, the economy was undeveloped, and the population lived in a largely traditional, subsistence world.

The political vacuum in East Timor, created in the aftermath of the 1974 coup in Portugal, was rapidly filled by the assimilated elite of Dili, and a number of political organizations emerged. Principal among these was Fretilin – an acronym for Frente Revolucionaria de Timor Leste Independente, or 'Revolutionary Front for an Independent East Timor' – that established itself in the course of the summer of 1974. As its name suggests, the general ideological orientation of Fretilin was 'militantly anti-colonialist' (*New Left Review* 91, May-June 1975: 76). Fretilin was at that stage dominated by intellectuals who had been 'politicized' by the national-liberation struggles in Portuguese Africa, the events surrounding the collapse of the Portuguese Empire, and by the radical ideas that had risen to the surface during these events. Fretilin had not, at the time it effectively took power in East Timor in the autumn of 1975, yet formulated a firm guiding ideology. However, the Fretilin leaders were profoundly influenced by the political and social ideas of Amilcar Cabral, whom José Ramos Horta, one of the leading figures in Fretilin, described as 'the great African thinker and revolutionary leader of Guinea-Bissau and Cape Verde' (Ramos Horta 1987: 35). Quite apart from the influence that he exercised over Fretilin, the thinking of Amilcar Cabral has remained important because of the manner in which it bridged the gap between the Left's past adherence to the general Marxist world view, and its more recent concern with issues of culture and identity.

Given the common experience, in Guinea-Bissau and East Timor, both of Portuguese rule and of extreme underdevelopment, it is not surprising that the Fretilin leaders should have gravitated to the political ideas of Amilcar Cabral. East Timor also shared with the Portuguese African territories a dilemma engendered by the contradiction of Portuguese colonial policy: that a highly-educated and Westernized *assimilado* elite – tiny in number – had been created in a society that was only just beginning to emerge from a subsistence economy and a completely traditional world.

At the root of Amilcar Cabral's political vision – articulated in a series of lectures and articles written between 1966 and 1970 (Cabral 1980) – was a desire to restore what might be called 'indigenous integrity' to the colonized world, but to achieve this within a broadly Marxist and therefore 'progressive' framework. For Cabral this involved the 'decolonializing' of Marxism itself, and of its European-dominated notion that 'history' proper only began with the class struggle. In an effort to restore historical validity to even the most undeveloped subsistence societies, in which the differentiation of economic function into classes had hardly begun, Cabral argued that the Marxist theory of history should broaden its perspective, and take into account both *pre*-class and *post*-class societies. Only if it did this, continued Cabral, could Marxism hope to comprehend and resolve the dilemmas facing anti-colonial struggles in areas such as Africa, where virtually pre-class subsistence economies coexisted with fully-modernized industrial sectors within the same societies, and where the goal of national-liberation movements was not merely to end colonialism, but also to build socialist societies out of social forces representing virtually opposite poles of historical development (Cabral 1980: 126).

Just as Cabral attempted to restore validity to the pre-class historical phase, and thereby eradicate the notion that colonialism 'gave' a history to 'primitive' colonial regions, so he tried to defend the validity of indigenous cultures. He challenged the crude interpretation of Marxism which asserted that culture should be understood in purely materialist terms, as simply representing the collective modes of thought of a particular class at a particular historical stage. Cabral argued that culture was the cumulative inheritance of a unique society, and, furthermore, that these cumulative inheritances from different human societies were all essential parts of the 'common heritage of all mankind' (Cabral 1980: 150).

Cabral shared with other Marxist thinkers the view that imperialism, far from liberating the colonial world from backwardness, had trapped it in a condition of semi-backwardness and – insofar as there *was* any development within the economy – complete dependency. However, Cabral's concern was focused beyond the 'distorted' economy that was created by colonialism to the distortion of indigenous culture, arguing that the colonial distortions of the economy, the society and culture were completely interrelated. On the one side, colonialism deliberately created a Westernized, economically and politically privileged class that was entirely divorced from traditional culture; on the other, the mass of the populace were fossilized in a customary society, dominated by traditional hierarchies subservient to colonial rule, in which all chances of organic social or cultural change and development were stunted (Cabral 1980: 142–45).

Cabral argued that the negotiated independence agreements that had begun throughout Africa in the late 1950s provided no solution to this status of backwardness and dependency. In effect, these agreements constituted a deal reached between the outgoing colonial power, the Westernized elite that owed their authority and wealth to their commercial contacts with the colonial metropolis, and the traditional leaders of the rural hinterland, who ensured that their authority remained more or less intact (Cabral 1980: 129, 134). In the guise of neo-colonialism, therefore, the 'putrid' force of 'imperialist domination' continued to 'decay in the heart of mankind' (Cabral 1980: 154).

True national liberation, therefore, necessitated revolution. Both the process of revolution itself, and the achievement of the primary goal of revolution – the total removal of colonial power and influence within a society – were necessary preludes to the reconquest by a people of their own history, and of indigenous integrity in the economic, social and cultural fields (Cabral 1980: 123–24). Cabral agreed with the Vietnamese, Cambodian, Chinese and indeed Western Marxists of the time that national liberation could only be achieved when 'the national productive forces have been completely freed from all and any kind of foreign domination' (Cabral 1980: 130). He particularly emphasized, however, the primary role that cultural resistance to assimilation and the struggle for indigenous cultural rediscovery could play in developing 'political consciousness' in a colonized people (Cabral 1980: 140–43).

In a sense, therefore, national *liberation* was also a work of national *restoration*. National liberation involved economic, social and cultural liberation, and this was the necessary prelude to the healing of the distortions brought about by colonial rule in all these areas, and the restoration thereby of indigenous integrity. But it was absolutely central to Amilcar Cabral's political vision that this restoration did not involve in any way a return to the general condition and mentality of backwardness that prevailed before colonial rule had been imposed. In order to avoid this danger, it was vital for what Cabral called a 'revolutionary vanguard' to gain control of the national-liberation movement by forging an alliance between the radical section of the educated elite and the mass of the population living in the rural hinterland (Cabral 1980: 132). This alliance would constitute a revolutionary alternative to the 'neo-colonialist' alliance between conservative *assimilados* and the traditional 'feudal' leadership of the countryside (Cabral 1980: 146).

Cabral argued that it should be the task of this 'revolutionary vanguard' to ensure, first, that the 'progressive' elements of traditional culture be separated from the 'reactionary' elements; and, second, that diverse traditional cultures within a society should be encouraged to move towards a harmonious 'confluence'. The ultimate objective was the regeneration and moulding of a culture that was indigenous, 'popular' and, ultimately, 'national' (Cabral 1980: 146–49). This, insisted Cabral, would be a two-way process. It would not simply be a matter of the revolutionary vanguard 'discovering' the aspirations of the peasantry and shaping their political programme accordingly. Rather, the revolutionary cadres would have to reconnect 'innately', as it were, with that indigenous culture from which their privileged status and education had severed them. Only after they themselves had ended the cultural alienation created by colonialism, and had learned to inhabit the same cultural world and speak the same cultural language as the peasantry, would they be able reciprocally to educate the peasantry, guide their cultural outlook along progressive paths, and enlarge their world-view (Cabral 1980: 152–54).

Like Frantz Fanon (Fanon 1967: 116–18) and other national-liberation theorists of his time, Cabral believed that this cultural reintegration between the elite and the masses could only take place in the context of armed struggle. Only armed struggle could bring about complete and genuine independence; but in addition, the very process of armed struggle could force elite and masses to work and fight together in what would be 'a veritable forced march along the road to cultural progress' (Cabral 1980:

153). Armed struggle, in fact, was necessary for the *psychological* transformation from a dependent to a truly independent mentality.

The trend of Amilcar Cabral's political and social thought matched both the general climate of anti-colonial analysis that prevailed when East Timor was 'politicized' in 1974–75, and the actual condition of East Timorese society. In East Timor, as in Portuguese Africa, a tiny Westernized elite was leading to independence an undeveloped society still instinctively deferential to the local traditional chiefs or *liurai*. During the course of 1974 and 1975, the Fretilin leadership saw their foremost task as that of politicizing and mobilizing the population, in order to achieve an independence from Portugal that was complete, not partial.

Like Amilcar Cabral, the Fretilin leadership put particular emphasis on the cultural agenda. They saw the restoration of indigenous integrity, of which cultural integrity was an essential ingredient, as the ultimate goal of national liberation. In this respect, therefore, Fretilin's outlook on culture was entirely different from the ultra-Maoist attitude of the Khmer Rouge, whose intention was to obliterate all traces of pre-proletarian culture. In East Timor, from mid 1974 onwards, a concerted effort was made to enhance the status of indigenous culture. Handbooks were printed in the Tetum language – the most widespread indigenous language – as part of an intensive literacy campaign; and in the furtherance of the same general campaign to restore indigenous culture, traditional Timorese music was played daily on the radio (Borja da Costa 1976: 12–13).

The poetry of one of the Fretilin leaders, Francisco Borja da Costa, illustrates this cultural endeavour, *à la* Cabral, to restore and at the same time to revolutionize traditional culture. His poems written in the Tetum language have a strongly Brechtian character. Through the use of Tetum, they try to represent and understand from within, as it were, the mentality and outlook of the peasants, and the peasants' – rather than the intellectuals' – perspective on the oppression and poverty that encircled their world (Borja da Costa 1976: 29–31).

THE PARADOXES OF ANTI-COLONIALISM

In 1975, China warned Vietnam against being so absorbed by the struggle against the American 'wolf' at their front door, that they ignored the even greater threat to their independence posed by the Russian 'tiger' entering their back door. This metaphor could have been applied far more appropriately to the situation of East Timor in the same year. The Portuguese decolonized the territory faster than Fretilin was able to build up its anti-colonial struggle; and, when Indonesia invaded East Timor in December 1975 and subsequently set about incorporating the territory as a province of the Indonesian Republic, Fretilin found itself saddled with an anti-colonial ideology that was wholly inappropriate to the new situation it faced. In fact, it could be argued that a campaign to restore 'indigenous integrity' and liberate East Timor from the economic and cultural shackles of Portuguese imperialism would naturally have led to cultural integration between the two halves of Timor that had been arbitrarily severed by colonial rule. A fiercely anti-colonial strategy of restoring indigenous integrity did not justify – but did point in the direction of – some form of integration with Indonesia.

Just as the anti-colonial ideology of Fretilin proved to be inappropriate to the circumstances it faced in 1975, so did its Marxist revolutionary rhetoric. This rhetoric gave Indonesia an excuse to crush a Fretilin regime that it, its allies in the West, and other anti-communist states of Southeast Asia saw as a potential Southeast Asian Cuba that might destabilize the region. Subsequently – but too late – Fretilin leaders toned down and to an extent disowned the revolutionary ideology they had espoused in the 1974–75 period.

Yet, paradoxically, it was precisely the revolutionary credentials of Fretilin that ensured substantial support for their cause in the West. By 1975, the Western Left – those, in any case, who generally subscribed to the Marxist world-view – not only regarded anti-colonial movements as an essential front in the clash with global capitalism; they saw the active national-liberation movements of the Third World as the principal force in the revolutionary tide that would eventually overwhelm the capitalist system. This attitude became even more pronounced in the decade after 1975, during which time the Western Left lost any remaining confidence they had had in the revolutionary role of the established communist states of Europe or East Asia, and realized that the Paris 'events' of 1968 had been more of an intellectual fashion show than a serious indication of revolutionary trends in the West.

Despite the decline of Marxism as a global ideological force after its high point in the mid 1970s, the interest of the Western Left in the Third World – relieved as it now was of the need to apply a 'correct' Marxist perspective – was greatly invigorated, though increasingly centred on questions of culture and identity. In a new alliance between the Western Left and sections of Western liberalism, campaigns for ecological protection, cultural survival, racial equality, human rights, and the rights of minorities proliferated, and separatist movements that would in the early anti-colonialist days have been stigmatized as a hangover of the colonial era – like those of the Tibetans, the Karens, or the West Papuans – were now given a much wider measure of support. Conversely, post-colonial regimes were now subject to criticism in a way that they had never been before. However, although the Marxist trappings were now dropped, the main adversary was still perceived – by the Western and non-Western Left alike – to be 'global capitalism'. Hence the general perspective of these movements remained fundamentally anti-colonial and anti-Western. Consequently, those regimes that were regarded as closely linked to the West, and locked into the global capitalist system, began to come under particular attack. This does help to explain why, although Marxists around the world, along with the Indonesian Left, had actually supported the Indonesian annexation of western New Guinea and aggression in Borneo in the early 1960s, the same leftist alliance, after 1975, campaigned against the Indonesian annexation of East Timor.

It is easy, therefore, to see why the cause of East Timor benefited greatly from its link with the Western Left. Paradoxically, however, it was precisely campaigns such as that for the liberation of East Timor that were held up by the political elites of Asian states as instances of Western colonialism operating under a new guise. It was argued that Western concepts of democracy and individual rights, masquerading as 'universal' human rights, were now being imposed on Asia in order to destabilize and weaken regimes, and undermine both their value-systems and – in the case of demands for trade union rights and so forth – their economic competitiveness. The debate over 'Asian values', in fact, arose as a reaction to what was seen as an attempt – illustrated by the kind of campaigns noted above – to impose 'neo-colonialist' Western ideological hegemony.

This book will not intrude into the period beyond 1980. But it is important to note that the long shadow cast by anti-colonialism has reached into the modern era in Southeast Asia. At the same time, the definitions of anti-colonialism have become confused, and clearly inadequate as a guideline for understanding or resolving the modern political problems of the region. The classic anti-colonial statement embodied in United Nations Resolutions 1514 and 1541, passed in December 1960, combined an assertion of the universal right to self-determination with another assertion that the 'national unity and territorial integrity' of nations should be respected (Djonovich 1974: 188–89). The implication was that, in the process of decolonization, the right to self-determination could only be exercised if it did not violate the 'national unity and territorial integrity' of a national entity. This raises the question of how, in the context of decolonization, 'territorial integrity' should be defined. Should it be based on what might be called the 'Amilcar Cabral principle', that of indigenous cultural integrity? In that case, there would be a strong argument for the independence of Tibet, but a less convincing one for the independence of East Timor. Should it, rather, be based on the shape of pre-colonial states? This, of course, would involve complex historical disputes, and deny the rights of regions that had been part of pre-colonial states, but had had an attested tradition of opposition to those pre-colonial states – as, for example, the Karens of Burma. Or should 'territorial integrity' be defined by the borders that had been created by colonial rule? In which case, the independent rights of the East Timorese would be clear, but those of Aceh and West Papua/Irian Jaya would be denied.

In general, these questions of national identity and national rights are as complicated and difficult to resolve in Europe as they are in the post-colonial world. In Asia, however, these issues, and the question of the relationship between Western and Asian 'values', or between globalism and the maintenance of the integrity of local cultures, are still seen through what might be called the anti-colonial 'prism'. As long ago as the 1920s and 1930s, the Vietnamese conservative thinker Pham Quynh tried to open up a dialogue on genuinely equal terms between Western and Asian political ideas and values, in order to discover what in the end was universal, and what was particular, and to establish some kind of fruitful relationship between these universal and particular values. This endeavour was crushed between the twin forces of colonial obduracy and radical anti-colonialism. It would perhaps be fruitful to reconsider the thinking of people like Pham Quynh and Soetan Sjahrir, who – despite the fact that they occupied opposite poles of the ideological spectrum – envisaged a time when, not just the economic systems, but the world-views of the West *and* Asia would be genuinely post-colonial, in the sense of being 'post anti-colonial'.

Bibliography

Note: This bibliography is restricted to sources cited in the text. Some commentary is included for the benefit of readers who may not have access to the compilations of speeches and papers cited, and so may wish to seek other sources for the same material.

Abu Bakar Hamzah (1981) *Al-Imam: its role in Malay Society 1906–1908*, MPhil Dissertation, University of Kent at Canterbury. (Contains translated articles from *Al-Imam*.)

Aceh (1953) 'Manifesto of the Aceh Rebels', in Feith, H. and L. Castles (eds) (1970), 211–13.

Aidit, D.N. (1955) *The Road to People's Democracy for Indonesia: report delivered by D.N. Aidit, General-Secretary of the Central Committee of the PKI to 5th. National Congress of the PKI* (March 1954), Jakarta: Jajasan 'Pembaruan'.

—— (1957) 'Indonesian Society and Revolution' (1957), in Feith, H. and L. Castles (eds) (1970), 247–51.

—— (1963) 'Political report to plenary meeting of the PKI Central Committee' (December 1963), 23–26 , in Feith, H. and L. Castles (eds) (1970), 266–70.

Alisjahbana, S. Takdir (1966) *Indonesia: Social and Cultural Revolution*, Kuala Lumpur: Oxford University Press.

Anon. (1974) *The Watchmaker of Dien Bien Phu: a collection of Vietnamese short stories 1945–1965*, Hanoi: Foreign Languages Publishing House.

Anwar, Chairil (1974) *The Complete Poems* (edited and translated by Liaw Yock Fang, with the assistance of H.B. Yassin), Singapore: University Education Press.

Armstrong, John P. (1964) *Sihanouk Speaks*, New York: Walker and Co. (contains articles by Sihanouk which appeared in *Réalités Cambodgiennes*, 24 May-13 September 1958, and Sihanouk's abdication speech, March 1955).

Aung San (1945) 'Speech in Rangoon' (29 August 1945), in Silverstein J. (ed.) (1993), 77–93.

—— (1946a), 'Problems for Burma's Freedom: an inaugural address at a convention of the Anti-Fascist People's Freedom League' (January 1946), in Silverstein J. (ed.) (1993), 93–112.

—— (1946b) 'Critique of British Imperialism' (16 May 1946), in Silverstein J. (ed.) (1993), 112–39.

—— (1946c) 'The situation and tasks: presidential address to AFPFL Supreme Council Session' (August 1946), in Silverstein J. (ed.) (1993), 142–48.

—— (1946d) 'Report of speech at the opening of the Supreme Council of the AFPFL' (1 November 1946), in Tinker H. (ed.) (1984), vol. 2, 104.

—— (1947a) 'Radio Address' (4 February 1947), in Silverstein J. (ed.) (1993), 54–56.

—— (1947b) 'Address at Convention held at the Jubilee Hall, Rangoon' (23 May 1947), in Silverstein J. (ed.) (1993), 151–61.

Ba Maw (1943) 'Declaration of Independence' (1 August 1943), in Trager F. (ed.) (1971), 164–68.

—— (1944) 'Burma's New Order Plan' (September 1944), in Trager F. (ed.) (1971), 171–76.

—— (1968) Breakthrough in Burma: memoirs of a Revolution, 1939–1946, New Haven: Yale University Press.

Ba Tin (1948) 'On the present political situation in Burma and our tasks' (March 1948), in Fleischmann K. (ed.) (1989), 83–121. (The 'Goshal Thesis'.)

Bandung (1955) Asia-Africa Speaks from Bandung, Republic of Indonesia: Ministry of Foreign Affairs. (Contains speeches by Carlos Romulo of the Philippines Delegation, and Wan Waithayakon of the Thai Delegation.)

Bao Dai (1980) Le Dragon d'Annam, Paris: Plon.

Benda, Harry J., James K. Irikura, Koichi Kishi (eds) (1965) Japanese Military Administration in Indonesia: Selected Documents, New Haven: Translation Series no. 6, Southeast Asian Studies, Yale University. (Contains Japanese military orders relating to Java, Sumatra and the eastern islands; and general statements of policy of the Japanese government.)

Bong Souvannouvong (1961) Doctrine Lao, ou Socialisme Dhammique, Geneva: L'imprimerie Atar.

Borja da Costa, Francisco (1976) Revolutionary Poems in the Struggle against Colonialism: Timorese Nationalist Verse (edited by Jill Jolliffe, translated by Mary Ireland), Sydney: Wild and Woolley. (See especially two Tetum poems translated into English as 'Poor People' and 'What is the Reason?'.)

Brecht, Bertolt (1976) Poems: volume 2, 1929–1938 (edited and translated by John Willett and Ralph Manheim), London: Eyre Methuen.

BSPP (1962) Burma Socialist Programme Party, 'The Constitution of the Burma Socialist Programme Party for the transitional period of its construction' (4 July 1962), see Appendix 2 in BSPP (1963).

—— (1963) The System of the Correlation of Man and His Environment: The Philosophy of the Burma Socialist Programme Party, Union of Burma: BSPP.

Bukharin, N. (1928) 'Speech to Sixth Congress of the Third International' (1928), in Carrère d'Encausse, H. and Stuart R. Schram (eds) (1969), 232–33.

Cabral, Amilcar (1980) Unity and Struggle: Speeches and Writings, London, Heinemann. (Writings of Amilcar Cabral cited cover the period 1966–1970).

Carey, Peter and G. Carter Bentley (eds) East Timor at the Crossroads: the forging of a nation, London: Cassell.

Carney, Timothy M. (1988) Communist Party Power in Kampuchea (Cambodia): Documents and Discussion, Ithaca, New York: Department of Asian Studies, Southeast Asia Program, Cornell University.

Carrère d'Encausse, Hélène and Stuart R. Schram (eds) (1969) Marxism and Asia, London: Penguin. (A collection of Comintern and other documents relating to international communist policy towards Asia.)

CCP (1966) Central Committee of the Chinese Communist Party, 'Decision concerning the Great Proletarian Cultural Revolution' (August 1966), in Chai, Winberg (ed.) (1972), 403–16.

—— (1972) Chinese Communist Party, Serving the People with Dialectics: Essays on the Study of Philosophy by Workers and Peasants, Peking: Foreign Languages

Press. (Contains sections on: 'Solving the Particular Contradiction of Onions'; 'Raising Peanut Yields'; 'Weather Keepers for the Revolution'.)

Chai, Winberg (ed.) (1972) *Essential Works of Chinese Communism*, New York, Bantam Books.

Chandler, David P., Ben Kiernan and Chantou Boua (eds) (1988) *Pol Pot Plans the Future: Confidential Leadership Documents from Democratic Kampuchea, 1976–1977*, New Haven, Conn.: Monograph Series 33, Yale University, Southeast Asian Studies.

Cheah Inn Kiong (1938) 'Speech by President of the Straits Chinese British Association (SCBA)' at meeting held 7 September 1938 (Typescript), Penang, Malaysia: University Library of Universiti Sains Malaysia: Microfilm 233.i.

Christie, Clive J. (1996) *A Modern History of Southeast Asia: Decolonization, Nationalism and Separatism*, London: I.B. Tauris.

—— (1998a) *Race and Nation: A Reader*, London: I.B. Tauris.

—— (1998b) *Southeast Asia in the Twentieth Century: A Reader*, London: I.B. Tauris.

Cole, Allan B. (ed.) (1956) *Conflict in Indochina and International Repercussions: A Documentary History 1945–1965*, Ithaca, New York: Cornell University Press. (Contains, among other documents, 'Declaration of the Provisional French Government concerning Indochina', 24 March 1945, 5–6; and policy statements by Ngo Dinh Diem.)

Coté, Joost (ed.) (1992) *Letters from Kartini: An Indonesian Feminist, 1900–1904*, Clayton, Victoria: Monash University Institute, Monash University. (Includes Kartini's memorandum entitled, 'Give the Javanese an Education!', 1903, 529–47.)

CPB (1946a) Communist Party of Burma, 'Statement of the Central Committee of the Communist Party of Burma' (13 July 1946), in Fleischmann, Klaus (ed.) (1989), 11–15.

—— (1946b) 'Statement of the Politburo of the Communist Party of Burma' (27 September 1946), in Fleischmann, Klaus (ed.) (1989), 21–30.

CPK (1976/II) Communist Party of Kampuchea, 'Excerpted report on the leading views of the Comrade representing the Party organization at a zone level' (Document II, June 1976), in Chandler, David et al. (eds) (1988), 9–35.

—— (1976/III) 'The Party's Four Year Plan to build socialism in all fields, 1977–1980' (Document III, July-August 1976), in Chandler, David et al. (eds) (1988), 36–119.

—— (1976/IV) 'Preliminary explanation before reading the plan, by the Party Center' (Document IV, 21 August 1976), in Chandler, David et al. (eds) (1988), 120–63.

—— (1976/VI) 'Report of activities of the Party Center according to the general political tasks of 1976' (Document VI, 20 December 1976), in Chandler, David et al. (eds) (1988), 177–212.

—— (1977/VII) 'Abbreviated lesson on the history of the Kampuchean Revolutionary Movement led by the Communist Party of Kampuchea' (Document VII, probably 1977), in Chandler, David et al. (eds) (1988), 213–26.

CPSU (1960) Communist Party of the Soviet Union, 'Statements of the November 1960 Moscow Conference of Communist and Workers' Parties', in Carrère d'Encausse, Helen and Stuart Schram (eds) (1969), 306–9.

De Gaulle, General Charles (1960) *Salvation 1944–1946*, London: Weidenfeld and Nicolson. (The last volume of his *War Memoirs*.)

Decoux, Jean (1949) *A la barre de l'Indochine: Histoire de mon Gouvernement Général (1940–1945)*, Paris: Librairie Plon.

Dharmapala, Anagarika (1965) *Return to Righteousness* (edited by Ananda Guruge), Ceylon: Ministry of Education and Cultural Affairs.

Djonovich, Dusan J. (1974) *United Nations Resolutions*, Series 1, Resolutions adopted by the General Assembly, Vol. VIII (1960–1962), New York: Oceana Publications.

Donnell, John C. (1961) 'Personalism in Vietnam', in Wesley R. Fishel (ed.) *Problems of Freedom: South Vietnam since Independence*, New York: Free Press of Glencoe, 26–67.

Donohue, John J. and John L. Esposito (eds) (1982) *Islam in Transition: Muslim Perspectives*, New York: Oxford University Press. (Contains selected writings of Jamal al-Din Afghani and Muhammad Abduh.)

Du Croo, M.H. (1943) *Marechausee in Atjeh*, Maastricht: N. V. Leiter-Nypels. (Contains 'surrender' document of Acehnese leaders.)

Ducoroy, Maurice (1949) *Ma Trahison en Indochine*, Paris: Les Editions Internationales.

Eutrope, E. (1957) 'Avant-Propos' in *Bulletin des 'Amis du Laos'* 1 (July 1937): ix-xi, Hanoi.

Fall, B.B. (1967) *The Two Vietnams: A Political and Military Analysis*, New York: Praeger. (Contains 'Manifesto of the Eighteen' addressed to Ngo Dinh Diem in appendix II, 435–41.)

―― (ed.) (1968) *Ho Chi Minh on Revolution*, New York: Signet Books. (Contains Ho Chi Minh's 'The Path which Led me to Leninism', 1960, 23–25.)

Fanon, Frantz (1967) *The Wretched of the Earth*, Harmondsworth: Penguin.

Feith, Herbert and Lance Castles (eds) (1970) *Indonesian Political Thinking 1945–1965*, Ithaca, New York: Cornell University Press. (A vital documentary resource.)

Fleischmann, Klaus (ed) (1989) *Documents on Communism in Burma, 1945–1977*, Hamburg: Mitteilungen des Instituts fur Asienkunde.

Freidus, Alberta Joy (1977) *Sumatran Contributions to the Development of Indonesian Literature 1920–1942*, Honolulu: University Press of Hawaii.

Garcia, Mauro (ed.) (1965) *Documents of the Japanese Occupation of the Philippines*, Manila: The Philippine Historical Association. (Contains Filipino documents and statements during the occupation period, including 'The Filipinos' Credo', issued over the signature of José Laurel on 14 November 1943; a 'Manifesto' issued by the Philippine Council of State on 13 February 1943; and Claro M. Recto's letter to Lieutenant-General T. Wati of 20 June 1944.)

Gellhorn, Martha (1967) *The Face of War*, London: Sphere Books. (As a war reporter, Martha Gellhorn wrote an extremely hostile article on the Indonesian Revolution in January 1946.)

Gunn, Geoffrey C. (ed.) (1995) *Tan Malaka's Naar de Republiek Indonesia: A Translation and Commentary*, Nagasaki: np (Contains Tan Malaka's book, entitled in English *Towards an Indonesian Republic*, published in Canton in 1925.)

Hasjmy, Ali (ed.) (1971) *Hikayat Prang Sabi: Mendjiwai Perang Aceh Lawan Belanda*, Banda Atjeh: Pustaka Faraby.

―― (ed.) (1976) *Peranan Islam dalam Perang Aceh dan Perjuangan Kermerdekaan Indonesia*, Jakarta: Bulan Bintang.

―― (1989) *30 Tahun Daerah Istimewa Aceh*, Typescript. (Contains text of *Fatwa* issued by four *ulama* on 15 October 1945.)

Hatta, Mohammad (1923) 'Indonesia in the Middle of the Asian Revolution', in Hatta, Mohammad (1972), 17–26.

―― (1926) 'The Economic World Structure and the Conflict of Power', in Hatta, Mohammad (1972), 36–57.

—— (1928) 'Indonesia Free', a speech delivered at the Court of Justice in the Hague (9 March 1928), in Hatta, Mohammad (1972), 203–97.

—— (1930) 'The Objectives and Policy of the National Movement in Indonesia', in Hatta, Mohammad (1972), 103–43.

—— (1960a) *Past and Future*, an address delivered at Gajah Mada University, Jogjakarta (27 November 1956), Ithaca, New York: Modern Indonesia Project, Southeast Asia Program, Department of Far Eastern Studies, Cornell.

—— (1960b) *Demokrasi Kita*, Djakarta: Pandji Masjarakat.

—— (1968) 'Asian Countries in a Changing World' (12 June 1968), in Hatta, Mohammad (1972), 582–92.

—— (1972) *Portrait of a Patriot*, The Hague and Paris: Mouton. (A collection of the writings and speeches of Mohammad Hatta.)

Ho Chi Minh (1925) 'Problems of Asia', in Ho Chi Minh (1960), 133–36.

—— (1930) 'Appeal made on the occasion of the founding of the Communist Party of Indochina' (1930), in Ho Chi Minh (1961), vol. 2, 145–48.

—— (1945a) 'Declaration of Independence of the Democratic Republic of Vietnam' (2 September 1945), in Ho Chi Minh (1961), vol. 3, 17–21.

—— (1945b) 'Message to the People's Executive Committees at all levels' (October 1945), in Ho Chi Minh (1961), vol. 3, 32–35.

—— (1948) 'Twelve Recommendations' (5 April 1948), in Ho Chi Minh (1961), vol. 3, 146–47.

—— (1960) *Selected Works*, volume 1, Hanoi: Foreign Languages Publishing House. (Contains Ho Chi Minh's articles on the national and colonial question, 1920–1924.)

—— (1961) *Selected Works*, volumes 2 and 3, Hanoi: Foreign Languages Publishing House.

—— (1965) Statement by Ho Chi Minh (15 May 1965), in Central Committee of the Communist Party of Vietnam (1995) *President Ho Chi Minh's Testament*, Hanoi: np, 35–39.

—— (1994) *Selected Writings 1920–1969*, Hanoi: The Gioi Publishers.

Hu Shih (1919) 'The Significance of the New Thought' (1919), in Ssu-yu Teng and John K. Fairbank (eds) (1969), 252–55.

—— (1922) 'On the Literary Revolution' (1922), see Ssu-yu Teng and John K. Fairbank (eds) (1969), 255–56.

ICP (1930), Indochina Communist Party, 'Political Theses of the Indochinese Communist Party' (1930), in *An Outline History of the Viet Nam Workers' Party, 1930–1970*, Hanoi: Foreign Languages Publishing House, 105–11.

Jameson, Neil L. (1993) *Understanding Vietnam*, Berkeley: University of California Press. (Contains illustrative passages from the inter-war writings of Dao Duy Anh and Tran Trong Kim.)

Jaurés, Jean (1908) *Studies in Socialism*, translated by Mildred Minturn, London: Independent Labour Party.

Kahin, George McT. (1956) *The Asian-African Conference: Bandung, Indonesia, April 1955*, Ithaca, New York: Cornell University Press. (Contains opening speech by Sukarno, 18 April 1955; speech by Prime Minister Nehru of India, 22 April 1955; and text of final communiqué, 24 April 1955.)

Katay don Sasorith (1953) *Le Laos: son évolution politique, sa place dans l'Union française*, Paris: Berger-Levrault. (Contains essay written by Katay don Sasorith in 1938, entitled 'Etude Annexe du Statut politique du Laos et de condition juridique des Laotiens', 141–51.)

Kennan, George F. (1947) 'The Sources of Human Conflict', first published in *Foreign Affairs* (July 1947), in Richard Hofstadter (ed.) (1958) *Great Issues in American History*, New York: Vintage Books, Random House, vol. 2, 420–27.

Khieu Samphan (1979) *Cambodia's Economy and Society* (translated with an introduction by Laura Summers), Ithaca, New York: Data Paper III, Southeast Asia Program, Cornell University.

Krushchov, N.S. (1961) *On Peaceful Coexistence*, Moscow: Foreign Languages Publishing House.

Landon, Kenneth P. (1968) *Siam in Transition: A Brief Survey of Cultural Trends in the Five Years since the Revolution of 1932*, (originally published 1939), New York: Greenwood Press. (Contains a wide range of documents relating to the Thai Revolution of 1932, especially documents relating to the proposed National Economic Policy of Pridi, 260–93.)

Laos (1949) 'A Constitution of the Kingdom of Laos' (11 May 1947, amended 14 September 1949), in Department of External Affairs, Australia (1970) *Laos: Selected Documents on International Affairs*, Canberra: Department of External Affairs.

Le Duan (1977a) *Selected Writings*, Hanoi: Foreign Languages Publishing House. (Contains 'Forward to the Future', 15 May 1975, 525–40.)

—— (1977b) 'The October Revolution and the Vietnamese People's Struggle for National Independence and Socialism' (20 October 1977), in *Vietnam Courier*, No. 67 (December 1977): 2–6.

Le Van Tuan (1942) 'Les Mandarins Tonkinois à Phan-Thiet', originally published in *Indochine Hebdomadaire*, 97 (1942), included in collection entitled *Mandarins et Lettrés au Viet-Nam: leur examens et concours, leurs grandeurs et servitudes: un grand choix de textes de 1880 à 1969*, Saigon: Viet Nam Panorama, 96–102.

Leblond, Marius (1941) 'L'empire et la France du Pétain', in André Bellesort et al. (1941) *France 1941: la révolution nationale constructive: un bilan et un programme* Paris: éditions Alsace, 146–64.

Lee Kuan Yew (1963a) Speech at the Singapore National Union of Journalists (24 May 1963), in Lee Kuan Yew (nd) *Malaysia Comes of Age*, Singapore: Ministry of Culture, 1–11.

—— (1963b) Speech given at dinner of Foreign Correspondents' Association at the Adelphi Hotel (25 October 1963), in Lee Kuan Yew (nd) *Malaysia Comes Of Age*, Singapore: Ministry of Culture, 12–27.

—— (1965a) *The Battle for a Malaysian Malaysia*, Singapore: Ministry of Culture. (Contains press conference, 3 June 1965.)

—— (1965b) 'Southeast Asia in Turmoil' (7 March 1965), in Lee Kuan Yew (nd) *Malaysia: Age of Revolution*, Singapore: Ministry of Culture, 1–20.

—— (1965c) 'Future of Malaysia' (24 March 1965), in Lee Kuan Yew (nd) *Malaysia Comes of Age*, Singapore: Ministry of Culture, 33–48.

—— (1965d) *Socialist Solution for Asia: A Report of the 1965 Asian Socialists' Conference in Bombay*, Singapore: Ministry of Culture. (Contains speeches and statements of Lee Kuan Yew at the conference.)

—— (1966a) Speech in Stockholm at a Congress of the Socialist International (7 May 1966), in Lee Kuan Yew (nd) *Socialism and Reconstruction in Asia*, Singapore: Ministry of Culture, 18–36.

—— (1966b) Speech at Socialist International Congress at Uppsala (27 April 1966), in Lee Kuan Yew (nd) *Socialism and Reconstruction in Asia*, Singapore: Ministry of Culture, 1–16.

Lenin, V.I. (1902) 'What is to be Done? Burning Questions of Our Movement', in V.I. Lenin (1947) *Selected Works Volume 1*, Moscow: Foreign Languages Publishing House, 147–269.

—— (1914) 'The Rights of Nations to Self-Determination', in V.I. Lenin (1947) *Selected Works Volume 1*, Moscow: Foreign Languages Publishing House, 552–98.

—— (1917) 'Imperialism, the Highest Stage of Capitalism', in V.I. Lenin (1947) *Selected Works Volume 1*, Moscow: Foreign Languages Publishing House, 630–725.

—— (1919) 'The Third International and its Place in History', in V.I. Lenin (1947), *Selected Works Volume 2*, Moscow: Foreign Languages Publishing House, 471–77.

—— (1920) 'Preliminary Draft of Theses on the National and Colonial Questions for the Second Congress of the Communist International', in V.I. Lenin (1947), *Selected Works Volume 2*, Moscow: Foreign Languages Publishing House, 654–58.

—— (1923) 'Better Fewer, but Better', in V.I. Lenin (1947), *Selected Works Volume 2*, Moscow: Foreign Languages Publishing House, 844–55.

Liang Ch'i-ch'ao (1902) 'The Renovation of the People', in Ssu-yu Teng and John K. Fairbank (eds) (1969), 220–23.

Lin Piao (1965) 'Long Live the Victory of the People's War!', in Chai, Winberg (ed.) (1972), 394–403.

Lu Hsun (1954) *Selected Stories*, Peking: Foreign Languages Press. (Especially 'Kung i-chi', 1919; 'Storm in a Teacup', 1920; 'In the Wineshop', 1924; and 'The Misanthrope', 1925.)

Lukacs, Georg (1972) *Lenin: A Study on the Unity of His Thought* (first published 1924), London: NLB.

Mahathir bin Mohamad (1970) *The Malay Dilemma*, Singapore: Donald Moore, for Asia Pacific Press.

Malaysia (nd) *Rukunegara*, Malaysia: Department of Information.

Malleret, Louis (1934) *L'Exotisme Indochinois dans la Littérature Française depuis 1860*, Paris: Larose Editeurs.

Mao Tse-tung (1937) 'On Contradiction', in Chai, Winberg (ed.) (1972), 75–93.

—— (1940) 'On New Democracy', in Chai, Winberg (ed.) (1972), 151–70.

—— (1942) 'Talks at the Yenan Forum on Arts and Literature', in Chai, Winberg (ed.) (1972), 191–202.

—— (1958) Article from *Peking Review*, 10 June 1958, in Schram, Stuart R. (1969), 351–52.

—— (1964) 'We must Prevent China from Changing Colour', in Schram, Stuart R. (1969), 367.

—— (1967) 'The Dead Still Rule Today', in Schram, Stuart R. (1969), 368.

Marr, David G. (ed.) (1975) *Reflections from Captivity: Phan Boi Chau's 'Prison Notes' and Ho Chi Minh's 'Prison Diary'* (translated by Christopher Jenkins, Tran Khanh Tuyet and Huynh Sanh Thong), Athens, Ohio: Ohio University Press.

—— (1979) 'Vietnamese Historical Reassessment', in Anthony Reid and David Marr (eds) (1979) *Perceptions of the Past in Southeast Asia*, Singapore: Heinemann, 313–39.

Marx, Karl and F. Engels (1975) *The First Indian War of Independence, 1857–1859*, Moscow: Progress Publishers.

Mounier, Emmanuel (1952) *Personalism*, Notre Dame, Indiana: University of Notre Dame Press.

—— (1956) *The Character of Man* (translated by Cynthia Rowland), London: Rockliff. (Contains an outline of his psychological and philosophical ideas.)

Mus, Paul (1954) *Le Destin de l'Union Française: de l'Indochine à l'Afrique*, France: éditions du Seuil. (Contains text of Franco-Vietnamese convention of 1925, and the 'Testament' of Khai-Dinh, 1925.)

McClelland, J.S. (ed.) (1970) *The French Right: from de Maistre to Maurras*, London: Jonathan Cape. (Contains selections from the writings of Charles Maurras.)

McVey, Ruth T. (ed.) (1969) *Sukarno's Nationalism, Islam and Marxism*, Ithaca, New York: Modern Indonesia Project, Southeast Asia Program, Cornell University.

Narasu, P. Lakshmi (1907) *The Essence of Buddhism*, Madras: Srinivasa Varadachari.

Nasution, Abdul Haris (nd) *Fundamentals of Guerilla Warfare, and the Indonesian Defence System Past and Future*, Jakarta: Indonesian Service of the Indonesian Armed Forces.

Natsir, Mohammad (1954) *Some Observations Concerning the Role of Islam in National and International Affairs*, Ithaca, New York: Data Paper no. 16, Department of Far Eastern Studies, Cornell University.

—— (1956) Speech to Masyumi Party (7 November 1956), in Feith, H. and L. Castles (eds) (1970), 89–94.

—— (1957) Speech to the Constituent Assembly (12 November 1957), in Feith, H. and L. Castles (eds) (1970), 215–19.

New Left Review (1975): Editorial, *New Left Review* 91 (May-June 1975): 1–4, London.

Ngo Dinh Diem (1955a) 'New Year Message to the People', January 1955, in Cole, Allan B. (ed.) (1955), 210–14.

—— (1955b) 'Speech outlining tasks and principles', 21 March 1955, in Cole, Allan B. (ed.) (1955), 214–16.

—— (1955c) 'Message to Vietnam's Friends in the Free World following the victory over the Binh Xuyen Sect' (8 May 1955), in Ngo Dinh Diem (1956) *Major Policy Speeches of Ngo Dinh Diem*, Saigon: Press Office, Presidency of the Republic of Vietnam, 7–10.

—— (1955d) 'Speech at the reopening of the Dong Cam Dam', Tuy-Hoa (7 September 1955), in Ngo Dinh Diem (1956) *Major Policy Speeches of Ngo Dinh Diem*, Saigon: Press Office, Presidency of the Republic of Vietnam, 11–19.

—— (1956a) 'Message to the National Assembly' (17 April 1956), in Ngo Dinh Diem (1956) *Major Policy Speeches of Ngo Dinh Diem*, Saigon: Press Office, Presidency of the Republic of Vietnam, 25–28.

—— (1956b) 'Statement on the Second Anniversary of the Refugee Movement' (11 October 1956), in Ngo Dinh Diem (1956) *Major Policy Speeches of Ngo Dinh Diem*, Saigon: Press Office, Presidency of the Republic of Vietnam, 33–35.

Nguyen Khac Vien and Huu Ngoc (eds and trans) (nd) *Vietnamese Literature*, Hanoi: Foreign Languages Publishing House. (Contains some writings of Phan Chau Trinh.)

Nhouy Abhay (1959) 'Buddhism in Laos', in René de Berval (ed.) (1959) *Kingdom of Laos: The Land of the Million Elephants and of the White Parasol*, Saigon: France-Asie 237–56.

Noer, Deliar (1979) 'Yamin and Hamka: Two Routes to an Indonesian Identity', in Anthony Reid and David Marr (eds) (1979) *Perceptions of the Past in Southeast Asia*, Singapore: Heinemann, 249–62.

NSC (1952) National Security Council Statement of Policy, 'United States Objectives and Courses of Action with Respect to Southeast Asia' (1952), in Neil Sheehan (ed.) (1972) *The Pentagon Papers, as published by the New York Times*, New York: Bantam Books, 27–32.

Paget, Roger K. (ed.) (1975) *Indonesia Accuses! Soekarno's Defence Oration in the Political Trial of 1930* (translation and commentary by Roger Paget), Kuala Lumpur: Oxford University Press.

Pané, Armijn (1964) *Belenggu*, Djakarta: Pustaka Rakjat.

—— (1985) *Shackles* (translated by John H. McGlynn), Athens, Ohio: Monograph No. 67, Ohio Center for Southeast Asian Studies, University of Ohio.

Peking Review (1965), 14 May 1965 and 12 November 1965: published in Peking/ Beijing.

Pham-Quynh (1937) *Essais Franco-Annamites 1929–1932*, Hué: Editions Bui-Huy-Tin.

—— (1942) *Charles Maurras: Penseur Politique*, Hué: Imprimerie AJS.

Phoui Sananikone (1954) Speech (9 June 1954), in Department of External Affairs, Australia (1970) *Laos: Selected Documents on International Affairs*, Canberra: Department of External Affairs.

Phuc Thien (1956) *President Ngo-Dinh-Diem's Political Philosophy*, Saigon: Review Horizons. (Contains extensive extracts from speeches of Ngo Dinh Diem.)

Ramos Horta, José (1987) *Funu: The Unfinished Saga of East Timor*, Trenton, New Jersey: The Red Sea Press Inc.

Rathausky, Rima (ed.) (1963) *Documents of the August 1945 Revolution in Vietnam* (translated by C. Kiriloff), Canberra: ANU. (Contains documents of the *Viet Minh* movement during the period March to August 1945.)

Revolutionary Council of Burma (1962) 'The Burmese Way to Socialism' (30 April 1962), Appendix 1 in BSPP (1963) *The System of Correlation of Man and His Environment: The Philosophy of the Burma Socialist Programme Party*, Union of Burma: BSPP.

Rhys-Davids, T.W. and William Stede (1972) *The Pali Text Society's Pali-English Dictionary*, London: Routledge and Kegan Paul.

Rizal, José (1961) *Noli Me Tangere* (translated by Leon Guerrero), London: Longmans.

—— (1968) *El Filibusterismo* (translated by Charles E. Derbyshire, under the title *Reign of Greed*), Manila: Philippine Education Company.

Rochet, Charles (1946) *Pays Lao: Le Laos dans la Tourmente 1939–1945*, Paris: Jean Vigneau.

Roff, W.R. (1967) *The Origins of Malay Nationalism*, New Haven, Conn.: Yale University Press.

—— (ed.) (1978) *The Wandering Thoughts of a Dying Man: The Life and Times of Haji Abduh Majid bin Zainuddin*, Kuala Lumpur: Oxford University Press. (Memoirs of an eminent Malay teacher of the pre-Second World War period.)

Rostow, W.W. (1961) 'Guerilla Warfare in Underdeveloped Areas' (address given at US Army Special Warfare School, Fort Bragg, June 1961), in Marcus G. Raskin and Bernard B. Fall (eds) (1967) *The Viet-Nam Reader*, New York: Vintage Books, 108–16.

Sakirman (1960) Articles published in *Bintang Merah* (May-June, July-August 1960), in Feith, H. and L. Castles (eds) (1970), 122–27.

Saleh, Hasan (1956) *Revolusi Islam di Indonesia*, Banda Aceh: Pustaka Djihad.

Schram, Stuart R. (1969) *The Political Thought of Mao Tse-tung*, Harmondsworth: Penguin. (Contains diverse writings of Mao Tse-tung.)

Sihanouk, Norodom (1955) *La Grande Figure de Norodom Sihanouk: Telle Qu'elle est dépeinte par les documents de valeur historique découvertes dans les archives du Palais Royal*, Phnom Penh: Imprimerie du Palais Royal. (Contains addresses and declarations of Sihanouk, and correspondence between Sihanouk and French officials, April 1945 to September 1953.)

—— (1959) *Sihanouk and Cambodian Independence*, Phnom Penh: Ministry of Information. (Translation of a collection of articles published by Sihanouk in *Réalités Cambodgiennes*, March 1958, and 13 September 1958 to 5 January 1959.)

Silverstein, Josef (1993) *The Political Legacy of Aung San*, Ithaca, New York: Southeast Asian Program.

Sjahrir, Soetan (1949) *Out of Exile* (translated by Charles Wolf), New York: The John Day Company.

—— (1953) 'Nationalism and Internationalism' (1953), in Feith, H. and L. Castles (eds) (1970), 232–37.

—— (1968) *Our Struggle* (first published in 1945; translated, with an introduction, by Ben Anderson), Ithaca, New York: Modern Indonesia Project, Southeast Asian Program, Cornell University.

Song Ong Siang (1967) *One Hundred Years' History of the Chinese in Singapore* (first published in 1923), Singapore: University of Malaya Press.

SRV (1979) (Socialist Republic of Vietnam) *Chinese Aggression against Vietnam*, Hanoi: Foreign Languages Publishing House.

Stalin, J.V. (1947) *Marxism and the National and Colonial Question*, London: Lawrence and Wishart. (Contains most of Stalin's writings on the national question.)

—— (1953) *Problems of Leninism*, Moscow: Foreign Languages Publishing House.

Ssu Yu-teng and John K. Fairbank et al. (eds) (1969) *China's Response to the West: A Documentary Survey*, New York: Atheneum.

The Straits Chinese Magazine. (Available on microfilm in the Library of Universiti Sains Malaysia, Penang, Malaysia.)

Stuart-Fox, Martin and Mary Kooyman (1992) *Historical Dictionary of Laos*, Metuchen, NJ: The Scarecrow Press.

Sukarno (1945) 'The Birth of Pantja Sila' (1 June 1945), in Sukarno (1961), 3–21.

—— (1951) Speech (17 September 1951), in Feith, H. and L. Castles (eds) (1970), 59–62.

—— (1952) 'The Crisis of Authority' (17 August 1952), in Feith H. and L. Castles (eds) (1970), 74–78.

—— (1957a) 'Saving the Republic of the Proclamation' (21 February 1957), in Feith H. and L. Castles (eds) (1970), 83–89.

—— (1957b) *Marhaèn and Proletarian* (translated by Clair Holt), Ithaca, New York: translation series, Modern Indonesian Project, Southeast Asia Program, Department of Far Eastern Studies, Cornell University.

—— (1959) 'The Rediscovery of our Revolution' (17 August 1959), in Sukarno (1961), 39–76.

—— (1960a) 'Like an Angel that Strikes from the Skies' (17 August 1960), in Sukarno (1961), 79–118.

—— (1960b) 'To Build the World Anew' (30 September 1960), in Sukarno (1961), 121–49.

—— (1961) *Towards Freedom and the Dignity of Man: A Collection of Five Speeches by President Sukarno of the Republic of Indonesia*, Djakarta: Republic of Indonesia, Department of Foreign Affairs.

—— (1964) 'A Year of Living Dangerously' (17 August 1964), in C.J. Christie (1998) *Southeast Asia in the Twentieth Century: A Reader*, London: I.B. Tauris, 239–46.

—— (1965) *Reach to the Stars: A Year of Self-Reliance*, (17 August 1945), Djakarta: Republic of Indonesia, Department of Information.

Sun Yat-sen (1905) 'Manifesto of the T'ung-Meng-Hui' (1905), in Ssu-yu Teng and John K. Fairbank (eds) (1969), 227–29.

Summary of World Broadcasts (*SWB*), 'Part 3: The Far East', Reading: Monitoring Service of the British Broadcasting Corporation (BBC).

Tagore, Rabindranath (1917) *Nationalism*, London: MacMillan.

Tan Cheng Lock (1926) Speech at Meeting of Legislative Council, Straits Settlements (1 November 1926), in Tan Cheng Lock (1947), 88–94.

—— (1932) Memorandum to Sir Samuel Wilson (December 1932), in Tan Cheng Lock (1947), 74–88.

—— (1934) Speech at Meeting of Legislative Council held in Malacca (12 February 1934), in Tan Cheng Lock (1947), 95–109.

—— (1943) Memorandum on the Future of Malaya (1 November 1943), in Tan Cheng Lock (1947), 10–42.

—— (1944) Comments on the Association of British Malaya's Memorandum on the Reconstruction of Malaya (4 June 1944), in Tan Cheng Lock (1947), 54–60.

—— (1945) 'Memorial Relating to Malaya submitted to His Majesty's Secretary of State for the Colonies' (1945), in Tan Cheng Lock (1947), 61–73.

—— (1946a) Speech at the Malacca Chinese Chamber of Commerce (12 October 1946), in Tan Cheng Lock (1947), 122–30.

—— (1946b) Memorandum on the future of the Chinese in Malaya (20 December 1946) (Typescript), Penang, Malaysia: Library of Universiti Sains Malaysia, microfilm 240.3.

—— (1946c) Speech at Public Meeting under the auspices of the Pan-Malayan Council of Joint Action (23 December 1946), in Tan Cheng Lock (1947), 132–36.

—— (1946d) Speech (2 April 1946), in Tan Cheng Lock (1947), 113–20.

—— (1947) *Malayan Problems from a Chinese Point of View*, Singapore: Tannsco. (A collection of Tan Cheng Lock's speeches in the period 1923–1946.)

Taylor, John G. (1995) 'The Emergence of a Nationalist Movement in East Timor', in Carey, Peter and G. Carter Bentley (eds) (1995), 21–41.

Thailand (1950) Text of Economic and Technical Agreement between the Government of Thailand and the Government of the United States of America (8 September 1950), in Thak Chaloemtiarana (1978).

Thak Chaloemtiarana (ed.) (1978) *Thai Politics 1932–1957*, volume 1, Bangkok: Social Science Association of Thailand, Thammasat University. (Contains documents relating to the Thai Revolution of 1932; texts of radio broadcasts relating to Thai identity and culture, 1941–1942; the *Thai Ratthaniyom* decrees from March 1940 to January 1942; and text of the 'National Cultural Maintenance Act', 4 October 1940.)

Thein Pe (1946) Party Conference Report (20 July 1946), in Fleischmann, Klaus (ed.) (1989), 16–20.

Third International (1928) 'Theses on the Revolutionary Movement in the Colonies and Semi-Colonies' (Sixth Congress of the Third International, 1928), in Carrère d'Encausse and Stuart R. Schram (eds) (1969), 237–39.

Tinker, Hugh (ed.) (1983) *Burma: The Struggle for Independence, 1944–1948, volume 1*, London: HMSO.

—— (ed.) (1984) *Burma: The Struggle for Independence, 1944–1948, volume 2*, London: HMSO. (Contains AFPFL correspondence and decisions during the period of negotiations over independence.)

Trager, Frank (ed.) (1971) *Burma: Japanese Military Administration, Selected Documents 1941–1945* (translated by Won Zoon Woon), Philadelphia: University of Pennsylvania Press.

Truman, Harry (1947) 'The Truman Doctrine' (address by President Truman to Joint Session of Congress, 12 March 1947), in Richard Hofstadter (ed.) (1958) *Great Issues in American History, volume 2, 1864–1957*, New York: Vintage Books, 414–15.

Truong Chinh (1946) 'The August Revolution' (1946), in Truong Chinh (1963) *Primer for Revolt: The Communist Takeover in Vietnam*, New York: Frederick A. Praeger, 1–80.

—— (1947) 'The Resistance Will Win' (1947), in Truong Chinh (1963) *Primer for Revolt: The Communist Takeover in Vietnam*, New York: Frederick A. Praeger, 81–211.

—— (1977) 'The Basic Features of the Line of the Great October Revolution' (5 November 1977), *Vietnam Courier* 67 (December 1977): 23–26.

Truong Chinh and Vo Nguyen Giap (1974) *The Peasant Question* (written 1937–38, translated by Christine Pelzer White), Ithaca, New York: Data Paper 94, Southeast Asia Program, Department of Asian Studies, Cornell University.

Tullié, A.-R. (1937) 'Notre but: nos projets', in *Bulletin des 'Amis du Laos'* 1 (July 1937): 1–12.

U Nu (1947) 'Seeds of the Freedom of the Burmese Masses' (24 September 1947), in Tinker, Hugh (ed.) (1984) *Burma: The Struggle for Independence, volume 2, 1944–1948*, London: HMSO, 769–71.

—— (1953a) *Burma Looks Ahead* (speeches by U Nu, 19 July 1951 to 4 August 1952), Rangoon: Ministry of Information, Government of the Union of Burma.

—— (1953b) *What is Revolution?* Rangoon: Government Printing and Stationery. (Speech delivered on the eighth Anniversary of Resistance Day, 27 March 1953.)

—— (1957) *The People Win Through* (with an introduction by Edward Hunter), New York: Taplinger. (This is a polemical play on the communist revolt in Burma, written by U Nu in 1950, and subsequently broadcast by Burmese radio. In the 1950s, it became a key educational text in Burmese schools.)

—— (1958) *Seven Point Programme*, Rangoon: Directorate of Information.

Veur, Paul W. van der (ed.) (1987) *Towards a Glorious Indonesia: Reminiscences of Dr. Soetomo* (translated by Suharni Soemarno and Paul W. van der Veur), Athens, Ohio: Monographs in International Studies, Southeast Asia series no. 81, Ohio University.

Vichitr/Wichit Vadakarn (1941) *Thailand's Case*, Bangkok: Thai Commercial Press. (See especially chapter 5, analyzing the main characteristics of the Thai race, 121–37.)

Vietnam Courier (1977–1979), published in Hanoi.

Wen Ching (1901) *The Chinese Crisis from Within*, London: Grant Richards. (Wen Ching was the pseudonym of Lim Boon Kheng.)

Wiranata Koesoema, R.A.A. (1948) Extract from 'Islamic Democracy in Theory and Practice' (translated from the original Dutch), in Feith, H. and L. Castles (eds) (1970), 221–26.

Zhdanov, A.A. (1947) *On the International Situation*, London: W.P. Coates.

Zhukov, G. (1958) 'The Collapse of the Colonial System of Imperialism' (August 1956), in Carrère d'Encausse, Helen and Stuart R. Schram (eds) (1969), 287–91.

Index